W9-BQX-006

Craig A. Everett, PhD
Editor

Divorce
and the Next Generation:
Perspectives for Young Adults
in the New Millennium

Divorce and the Next Generation: Perspectives for Young Adults in the New Millennium has been co-published simultaneously as *Journal of Divorce & Remarriage*, Volume 34, Numbers 3/4 2001.

Pre-publication
REVIEWS,
COMMENTARIES,
EVALUATIONS . . .

"**O**ne of the best investments you can make for your research library. . . . Contains many studies that will serve as reference tools for years to come. In fact, this book is so complete that it will likely be used like an encyclopedia by many researchers interested in family issues."

William Jeynes, PhD
Assistant Professor
Hillsdale College, Michigan

More pre-publication
REVIEWS, COMMENTARIES, EVALUATIONS . . .

"**W**ell written. . . . I highly recommend this volume. . . . Well
suited to the academic classroom, the
informed clinician's shelf, and researchers and members of the profession in general. Particularly helpful is
the book's ability to delineate the ways
in which the affects of divorce differ
among various social groups."

Vicki L. Loyer-Carlson, PhD
Marriage and Family Therapist
Private Practice
Tucson, Arizona

The Haworth Clinical Practice Press
An Imprint of The Haworth Press, Inc.

Divorce and the Next Generation: Perspectives for Young Adults in the New Millennium

Divorce and the Next Generation: Perspectives for Young Adults in the New Millennium has been co-published simultaneously as *Journal of Divorce & Remarriage*, Volume 34, Numbers 3/4 2001.

The *Journal of Divorce & Remarriage* Monographic "Separates"

(formerly the *Journal of Divorce* series)*

Below is a list of "separates," which in serials librarianship means a special issue simultaneously published as a special journal issue or double-issue *and* as a "separate" hardbound monograph. (This is a format which we also call a "DocuSerial.")

"Separates" are published because specialized libraries or professionals may wish to purchase a specific thematic issue by itself in a format which can be separately cataloged and shelved, as opposed to purchasing the journal on an on-going basis. Faculty members may also more easily consider a "separate" for classroom adoption.

"Separates" are carefully classified separately with the major book jobbers so that the journal tie-in can be noted on new book order slips to avoid duplicate purchasing.

You may wish to visit Haworth's website at . . .

http://www.HaworthPress.com

. . . to search our online catalog for complete tables of contents of these separates and related publications.

You may also call 1-800-HAWORTH (outside US/Canada: 607-722-5857), or Fax: 1-800-895-0582 (outside US/Canada: 607-771-0012), or e-mail at:

getinfo@haworthpressinc.com

Divorce and the Next Generation: Perspectives for Young Adults in the New Millennium, edited by Craig A. Everett, PhD (Vol. 34, No. 3/4, 2001). *"Provides important insights into the controversy surrounding parented divorce. . . . Addresses the impact of divorce on intimate relationships development in adolescents." (Dr. Patrick C. McKenry, Professor, The Ohio State University, Department of Human Development and Family Science, Columbus, Ohio)*

Child Custody: Legal Decisions and Family Outcomes, edited by Craig A. Everett, PhD (Vol. 28, No. 1/2, 1998). *"A library must for all family therapists, attorneys, and judges who work with families impacted by divorce. . . . This interesting and scholarly book will help professionals working in the field of divorce put some theory behind their interventions!" (Madge Holmes, PhD, Psychology Coordinator, Chapman University, Monterey, California)*

Divorce and Remarriage: International Studies, edited by Craig A. Everett, PhD (Vol. 26, No. 3/4, 1997). *Gives you important recent research on divorce and remarriage reflecting international and cultural patterns and research issues.*

Understanding Stepfamilies: Their Structure and Dynamics, edited by Craig A. Everett, PhD (Vol. 24, No. 1/2, 1996). *Contributing authors offer unique theoretical approaches to understanding stepfamily typologies and behaviors.*

The Economics of Divorce: The Effects on Parents and Children, edited by Craig A. Everett, PhD (Vol. 22, No. 1/2, 1994). *Focuses on the issues of work, employment, and financial support after divorce and how these issues affect the parents, children, and home environments of divorced families.*

The Stepfamily Puzzle: Intergenerational Influences, edited by Craig A. Everett, PhD (Vol. 19, No. 3/4, 1993). *"Offers the clinician valuable insights. . . . Deals with many aspects of stepfamily functioning and factors that influence stepfamily life. It would be an asset to any therapist working with stepfamilies." (Journal of Family Psychotherapy)*

Divorce and the Next Generation: Effects on Young Adults' Patterns of Intimacy and Expectations for Marriage, edited by Craig A. Everett, PhD (Vol. 18, No. 3/4, 1993). *"Contains ample interesting information. . . . Particularly useful for clinicians who work in the area of divorce." (The Canadian Family Psychologist)*

The Consequences of Divorce: Economic and Custodial Impact on Children and Adults, edited by Craig A. Everett, PhD (Vol. 16, No. 1/2/3/4, 1992). *"A wealth of findings relevant for therapists working with families or couples grappling with divorce. . . . Experienced and inexperienced therapists alike will find something of interest in this book." (The British Journal of Psychiatry)*

Marital Instability and Divorce Outcomes: Issues for Therapists and Educators, edited by Craig A. Everett, PhD (Vol. 15, No. 1/2, 1991). *"I would recommend the book to those desiring exposure to a wide variety of information about marital instability and divorce outcomes." (Journal of Marriage and the Family)*

Women and Divorce/Men and Divorce: Gender Differences in Separation, Divorce, and Remarriage, edited by Sandra S. Volgy, PhD (Vol. 14, No. 3/4, 1991). *"Opens the door to studies which will compare similar variables for each gender." (Dale Brotherton, PhD, Associate Professor, Montana State University; Clinical Member, AAMFT)*

Children of Divorce: Developmental and Clinical Issues, edited by Craig A. Everett, PhD* (Vol. 12, No. 2/3, 1989). *"An excellent book covering a number of aspects of divorce. . . . The book gives a good feeling of the complexity of the effects of divorce on children and the roles of related variables." (The Brown University Family Therapy Letter)*

Minority and Ethnic Issues in the Divorce Process, edited by Craig A. Everett, PhD* (Vol. 11, No. 2, 1988). *This important book provides rare insights into the unique factors involved in the divorce process for minority and ethnic populations.*

The Divorce Process: A Handbook for Clinicians, edited by Craig A. Everett, PhD* (Vol. 10, No. 1/2, 1987). *"The book's strength lies in the descriptive papers which provide reports of empirical studies . . . exploring the boundaries and characteristics of the divorcing and remarried populations and their families." (Australian Psychologist)*

Divorce Mediation: Perspectives on the Field, edited by Craig A. Everett, PhD* (Vol. 8, No. 3/4, 1985). *"This book has something to offer mediators and non-mediators, and students and professionals alike. It provides a descriptive overview of a new and growing profession." (The Family Psychologist)*

Therapists, Lawyers, and Divorcing Spouses, edited by Esther Oshiver Fisher, PhD, EdD, and Mitchell Salem Fisher, MHL, PhD, JD* (Vol. 6, No. 1/2, 1982). *Experts explore the need for cooperation between the law and helping professions in order to lessen the trauma of the divorce process.*

Impact of Divorce on the Extended Family, edited by Esther Oshiver Fisher, PhD, EdD* (Vol. 5, No. 1/2, 1982). *A valuable study of the various impacts of divorce on the extended family of the divorced or divorcing couple.*

Published by

The Haworth Clinical Practice Press™, 10 Alice Street, Binghamton, Ny 13904-1580 USA.

The Haworth Clinical Practice Press™, is an imprint of The Haworth Press, Inc., 10 Alice Street, Binghamton, NY 13904-1580 USA.

Cover design by Thomas J. Mayshock Jr.

Divorce and the Next Generation: Perspectives for Young Adults in the New Millennuim has been co-published simultaneously as *Journal of Divorce & Remarriage™*, Volume 34, Numbers 3/4 2001.

Library of Congress Cataloging-in-Publication Data

Divorce and the next generation : perspectives for young adults in the new millennium / Craig A. Everett, editor.
    p. cm.
    Published also as v. 34, no. 3/4, 2001 of Journal of divorce & remarriage.
    Includes bibliographical references and index.
    ISBN 0-7890-1411-4 (alk. paper)–ISBN 0-7890-1412-2 (alk. paper)
    1. Young adults–Psychology. 2. Interpersonal relations. 3. Children of divorecd parents–Psychology. 4. Parent and child. I. Everett, Craig A. II. Journal of divorce & remarriage.
HQ799 . 5. D57 2001
305 . 242–dc21

                                           2001039833

Divorce
and the Next Generation:
Perspectives for Young Adults
in the New Millennium

Craig A. Everett, PhD
Editor

Divorce and the Next Generation: Perspectives for Young Adults in the New Millennium has been co-published simultaneously as *Journal of Divorce & Remarriage*, Volume 34, Numbers 3/4 2001.

The Haworth Clinical Practice Press
An Imprint of
The Haworth Press, Inc.
New York

Indexing, Abstracting & Website/Internet Coverage

This section provides you with a list of major indexing & abstracting services. That is to say, each service began covering this periodical during the year noted in the right column. Most Websites which are listed below have indicated that they will either post, disseminate, compile, archive, cite or alert their own Website users with research-based content from this work. (This list is as current as the copyright date of this publication.)

Abstracting, Website/Indexing Coverage . . . . Year When Coverage Began

- *Academic Search Elite (EBSCO)* **1996**
- *Applied Social Sciences Index & Abstracts (ASSIA) (Online:*
  ASSI via Data-Star) (CD-Rom: ASSIA Plus)
  <http://www.bowker-saur.co.uk> **1993**
- *CNPIEC Reference Guide: Chinese National Directory*
  of Foreign Periodicals **1995**
- *Contemporary Women's Issues* **1998**
- *e-psyche, LLC <www.e-psyche.net>* **2001**
- *Expanded Academic ASAP <www.galegroup.com>* **1992**
- *Expanded Academic Index* **1995**
- *Family Studies Database (online and CD/ROM) <www.nisc.com>*. . . . **1996**
- *FINDEX <www.publist.com>* **1999**
- *GenderWatch <www.slinfo.com>* **1999**
- *Guide to Social Science & Religion in Periodical Literature* **1999**
- *Index Guide to College Journals (core list compiled by integrating*
  48 indexes frequently used to support undergraduate programs
  in small to medium sized libraries) **1999**
- *Index to Periodical Articles Related to Law* **1990**

(continued)

Special Bibliographic Notes related to special journal issues (separates) and indexing/abstracting:

- indexing/abstracting services in this list will also cover material in any "separate" that is co-published simultaneously with Haworth's special thematic journal issue or DocuSerial. Indexing/abstracting usually covers material at the article/chapter level.
- monographic co-editions are intended for either non-subscribers or libraries which intend to purchase a second copy for their circulating collections.
- monographic co-editions are reported to all jobbers/wholesalers/approval plans. The source journal is listed as the "series" to assist the prevention of duplicate purchasing in the same manner utilized for books-in-series.
- to facilitate user/access services all indexing/abstracting services are encouraged to utilize the co-indexing entry note indicated at the bottom of the first page of each article/chapter/contribution.
- this is intended to assist a library user of any reference tool (whether print, electronic, online, or CD-ROM) to locate the monographic version if the library has purchased this version but not a subscription to the source journal.
- individual articles/chapters in any Haworth publication are also available through the Haworth Document Delivery Service (HDDS).

Divorce and the Next Generation: Perspectives for Young Adults in the New Millennium

CONTENTS

EMOTIONAL AND MENTAL HEALTH ISSUES

ABOUT THE EDITOR

Craig A. Everett, PhD, is a marriage and family therapist in private practice in Tucson, Arizona, and Director of the Arizona Institute of Family Therapy. In addition to more than 20 years of experience in clinical practice, he was formerly President of the American Association for Marriage and Family Therapy. Dr. Everett's previous positions include Director of Family Therapy Training and Associate Professor at both Florida State University and Auburn University. He has been the editor of the *Journal of Divorce & Remarriage* since 1983 and is an editorial board member of six professional journals.

Introduction

There have been many studies which have identified and tracked the post-divorce adjustment of children and adolescents. However, there are more subtle concerns as to whether the patterns of family conflict, marital animosity, and divorce will be transmitted to the next generation of adolescents and young adults who are now developing intimate attachments and beginning to select mates. Some of these children of divorce seem to rush into a marriage as an escape from their unhappy family experiences or in pursuit of a magical "fix" for the intimacy they may have missed growing-up. Others appear to pursue unhappy serial relationships, replicating mate selection patterns from their families of origin with domestic violence and alcoholism present. Even others often seem confused about their commitments and expectations for marriage and parenthood.

A previous volume, *Divorce and the Next Generation: Effects of Young Adults' Patterns of Intimacy and Expectations for Marriage,* published in 1993, addressed the issue of "how the experience of divorce in one generation may influence the next generation's approach to and preparedness for marriage." It is clear to researchers, clinicians, and educators that the common place experience of divorce among parents leaves a sweeping legacy of issues for the children in areas of self-esteem, security, identity, peer relationships, views of intimacy, and their own anticipation of marriage.

Many studies continue to assess the post-divorce adjustment of children and adolescents, particularly with regard to concerns for their social and academic achievements. However, few studies address issues that can be viewed as somewhat predictive of these children's

[Haworth co-indexing entry note]: "Introduction." Everett, Craig A. Co-published simultaneously in *Journal of Divorce & Remarriage* (The Haworth Clinical Practice Press, an imprint of The Haworth Press, Inc.) Vol. 34, No. 3/4, 2001, pp. 1-2; and: *Divorce and the Next Generation: Perspectives for Young Adults in the New Millennium* (ed: Craig A. Everett) The Haworth Clinical Practice Press, an imprint of The Haworth Press, Inc., 2001, pp. 1-2. Single or multiple copies of this article are available for a fee from The Haworth Document Delivery Service [1-800-342-9678, 9:00 a.m. - 5:00 p.m. (EST). E-mail address: getinfo@haworthpressinc.com].

expectations of adult intimate relationships, as well as of their overall emotional well-being in the future. This second volume will provide an ongoing look at these issues.

Many of these studies rely upon "captive" populations from college and high school settings. Despite these inherent limitations, the studies nevertheless provide a window to view how this next generation of adolescents and young adults from divorced families are functioning emotionally in their primary milieu and how they are performing in the formative stages of developing intimate relationships. Of particular note in this volume are studies on gender perceptions, self-esteem, attitudes toward romantic and intimate relationships, and mental health. It is hoped that these findings will not only stimulate further research but will provide helpful data to clinicians and family life educators.

Craig A. Everett
Tucson, AZ

INTRODUCTORY ISSUES

How Young Adults Perceive Parental Divorce: The Role of Their Relationships with Their Fathers and Mothers

Shmuel Shulman
Miri Scharf
Daniel Lumer
Offer Maurer

SUMMARY. The aim of this study was to examine the extent to which perception of parental divorce among young adults is related to their recounting of the relationships with their parents. Interviews were held

Shmuel Shulman, PhD, is Associate Professor, Department of Psychology, Bar Ilan University, Israel. Miri Scharf, PhD, is Lecturer at the Faculty of Education, University of Haifa, Israel. Daniel Lumer, MA, is Clinical Child Psychologist and has completed his studies at the Department of Psychology, Bar Ilan University, Ramat Gan, Israel. Offer Maurer, BA, is a doctoral student in clinical psychology at the Department of Psychology, Bar Ilan University, Ramat Gan, Israel.

Address correspondence to: Shmuel Shulman, Department of Psychology, Bar Ilan University, 52900 Ramat Gan, Israel (E-mail: shulman@mail.biu.ac.il).

[Haworth co-indexing entry note]: "How Young Adults Perceive Parental Divorce: The Role of Their Relationships with Their Fathers and Mothers." Shulman, Shmuel et al. Co-published simultaneously in *Journal of Divorce & Remarriage* (The Haworth Clinical Practice Press, an imprint of The Haworth Press, Inc.) Vol. 34, No. 3/4, 2001, pp. 3-17; and: *Divorce and the Next Generation: Perspectives for Young Adults in the New Millennium* (ed: Craig A. Everett) The Haworth Press, Inc., 2001, pp. 3-17. Single or multiple copies of this article are available for a fee from The Haworth Document Delivery Service [1-800-342-9678, 9:00 a.m. - 5:00 p.m. (EST). E-mail address: getinfo@haworthpressinc.com].

3

with 51 (30 female and 21 male) Israeli young adults involved in a romantic relationship and whose parents had divorced. Participants were asked to talk about how they felt about and understood the divorce currently. In addition, subjects were asked to talk about their relationships with their mothers and fathers. Analyses of young adults' recounts showed the perception of divorce to be multifaceted. They did not describe high levels of anger or current sense of loss but recalled past loss. Yet despite the recalled past loss, young adults described the divorce in an integrative manner. The quality of relationships with fathers more than with mothers was associated with how parental divorce was perceived. Quality of paternal presence during childhood as well as maturity of current relationship with the father, though lower than that with the mother, were related not only to lower levels of anger or sense of loss in the past, but also to a more integrative perception of the divorce and lower sense of current loss. The special role of fathers after divorce is discussed. *[Article copies available for a fee from The Haworth Document Delivery Service: 1-800-342-9678. E-mail address: <getinfo@ haworthpressinc.com> Website: <http://www.HaworthPress.com> © 2001 by The Haworth Press, Inc. All rights reserved.]*

KEYWORDS. Parental divorce, young adults, parent-child relationships, fathers

Recent research has started to deal with the long-term impact of childhood family disruption on young adults' adjustment. In a longitudinal study, Wallerstein (1991) reported that almost half of the young adults raised in divorced families were worried, underachieving, self-deprecating, and sometimes angry young men and women. In addition, they revealed problems in their relationships that included early marriages that ended in divorce. Zill, Morrison, and Coiro (1993) also found in young adults from disrupted families poorer relationships with their parents, as well as elevated levels of emotional distress, problem behavior, and a higher chance of dropping out of high school. Other studies pointed to the negative impact of parental divorce on expectations and attitudes about marriage (Gabardi & Rosen, 1991). Young adults whose parents had divorced were more likely to believe that love relationships would not last (Southworth & Conard, 1987), and were more pessimistic about marriage (Jennings, Salts & Smith, 1991). When describing their current dating partners, 82 percent of young adults whose parents had divorced indicated that they did not fully trust their partner (Duran-Aydintug, 1997).

This study attempted to understand why divorce continues to be troubling for children and what might alleviate the sense of loss. Ideas originating in attachment theory suggest that it is not just the loss or trauma that affects an individual's behavior; it is also important to know how the trauma is appraised and represented in order to assess its subsequent impact on an individual. In line with this assumption, this study focused on how young adults perceived, understood, and attributed meaning to their parents' divorce, which they had experienced when they were children. In particular, we explored the extent to which the nature and quality of relationships with parents in the divorced family was related to the way the divorce was understood by young adults.

Several conditions and reasons have been suggested to explain why divorce might be troubling for later adjustment of children. Studies on adult children of divorce showed that women were more burdened by memories of the breakup of the marriage (Wallerstein, 1991). Sanders, Halford, and Behrens (1999) found that couples in which the woman's parents had divorced showed more negative communication during conflict discussions. The age of the child at the time of divorce was also described as affecting the impact of parental marital disruption. Earlier studies claimed that the younger the child at the time of divorce, the more severe the child's reactions were (Hetherington, 1979; Kurdrek & Sieski, 1980). The authors of these studies suggested that older children had more cognitive capabilities to understand divorce and its meaning. Recent findings, however, show that in the long run, young adults who were younger than six when their parents divorced showed better adjustment than those whose parents divorced when they were six or older (Grant, Smith, Sinclair & Salts, 1993).

A number of studies found that intense interpersonal conflict between divorced parents was destructive to young people's ability to form intimate relationships (Franklin, Janoff-Bulman, & Roberts, 1990; Hayashi & Strickland, 1998). Conflicts erode the quality of relationships the child can have with either parent by forcing the child into loyalty triangles, thus exposing him or her to a less than adaptive model of close relationships. Persistence of conflict between parents even after divorce further interferes with children's adjustment and the development of communication skills (Katler, 1987; Sanders et al., 1999). Together, these studies suggest that demographic factors such as gender or age at the time of divorce or the severity of parental conflict prior to or after the divorce will affect how the experience of divorce is consolidated by an individual.

Applying a social constructionism approach, Kurdek (1993) suggested that the appraisal of the events is more important that their mere occurrence. Applied to the study of divorce, this approach considers individuals, in particular young adults, as active in interpreting their past experience and their ability to cope with and contend with negative memories (Arditti & Prouty, 1999).

Attachment theory, and more specifically Main's (Main, Kaplan, & Cassidy, 1985; Main & Hesse, 1990) deliberations on adults' attachment representation, shed further light on the phenomenon of adults' resolution of childhood loss or trauma. Pearson, Cohn, Cowan, and Cowan (1994) identified an adult attachment type they termed "earned security." These individuals described their parents as rejecting or neglectful. However, unlike adults classified as insecure, they were able to overcome their difficult childhood and had a coherent perspective of it. As parents, the earned-secures, like the continuous-secures, demonstrated more warmth and structure with their preschool children than did their insecure counterparts.

Pianta, Marvin, Britner, and Borowitz (1996) examined maternal representations of the trauma of giving birth to a disabled child. The birth of a disabled child is a period of great stress for parents, disruption of family routine, and above all a challenge to parental expectations for the child and increased feelings of guilt. Some parents are able to resolve this trauma after a period of time. The resolution is reflected in re-orientation to the present and future, a realistic view of the child's condition and skills, a balanced view of the impact on themselves, and the capacity to tell their story in a clear and coherent manner. Difficulty in resolution of the trauma is reflected inability to come to terms with the child's condition, an active search for a different diagnosis and for reasons why the trauma occurred, and an unbalanced perception of the impact on themselves (denial or victimization). When recounting their story, confusion and mental disorganization are predominant.

The ability to resolve a sense of loss depends on whether traumas have been repeated and occurring over long periods of time (Adam, Keller, & West, 1995). When parental conflict or animosity does not decrease and parents are emotionally unavailable for their children, marital disruption can be a source of continuous trauma for a child.

However, a supportive relationship with one parent despite the marital disruption may diminish the sense of loss and allow children to develop a more balanced understanding of the divorce. Pearson et al. (1994) described how a supportive relationship with one parent may counterbalance the difficulties with the other, and enable the child to earn a sense of security. Phelps, Belsky, and Crnic (1998) also showed that a secure attachment with one parent may compensate for the insecure attachment with the other parent.

Three major hypotheses were examined in this study. First, we hypothesized that the gender and age of the child during divorce would be related to the way the child, when a young adult, understood the parents' divorce. Young women would report a less integrative perception of parental divorce than young men. And young men, in contrast to young women, would report less a sense of loss. A less integrative perception of divorce would be reported by young adults who were younger when their parents divorced than by those who were older. We also assumed that the way parental divorce was understood would be related to the intensity of parental conflict during the divorce and in subsequent years. Finally, in line with the focus of this study, it was hypothesized that the quality of the resolution of the divorce trauma would be related to the quality of relationships with parents.

After the breakup of a marriage children more commonly stay with their mother. Yet statistics show that the vast majority of fathers remain continuously involved in their children's lives (Mott, 1990). Moreover, to conclude that relationships between fathers and their children after divorce become devitalized is incorrect and an over-generalization (Arditti & Prouty, 1999). In many cases fathers continue to remain close to their children despite objective obstacles, and maintain their contact and sense of emotional availability in different modes. Accordingly, in this study we explored the possible contribution of the quality of relationship with each parent to the way young adults perceived their parents' divorce and its impact on them.

METHOD

Participants

This study was based on data collected from 51 Israeli college students (30 females and 21 males) and was part of a larger project with students whose parents had divorced. Purposive sampling techniques were used, and the research team posted notices at two universities in the center of Israel. More women than men contacted the research team, so additional announcements were made in order to obtain the 21 male subjects.

Participants were not married, but had a romantic partner. The age range of the subjects was 19 to 29 years (mean = 23.9 years). Mean age reported at the time of parental divorce was 11.8 years. Twenty-three percent of the mothers remarried; 63 percent of fathers remarried. The average length of time participants reported living in a single-parent household was 10.3 years.

Measures and Procedure

Participants were interviewed and asked to talk about their parents' divorce: "Please describe your parents' divorce: what you remember from that time, any specific memories"; "What is the meaning of the divorce to you?" "How do you consider it today?" The verbal samples were tape-recorded and transcribed, and were rated independently by two raters on five scales developed in line with the salient topics found in the transcripts and with the theoretical assumption of this paper. The latter suggested an examination of an individual's ability to resolve the loss inflicted by the divorce and to perceive the divorce in a comprehensive manner. The five-point (1-low, 5-high) rating scales were as follows:

1. Integrative perception of the divorce: The degree to which the subject is aware of the complexity of the divorce, is able to understand it from mother's, father's, and children's perspective, and has a coherent view of the divorce. (A low point refers to description of facts, lack of reflective understanding, no insight; a high point refers to complex description of events, of parents' motives, and ability to understand events from different perspectives.)
2. Sense of loss in the past: The intensity of loss that the subject describes having experienced during the divorce and during childhood.
3. Sense of current loss: The intensity with which the subject currently experiences loss or not achieving goals in life due to parental divorce.

4. Anger: The intensity of anger or negative emotions when describing the divorce.
5. Lack of memory: The extent to which the subject is unable to remember details from the time of the divorce, and presents a very general and superficial description of the past events.

Agreement between raters ranged between .67 and .84. All disagreements were conferenced to consensus.

In addition, subjects were also asked to talk for five minutes about their mother and their relationship with her, and for additional five minutes about their father. The verbal samples were tape-recorded, transcribed, and were rated independently by two raters on the following five scales. Scales were developed in line with the salient topics found in the transcripts and with theoretical dimensions describing parent-child relationships as formulated in the attachment theory and family models. The five 5-point (1–low, 5–high) rating scales were as follows:

1. Mother/father–Quality of emotional presence during childhood: The extent to which a parent is described as being emotionally available during childhood.
2. Maturity level of current relationship with mother/father: The extent to which current relationship is interdependent, reality-oriented, and of mutual respect.
3. Idealization of mother/father: The extent to which a parent is perceived as ideal or almost perfect.
4. Devaluation of mother/father: The extent to which a parent is described as worthless and as a failure.
5. Role reversal–mother/father: The degree to which parent exploited the child, who played an adult role prematurely.

Agreement between raters ranged between .69 and .96. All disagreements were conferenced to consensus.

Parental Conflict

Items of this scale are adapted from ICQ-Interparental Conflict Questionnaire (Forehand & McCombs, 1989), which assesses frequency of parental conflict (quarrels, arguments, "heated" argument, etc.) at three points in time: during divorce, three years after divorce, and currently. Subjects were asked to indicate on a scale from 1 to 7 the frequency or intensity of the various indices of conflict. Alpha Cronbach of the inventory at the three points in time was .81, .64, and .56 respectively.

RESULTS

Young Adults' Perception of Parental Divorce

A MANOVA was conducted with 2 (gender) $\times$ 2 (age at parental divorce before or after age 12 years) levels of between subject and 5 (perception of parental divorce scales) levels of repeated measure within-subject independent variables. Perception of parental divorce was the dependent variable. A significant main effect emerged for perception of parental divorce, $F(4\ 48) = 24.78, p < .0001$. In addition, there were two-way interactions between age at parental divorce and perception of parental divorce, $F(4, 48) = 4.11\ p < .001$, and gender and perception of parental divorce, $F(4, 48) = 2.50, p < .06$. A follow-up ANOVA and Scheffe contrasts specified differences between perception of divorce scales, as well as age at divorce and gender differences on each perception of divorce scale.

The first set of follow-up ANOVA compared perception of divorce scales across age at divorce and gender and showed that young adults rated differently the perception of divorce scales. As can be seen in Figure 1, integrative perception of the divorce and sense of loss in the past were rated as highest. Sense of current loss was rated at intermediate level, whereas anger and lack of memory were rated the lowest.

The second set of follow-up comparisons revealed two significant differences with regard to age at divorce for sense of loss in the past and sense of current loss scales, $F\ (1, 49) = 5.00, p < .05$, and $F\ (1, 49) = 6.69, p < .01$, respectively. Young adults whose parent had divorced when they were younger than 12 years reported a higher sense of loss in the past and sense of current loss than young adults whose parents had divorced when they were older than 12 years; $M = 3.62\ (SD = 1.15)$ and $M = 3.08, SD = 1.08)$ versus $M = 2.75\ (SD = 1.43)$ and $M = 2.02\ (SD = 1.27)$.

The third set of follow-up comparisons revealed one significant

FIGURE 1. Indices of Perception of Parental Divorce

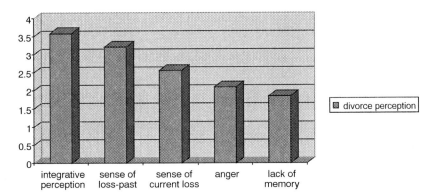

gender difference for the integrative perception of divorce scale, F $(1,49) = 4.31, p < .05$. Males reported a more integrative perception of parental divorce than did females, M = 3.91 (SD = 0.94) and M = 3.35 (SD = 1.13), respectively.

Perception of Parental Divorce and Parental Conflict

Pearson correlations between perception of parental divorce and level of parental conflict during divorce, five years after divorce and currently, were conducted. Results revealed only two significant correlations. Level of parental conflict during divorce was related to lower integrative perception of the divorce, $r = .30, p < .05$. In addition, level of current parental conflict was related to level of current sense of loss, $r = .29, p < .05$.

Perception of Parental Divorce and Quality of Relationships with Parents

Prior to an examination of the associations between perception of parental divorce and quality of relationships with mothers and fathers, t-tests were conducted to compare the quality of relationships with both parents. Means for mothers and for fathers across the five rating scales are presented in Figure 2. As can be seen, young adults described their mother as more emotionally available in the past and themselves as having more mature relationships currently. Fathers

FIGURE 2. Young Adults' Quality of Relationships with Mothers and Fathers

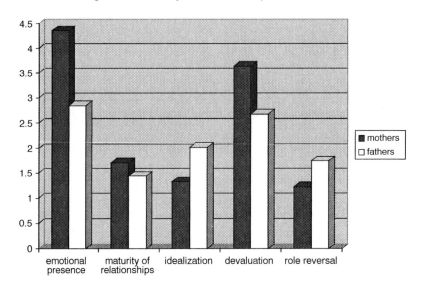

were more idealized than mothers but also more described as being involved in a relationship characterized by role reversal.

Pearson correlations between perceptions of parental divorce and quality of relationships with mothers and with fathers revealed similar patterns for males and females and therefore were collapsed for the analyses, which are presented here. No significant correlations between quality of relationship with mother and with father were found. The one exception was with regard to "role reversal." Role reversal with mother was significantly associated with role reversal with regard to father, $r = .27, p < .05$. Since living or not living with a parent could affect the quality of relationship with that parent, type of custody was controlled. Correlations of perception of parental divorce and quality of relationships with mother controlled for whether the young adult was or was not under maternal custody. Correlations of perception of parental divorce and quality of relationships with father controlled for whether the young adult was or was not under paternal custody.

Partial correlations between perceptions of parental divorce and quality of relationships with mother and with father are presented in Table 1. As can be seen, with regard to relationships with mothers, 5 out of 25 correlations were significant, whereas with regard to rela-

TABLE 1. Partial correlations between perceptions of parental divorce and quality of relationships with mothers and fathers

	Integrative perception	Sense of loss in the past	Sense of current loss	Anger	Lack of memory
Emotional presence–M	.09	−.07	−.12	−.06	−.02
Maturity of relationships–M	−.03	−.32*	−.20	−.26*	.14
Idealization–M	.07	.13	.20	.33*	−.02
Devaluation–M	.18	.24	.20	.38*	−.12
Role-reversal–M	.05	.00	.13	.36*	−.11
Emotional presence–F	.48**	−.32*	−.46**	−.33*	−.56**
Maturity of relationships–F	.29*	−.27*	−.45**	−.43**	−.33*
Idealization–F	.03	.17	.11	.18	−.10
Devaluation–F	−.18	.22	.64***	.57***	.01
Role-reversal–F	.14	.12	.19	.49**	−.35*

Note: + p < .10, *p < .05, **p < .01, ***p < .001

tionships with fathers 14 out of 25 correlations were significant. This proportion suggests that young adults' perception of parental divorce was more related to the quality of their relationship with father than with mother, X^2 (df = 1) = 6.86, $p < .01$.

As can be seen, quality of relationship with mother was mainly related to level of anger when describing the divorce. Higher idealization and devaluation of the mother as well as higher degree of role reversal were related to higher level of young adults' anger. In addition, maturity of current relationship with the mother was related to lower feelings of anger when describing the divorce, as well as lower sense of loss experienced in the past.

Quality of paternal presence during childhood as well as maturity of current relationship with the father, though lower than that with the mother, were related not only to lower levels of anger or sense of loss in the past but were also associated with a more integrative perception of the divorce and lower sense of current loss. In addition, maturity of current relationship with father and level of role reversal with regard to father were related to the extent to which the young adult was able to remember details from the time of the divorce. In sum, the quality of the relationship with the father was related to many indices of how parents' divorce was perceived by a young adult.

DISCUSSION

Results of this study suggest that young adults' perception of parental divorce is multifaceted and consists of feelings, recollections, and current state of mind. In this study, young adults did not describe high levels of anger or current sense of loss. They described the divorce in detail, and vividly emphasized the sense of loss they had experienced when the divorce took place. However, despite the recalled past loss, as young adults they were able to perceive the divorce in an integrative manner and understand it from the perspective of both parents. Generally, this suggests that young adults are probably capable of coming to terms with painful events from the past. This is similar to Pearson et al.'s (1994) descriptions of individuals who were able to overcome childhood difficulties in a less than optimal upbringing.

It was interesting to find that males showed a higher ability to recount an integrative description of the parental divorce. This can explain why women were found to be more affected by parental divorce even after they became adults (Sanders, Halford, & Behrens, 1999; Wallerstein, 1991). But our results cannot explain why women presented a less integrative perception of parental divorce; only a future study can further verify this finding.

Young adults whose parents divorced before they were 12-years-old described a higher sense of current and past loss. This is in line with previous studies indicating that the younger the child at the time of the divorce, the more severe the child's reactions will be in the future (Hetherington, 1979; Kudrek & Sieski, 1980). Past and present parental conflict also affected young adults' ability to overcome the impact of the divorce and integrate it.

The major finding of this study, however, is the fact that the quality of relationships with the father was an important factor in how the child would perceive the divorce when he or she became an adult. Note that only ten percent of the young adults in this study reported that they were raised in paternal custody. This suggests the centrality of the father even when the child no longer lives with him and even though fathers were described as less close.

Traditionally, divorced fathers were described as remote, showing lack of effort and involvement (Emery & Forehand, 1994; Shulman & Seiffge-Krenke,1997). Moreover, single fathers were described as less involved with their adult children (Marks, 1991) or even as having strained relationships with their adult children (Wallerstein & Lewis, 1998). Arditti and Prouty (1999) also reported on the basis of interview data that it was common among young adults to describe their fathers as disengaged or even lost. However, there were young people who described their active attempts they made to regain their fathers. In one case a young person's way of coping with diminishing paternal involvement was to say "I know he still cares" (p. 77). The relationship with the non-resident father may possibly be reactivated by the young adult. Arditti and Prouty state that "before jumping to conclusions about the inevitability of devitalized relationships, researchers and practitioners alike should consider the implications of nonresidence and infrequent contact. Relationships that continue to remain close despite these obstacles are worthy of in-depth, follow-up investigation. Fathers' attempts to maintain contact with children via letters, e-mail, telephone, and other means positively impact relationships and prevent disengagement (p. 77).

It is important to state that the results of this study, like those of many previous studies, are based on children's reports. Information based on fathers' reports may shed further light on how non-resident fathers feel about their children, and whether their feelings are acknowledged by the children. The question, however, is why the role of the father, who in most cases was not the custodial parent, is so important for how divorce is perceived. The father's remoteness perhaps does not reflect lack of interest or detachment. The child's knowledge that the father has a positive attitude toward him or her may compensate for the shorter periods of time they spend together (Shulman & Seiffge-Krenke, 1997) and facilitate the child's ability to perceive the divorce from the perspective of both parents.

A similar trend was reported among non-divorced families. Although mothers were found to have a more intimate relationship than fathers with their adolescent children, level of maternal intimacy did not predict positive adolescent functioning. Paternal intimacy, however, despite being less than maternal intimacy, did predict adolescent functioning (LeCroy, 1988).

The results of this study highlight the importance of father-child relationships after divorce. Though non-resident fathers are less involved with their children, their relationship is important for how the divorce will be recounted by the child when he or she reaches adulthood. A certain level of relationship with their fathers facilitates young adults' attainment of a more integrative view of the parental divorce, which could in turn help in the children's own close relationships.

REFERENCES

Adam, K. S., Keller, A. E. S., & West, M. (1995). Attachment organization and vulnerability to loss, separation, and abuse in disturbed adolescents. In S. Goldberg, R. Muir, & J. Kerr (Eds.), *Attachment theory, social, developmental, and clinical perspectives* (pp. 309-341). Hillsdale NJ: The Analytic Press.

Arditti, J. A., & Prouty, A. M. (1999). Change, disengagement, and renewal: Relationship dynamics between young adults and their fathers after divorce. *Journal of Marriage & Family Counseling, 25*, 61-81.

Duran-Aydintug, C. (1997). Adult children of divorce revisited: When they speak up. *Journal of Divorce & Remarriage, 27*, 71-83.

Emery, R. E., & Forehand, R. (1994). Parental divorce and children's well-being: A focus on resilience. In R.J. Haggerty, N. Garmezy, M. Rutter, & L. Shrrod (Eds.), *Risk and resilience in children and adolescents* (pp. 64-99). London: Cambridge University Press.

Forehand, R., & McCombs, A. (1989). The nature of interparental conflict of married and divorced parents: Implications for young adolescents. *Journal of Abnormal Child Psychology*, 235-249.

Franklin, K. M., Janoff-Bulman, R., & Roberts, J. E. (1990). Long-term impact of parental divorce on optimism and trust: Changes in general assumptions or narrow beliefs? *Journal of Personality and Social Psychology, 50*, 743-755.

Garbardi, L. & Rosen, A. (1991) Differences between college students from divorced and intact families. *Journal of Divorce & Remarriage, 15*, 175-191.

Grant, L. S., Smith, T. A., Sinclair, J. J., & Salts, C. J. (1993). The impact of parental divorce on college adjustment. *Journal of Divorce & Remarriage, 19*, 183-193.

Hayashi, G. M., & Strickland, B. R. (1998). Long-term effects of parental divorce on love relationships: Divorce as attachment disruption. *Journal of Social and Personal Relationships, 15*, 23-38.

Hetherington, E. M. (1979). Divorce: A child's perspective. *American Psychologist, 34*, 851-858.

Jennings, A. M., Salts, C. J., & Smith, T. A. (1991). Attitudes toward marriage: Effects of parental conflict, family structure, and gender. *Journal of Divorce & Remarriage, 17*, 67-79.

Katler, N. (1987). Long-term effects of divorce on children: A developmental vulner-ability model. *American Journal of Orthopsychiatry, 57,* 587-600.

Kurdek, L. A. (1993). Predicting marital dissolution: A 5-year prospective longitudi-nal study of newlywed couples. *Journal of Personality and Social Psychology, 64,* 221-242.

Kurdek, L. A. & Sieski, A. E. (1980). Children's perception of their parents' divorce. *Journal of Divorce, 3,* 339-378.

LeCroy, C. W. (1988). Parent-adolescent intimacy: Impact on adolescent function-ing. *Adolescence, 23,* 137-147.

Main, M., & Hesse, E. (1990). The parents of insecure-disorganized/disoriented infants: Observations and speculations. In M.T. Greenberg, D. Ciccheti, & E.M. Cummings (Eds.), *Attachment in the preschool years: Theory, research and inter-vention* (pp. 161-184). Chicago: University of Chicago Press.

Main, M., Kaplan, N., & Cassidy, J. (1985). Security in infancy, childhood, and adulthood: A move to the level of representation. In I. Bretherton & E. Waters (Eds.), *Growing points of attachment theory and research. Monograph of the Society for Research in Child Development, 50,* (1-2, serial no. 209), 66-104.

Mark, N. (1991). *Remarried and single parents in middle-adulthood: Differences in psychological well-being and relationships with adult children.* Madison, WI: University of Wisconsin, Center for Demography and ecology.

Mott, F. L. (1990). When a father is really gone? Paternal child contact in father absent homes. *Demography, 27,* 499-517.

Pearson, J. L., Cohn, D. A., Cowan, P. A., & Cowan, C.P. (1994). Earned- and continuous-security in adult attachment: Relation to depressive symptomatology and parenting style. *Development and Psychopathology, 6,* 359-373.

Phelps, J. L., Belsky, J., & Crnic, K. (1998). Earned security, daily stress, and parenting: A comparison of five alternative models. *Development and Psycho-pathology, 10,* 21-38.

Pianta, R. C., Marvin, R. S., Britner, P. A., & Borowitz, K. C. (1996). Mothers' resolution of their children's diagnosis: Organized patterns of caregiving repre-sentations. *Infant Mental Health Journal, 17,* 239-256.

Sanders, M. R., Halford, W. K., & Behrens, B. C. (1999) Parental divorce and premarital couple communication. *Journal of Family Psychology, 13,* 60-74.

Shulman, S. & Seiffge-Krenke, I. (1997). *Fathers and adolescents developmental and clinical approaches.* London: Routledge.

Southworth, S., & Conard, S. (1987). Post-divorce contact, relationship with father, and heterosexual trust in female college students. *American Journal of Orthopsy-chiatry, 57,* 371-382.

Wallerstein, J. S. (1991). The long-term effects of divorce on children: A review. *Journal of the American Academy of Child and Adolescent Psychiatry, 30,* 349-360.

Wallerstein, J. S., & Lewis, J. (1998). The long-term impact of divorce on children: A first report from a 25-year study. *Family and Conciliation Courts Review, 36,* 363-383.

Zill, N., Morrison, D. R., & Coiro, M. J. (1993). Long-term effects of parental divorce on parent-child relationships, adjustment, and achievement in young adulthood. *Journal of Family Psychology, 7,* 91-103.

Parental Divorce
and Children's Interpersonal Relationships:
A Meta-Analysis

Jenifer Kunz

SUMMARY. This meta-analysis involved 53 studies that compared the interpersonal relationships (parents, siblings, and peers) of children from divorced homes with those from continuously intact homes. Children from divorced homes had more positive sibling relationships than children from intact homes. Mixed-race samples of children had more negative interpersonal relationships than white samples of children. Younger children from divorced homes experienced a lower quality of mother-child relationship than older children. The quality of relationships are lower for studies conducted more recently when compared with those conducted in earlier decades. Larger samples and studies utilizing attitude measures yielded stronger evidence for a lower quality of interpersonal relationship. Effect sizes were stronger for clinical samples than in studies based on convenience or random samples. *[Article copies available for a fee from The Haworth Document Delivery Service: 1-800-342-9678. E-mail address: <getinfo@haworthpressinc.com> Website: <http://www.HaworthPress.com> © 2001 by The Haworth Press, Inc. All rights reserved.]*

KEYWORDS. Divorce, interpersonal relationships, children, peers, parents

Jenifer Kunz, PhD, is Associate Professor of Sociology, Department of Behavioral Sciences, West Texas A&M University, WTAMU Box 296, Canyon, TX 79016 (Email: jkunz@mail.wtamu.edu).

An earlier version of this paper was presented at the Southwestern Sociological Association Meetings in San Antonio, Texas.

[Haworth co-indexing entry note]: "Parental Divorce and Children's Interpersonal Relationships: A Meta-Analysis." Kunz, Jenifer. Co-published simultaneously in *Journal of Divorce & Remarriage* (The Haworth Clinical Practice Press, an imprint of The Haworth Press, Inc.) Vol. 34, No. 3/4, 2001, pp. 19-47; and: *Divorce and the Next Generation: Perspectives for Young Adults in the New Millennium* (ed: Craig A. Everett) The Haworth Clinical Practice Press, an imprint of The Haworth Press, Inc., 2001, pp. 19-47. Single or multiple copies of this article are available for a fee from The Haworth Document Delivery Service [1-800-342-9678, 9:00 a.m. - 5:00 p.m. (EST). E-mail address: getinfo@haworthpressinc.com].

The impact of divorce on children is an important area of study since every year there are over 1 million children in the United States whose parents separate (National Center for Health Statistics, 1990). For decades family professionals, political leaders, and parents have been concerned about how divorce affects children. Although family researchers have studied the effects of divorce on children's interpersonal relationships for nearly six decades, few firm conclusions have been reached.

Most of the research relating interpersonal relationships to family structure have assessed interpersonal relationships by using some measure of mother-child, father-child, sibling or peer relationship (Hertz-Lazarowitz, Rosenberg, and Guttmann, 1989; Hodges, London, & Colwell, 1990; Shapiro and Wallace, 1987; Wynn and Bowering, 1990). Because interpersonal relationships are critical to social competence, it is important to understand how such relations are affected by divorce.

In her sixty-year literature review of 347 empirical studies, Kunz (1992) concluded that the findings of many studies corroborated that divorce has *negative* consequences on children's interpersonal relationships (Hetherington, Cox, and Cox, 1976; Koch, 1961; Southworth and Schwarz, 1987; Wallen, 1954; Webster-Stratton, 1989). However, other studies demonstrate that interpersonal relationships of divorced children do not differ from those of children whose parents were not divorced (Amato, 1987; Compas and Williams, 1990; Hammond, 1979; Horns and Abbott, 1985; Shybunko, 1989). Still other studies have reported that divorce has a positive effect on children's interpersonal relationships (Brady, Ray, and Zeeb, 1986; Lopez, Campbell, & Watkins, 1988; Nelson, 1982; Nye, 1957). This study will conduct a meta-analysis of the relevant literature in order to clarify the inconsistent findings concerning divorce's impact on children's relationships with parents, siblings and peers.

The present analysis addresses two specific questions: first, how large are the differences between children in divorced and intact families on measures of interpersonal relationships? Second, are these differences larger for some domains of interpersonal relationships than for others?

Meta-analysis is a relatively new statistical technique in family sociology that allows the researcher to conduct a quantitative literature review (Hedges & Olkin, 1985). An effect size measure is computed for each study used in the analysis. Effect sizes express the results of studies in a common metric which enables the researcher to aggregate results across studies to attain general conclusions. Further, effect size can also be related to study characteristics such as size or race included in the sample or the type of analysis used. This allows one to test hypotheses about why studies show different effects.

The second purpose of this analysis is to study characteristics that help explain the variation in effect sizes. Characteristics such as race of sample and age of child can produce different results in studies. For example, Weinraub and Wolf (1983) studied white and African American children and found no significant difference in the quality of mother-child interaction between divorced and intact homes. On the other hand, Hertz-Lazarowitz et al. (1989) sampled 208 white boys and girls and determined that children from divorced families expressed lower levels of trust toward their mothers than those from intact families. Thus, race may affect the relationship between divorce and family relationships.

HYPOTHESES

In 1991, Amato and Keith (1991a) conducted a meta-analysis on 92 studies of parental divorce on the general well-being of children, and they have also recently conducted a meta-analysis of the effects of divorce on adult well-being (Amato & Keith, 1991b). Kunz (1995) has also conducted a meta-analysis on 65 studies that compared the intellectual functioning of children from divorced and intact homes. However, no one has conducted a meta-analysis on the effects of divorce on children's interpersonal relationships, which is the purpose of this paper.

Amato and Keith (1991a) examined ten study characteristics in their analysis: type and size of sample, number of items used to measure outcome, control variables, source of data, sex and age of child in sample, year data were collected, and country where the study was conducted. Kunz (1995) analyzed the following study characteristics: year data were collected, size of sample, age of child, type of sample, ethnicity or race, and source of information on the child. Specific study characteristics that we will examine are: ethnicity or race and age of children in sample, year study was conducted, type and size of sample, and type of measurement used.

Both Amato and Keith (1991a) and Kunz (1995) demonstrated that the consequences of parental divorce were more significant for whites than for mixed-race samples. Amato and Keith (1991b) also concluded that effect sizes were strongest for children in the middle age groups while Kunz (1995) concluded that effect sizes were larger for older children. However, the study conducted by Amato and Keith (1991a) focused on the effects of parental divorce on adult well-being and not specifically on younger children. Both Amato and Keith (1991a) and Kunz (1995) also discovered that for some outcomes, studies published more recently displayed weaker effect sizes than did studies carried out during earlier decades. Because Amato and Keith (1991a) only had two clinical samples for mother-child and father-child relationship outcomes they were not able to elaborate about clinical samples. Although Kunz (1995) found no overall pattern of consistency for type of sample, another study conducted by Amato and Keith (1991b) on the effects of divorce on adult well-being found that effect sizes were significantly stronger in clinical samples than in studies based on community samples. Amato and Keith's (1991a) data focusing specifically on children revealed that results from larger sample studies reported divorce was more detrimental on children's relationships with their mothers, but not their fathers. However, Kunz (1995) concluded that the negative impact of divorce was more substantial for smaller samples than for larger samples. Finally, neither Amato and Keith (1991a) nor Kunz (1995) addressed the type of measurement used in the analysis.

There are several explanations why children from divorced families might have weaker interpersonal relationships (Amato & Keith, 1991a; Kunz, 1995; McLanahan, 1989). One common explanation is the parental absence position. This position implies that if parents are significant resources for a child's development and socialization then two parents would have the advantage over one. However, when children experience a divorce, there is often less involvement with the noncustodial parent. Consequently, these children often experience a decrease in parental attention, assistance direction and supervision (Amato & Keith, 1991a; Kunz, 1995). This also supports the notion of Rollins and Thomas (1979) who said that a decrease in parental support and supervision might contribute to problems, such as less satisfying interpersonal relationships.

Economic disadvantage position is another explanation. This explanation assumes that it is the economic deprivation, and not the family structure per se, that affects the overall well-being of children in divorced families (Amato & Keith, 1991a; Kunz, 1995). Economic stress may, in turn, affect the development of children (Kunz, 1992). For example, children living in poverty might be negatively labeled by society and their peer group. Labeling theory suggests that these children might join deviant subcultures (Jones, Gallagher, & McFalls, 1995) which may, in turn, affect their interpersonal relationships.

Although this analysis will not test these theories, they will help to explain our findings. Based on these perspectives and previous research, we expect the following: (1) Children from divorced homes will experience more negative interpersonal relationships with their parents, siblings, and peer group than children from continuously intact homes; (2) divorce will be more detrimental to mixed-race samples in interpersonal relationships when compared to white samples of children; (3) younger children from divorced homes will experience more negative effects of divorce on their interpersonal relationships when compared to older children from divorced homes; (4) results of studies that are published earlier will have more negative consequences on interpersonal relationships than results of studies published more recently; (5) children who enter a clinical setting are more likely to have received support of counseling in their experience with the divorce; therefore, we predict that the results of studies concerning interpersonal relationships will be more positive among children in clinical when compared to nonclinical samples; (6) children included in larger samples will experience more negative consequences of divorce in their interpersonal relationships when compared to children included in smaller samples; and (7) results of attitude scale measures will have more negative consequences for children's interpersonal relationships than results of studies that used other types of measurement techniques.

METHODOLOGY

Meta-Analysis

This technique enables the researcher to conduct a quantitative literature review (Glass, McGaw, & Smith, 1981; Hedges and Olkin,

1985). One or more *effect sizes* are computed for each study. Each study can have more than one effect size. Because effect size represents the results of a study in a common metric, the results of many studies can be synthesized to reach general conclusions. Effect size can also be related to study characteristics, such as the type of sample or the specific measurement of the dependent variable. Thus, the researcher is able to ascertain, at least partially, why studies produce different results.

Selection of Studies

Fifty-three studies were analyzed in this meta-analysis. To be included in the meta-analysis, studies had to meet the following criteria. First, they had to contain a sample of children living in a single-parent family (through divorce or separation) as well as a sample from intact families. Second, they had to include at least one quantitative measure of interpersonal relationships. Third, information had to be present to allow for the computation of at least one effect size; this involved means and standard deviations, t-values, F-ratios, percentage differences, and chi-square values. Fourth, respondents had to be younger than 25 years of age. Children younger than 25 years of age were included because this study only focused on the effects of divorce on children and young adults. This was the same criteria that was used by Amato and Keith (1991a) and Kunz (1995).

Calculation of Effect Sizes

DSTAT: Software for the Meta-Analytic Review of Research Literatures (Johnson, 1989) was utilized to calculate an effect size. DSTAT utilizes five basic study statistics to compute effect sizes. These statistics include: (a) means and standard deviations, (b) t-tests, (c) F-tests, (d) percentage differences, and (e) chi-square values. The most common technique involved subtracting the mean score on the dependent variable for the intact group from that of the divorced group and dividing this difference by the pooled within-group standard deviation (Hedges & Olkin, 1985). If studies did not include means and standard deviations, then t-tests, F-tests, and chi-square values were calculated into effect sizes using the methods presented by the Hedges and Olkin (1985) publication. Percentage differences were calculated into effect sizes through the technique proposed by McNemar in 1962.

Statistics are converted into standardized effect sizes so they can be compared. The standardized effect size is g, which is the difference between divorced children and intact children depicted in standard deviation units. For those studies with small samples, the g statistic is known to overestimate the population effect size. Thus, g is converted to d, which corrects for this bias (Hedges, 1981; Hedges and Olkin, 1985). In this analysis, d-values are the measures of effect size.

Effect sizes were given signs to reflect the comparative interpersonal relationship of the divorced and intact groups. A negative sign manifested a lower level of interpersonal relationship for children in the divorced group in comparison to those children in the intact group while a positive sign indicated the opposite.

Separate effect sizes for each "independent sample" in a study were calculated. Independent samples exist when data are reported separately for subgroups of children, such as younger and older children, or boys and girls. The fifty-three studies reported data on 116 independent samples and involved 21,145 children and young adults.

Variables

Interpersonal relationship domains for each study were coded into the following six categories: (1) mother-child relationships; (2) father-child relationships; (3) family relationships; (4) sibling relationships; (5) peer group relationships; and (6) dating relationships. Although Amato and Keith (1991a) focused on children's well-being, the only interpersonal relationships they examined were mother-child and father-child relationships.

To facilitate comparing effect sizes across studies, the following study characteristics were coded for each study. Ethnicity indicated whether the samples were white, or samples with children from many different ethnic backgrounds (other). Age of children was divided into four categories: preschool-8 years, 9-12 years, 13-17 years, 18-25 years. The year data were reported were coded 1950-70s and 1980s. At the time of data collection, there were not many 1990 studies. Therefore, the 1990 studies were coded into the 1980s category. Type of sample included clinical, convenience, or random. Sample size was coded into three categories: small n = 14-99, medium n = 100-499, or large n = 500+. Type of measure used included attitude scales and other measures such as frequency of a specific behavior.

Analysis

Effect sizes across the interpersonal relationship domains were presented in a stem-and-leaf plot to reveal the shape of the frequency distribution of findings. This helped illustrate the degree of consistency among the findings of the various studies. Second, only one effect size per interpersonal relationship domain per sample was computed. Choices were made on a random basis. This is because significance testing requires that effect sizes be independent. When one study reported more than one interpersonal relationship domain it was necessary to choose between them. This was completed randomly. Thus, the number of effect sizes was reduced from 116 to 82. Another stem-and-leaf plot was created to reveal the new frequency distribution for the smaller number of relationships.

Finally, the mean effect size for different domains of interpersonal relations was calculated. Because effect sizes were not homogeneous, it was essential to analyze specific study characteristics to account for the differences in effect sizes. This was completed through comparing specific study characteristics to different findings.

FINDINGS

Overall Effect Sizes

The standardized effect size is d. This is the difference between divorced children and intact children represented in standard deviation units. Figure 1 presents a stem-and-leaf plot for effect sizes of divorce on children's interpersonal relations. The stem-and-leaf plot displays the actual observed value for each case. This is accomplished by reporting the observed value into two parts–the leading digit, called the stem, and a trailing digit, called the leaf. Each case is represented by a stem value and leaf value. There is a value for each finding reported in the 53 studies. For example, the effect size for the first study, -1.3, is reported in the first line. As noted above, effect sizes are given signs to reflect the comparative interpersonal relationship of the divorced and intact groups. A negative sign represents a lower level of interpersonal relationship for children in the divorced group in comparison to those in the intact group while a positive sign represents the opposite.

A small majority (53%) of effect sizes are negative. This means that a little more than half of the findings of the studies exhibited lower levels of interpersonal relationships for children of divorce when compared with children from intact families.

The average effect size is relatively weak. The mean is $-.04$ and the median $-.12$ for this distribution. In other words, across all studies and all interpersonal relationship domains, samples of children from divorced families of origin score about one-eighth of a standard deviation below samples of children from continuously intact families. This is a rather small difference. However, it should be noted that because the distributions represent effect sizes based on different interpersonal relationship domains, this conclusion is premature.

The shape of the frequency distribution in Figure 1 is a normal distribution. This confirms our earlier concern about inconsistent findings concerning divorce's relationship to interpersonal relationships.

Because significance testing requires that effect sizes be independent, when a study reported more than one interpersonal relationship domain it was necessary to choose between them. For example, one study might have reported three interpersonal relationship outcomes dealing with the father-child relationship. We randomly selected an

FIGURE 1. Stem-and-Leaf Plot for Effect Sizes of Divorce on the Interpersonal Relationships of Children in 56 Studies (N = 116)

First digit	Second digit
−1.	3
−1.	0
−0.	8888999
−0.	6666677777
−0.	44444445555
−0.	2222233333333333
−0.	011111111111111
0.	0
0.	1111111111
0.	222222233333333333
0.	4444455555555
0.	66667777
0.	88999
1.	0
1.	2

Example: The results of the first study was −1.3 while the second was −1.0.

outcome from each study. This decreased the number of effect sizes from 116 to 82. This distribution is presented in Figure 2. The results are similar to those in Figure 1. Sixty percent of effect sizes were negative as compared to 53 percent in Figure 1. The median effect size is − .16, or about one-sixth of a standard deviation. These results also demonstrate that the estimated effects of parental divorce are likely to be negative for children's interpersonal relationships.

Effect Sizes for Specific Domains of Interpersonal Relationships

The mean effect sizes for different domains of interpersonal relationships were calculated by weighting the effect sizes by their sample sizes, using Hedges and Olkin's (1985) methods and procedures outlined by Johnson (1989). The results are presented in Table 1.

The first column identifies the type of relationships while the second indicates the number of studies reporting relevant findings. Mean effect sizes are presented in the third column. All are negative except for relationships between brothers and sisters. All the differences between children from divorced families and from intact families are statistically significant at the .001 level. The strongest effects are for the father-child relationship (− .35) which is about one-third of a standard deviation. The mother-child relationship is relatively strong at − .13, which is about one-eighth of a standard deviation.

The last column in Table 1 contains the Hedges and Olkin (1985) "Q" statistic. This is a measure of effect size homogeneity. If the Q value is significant, it means that the amount of heterogeneity within a category is greater than expected by chance. This indicates whether or not the estimated effects of divorce are significantly stronger in some

FIGURE 2. Stem-and-Leaf Plot for Effect Sizes of Divorce on Interpersonal Relationships in Independent Samples (N = 82)

First digit	Second digit
− 1.	03
− 0.	55566667777888999
− 0.	011111111111122233333333444444
0.	0
0.	11122223333334444
0.	555555667777899
1.	2

TABLE 1. Mean Effect Sizes Across Six Domains of Interpersonal Relationships

Domain of Interpersonal Relationship	N	X̄ Effect Size	p	Q
Mother-child relationship	21	−.13	.001	106
Father-child relationship	15	−.35	.001	142
Family relationship	22	−.03	.001	180
Peer relationship	39	−.05	.001	201
Sibling relationship	08	.07	.001	41
Dating relationship	11	−.04	.001	51

Note: *N* refers to the number of effect sizes based on independent samples. A negative effect size indicates that the divorced group scores lower then the intact group in interpersonal relationships. *Q* is the Hedges and Olkin (1985) measure of heterogeneity.
***p < .001

studies than in others. If effect sizes are not homogeneous, it is important to analyze study characteristics (Johnson, 1989) to see if the differences in effect sizes between studies can be accounted for. All were statistically significant at the .001 level.

Between-Study Comparisons

Tables 2 through 7 report the amount of heterogeneity in effect sizes for interpersonal relationships accounted for by study characteristics. In Tables 2 through 7, the Q between-value represents the amount of heterogeneity that can be attributed to each study characteristic. It tests the significance of the difference in mean effect sizes across categories. The Q within-value reflects the degree of heterogeneity that remains within categories. Because the number of studies focusing on sibling relationship and dating relationship are relatively small, eight and eleven respectively, it was necessary to combine sibling relationship studies with family relationship studies. Dating relationship studies were combined with studies on peer relationships for this analysis.

The first study characteristic analyzed compared studies examining only white children to samples where more than one ethnic group was represented. Because 34 independent samples did not specify the race or ethnicity use in their analysis, only 48 effect sizes were included in this part of our analysis. Table 2 reveals that significant differences were found for all four domains of interpersonal relationships. We predicted that divorce would be more detrimental to mixed-race samples in interpersonal relationships when compared to white samples of

TABLE 2. Racial Differences in Effect Size

Domain of Interpersonal Relationship	N	X̄ Effect Size	Q–Between	Q–Within
All relationships			1	
White	24	− .27		3***
Other	24	− .30		111***
Mother-child relationship			3**	
White	05	− .19		27***
Other	05	− .38		15**
Father-child relationship			13***	
White	02	− .13		48***
Other	02	− .54		4
Family relationship			36***	
White	05	.25		47***
Other	08	− .23		40***
Peer relationship			30***	
White	12	− .44		141***
Other	09	− .15		22**

Note: *N* refers to the number of effect sizes based on independent samples. A negative effect size indicates that the divorced group scores lower than the intact group in interpersonal relationships. *Q* is the Hedges and Olkin (1985) measure of heterogeneity.
**p < .01   ***p < .001

children. However, effect sizes were larger for mixed-race samples in only three domains, all interpersonal relationships (− .30), mother-child relationships (− .38), and father-child relationships (− .54). Further, effect sizes were smaller for mixed-race samples in family relationship (− .23) and peer relationship (− .15). The only effect size that was positive was for white children in the family relationship domain. It is clear from this analysis that parental divorce has more serious consequences on mother-child, father-child, and family interpersonal relationships for the mixed-race samples. However, the mean effect size for white children in peer relationships is − .44. This is interesting because, although parental divorce has more serious consequences for mixed-race samples than white samples in family relationships, parental divorce is more detrimental for white children on peer relationships than mixed-race samples. The overall pattern suggests that divorce is more detrimental to mixed-race samples of children in their interpersonal relationships than white children samples.

Table 3 contains comparisons between preschool, 6 to 8-year-olds, 9 to 12-year-olds, 13 to 17-year-olds, and 18 to 25-year-olds. Because

TABLE 3. Age Differences in Effect Size

Domain of Interpersonal Relationship	N	X̄ Effect Size	Q–Between	Q–Within
All relationships			32***	
Preschool	11	.09		69***
06-08 years old	09	−.01		88***
09-12 years old	23	−.13		157***
13-17 years old	17	−.22		141***
18-25 years old	14	−.08		147***
Mother-child relationship			23***	
Preschool-12 years old	08	−.12		27***
13-17 years old	04	−.33		12*
18-25 years old	03	.12		33***
Father-child relationship			15***	
Preschool-12 years old	05	−.27		55***
13-17 years old	03	−.18		33***
18-25 years old	03	−.51		8*
Family relationship			10**	
Preschool-8 years old	10	.11		110***
09-17 years old	07	−.02		39***
18-25 years old	01	−.65		0
Peer relationship			31***	
Preschool-8 years old	06	.06		12*
09-12 years old	10	.04		32***
13-17 years old	07	−.32		46***
18-25 years old	07	−.11		24***

Note: N refers to the number of effect sizes based on independent samples. A negative effect size indicates that the divorced group scores lower than the intact group in interpersonal relationships. Q is the Hedges and Olkin (1985) measure of heterogeneity.
*p < .05   **p < .01   ***p < .001

some age categories contained only one independent sample, it was necessary to combine age categories within various relationships. For example, for both mother-child and father-child relationships the first age category includes preschoolers to children aged 12-years-old. Age is significantly associated with effect sizes in all domains, all relationships combined, mother-child, father-child, family, and peer relationships. We predicted that younger children from divorced homes will experience more negative effects of divorce on their interpersonal relationships when compared to older children from divorced homes. Overall there is some variability in the results for the age of child. Generally, it appears that effect sizes were more positive for preschoolers than for other age groups. For example, preschoolers in the all relationships domain (.09), family (.11), and peer relationship (.06) domain. This is somewhat surprising because Kunz (1992), in her review of 347 empirical studies, concluded that divorce is more detrimental for younger children than older children. However, this analysis is dealing particularly with the domain of interpersonal relationships and not with other aspects of the consequences of divorce. Overall, Table 3 demonstrates that the effects of studies of divorce were stronger and more negative for older children than for younger children.

Table 4 contains mean effect sizes for the year the data were collected. The year data were collected is an important study characteristic because of changes in the divorce rate over the past 40 years. Some suggest (Kunz, 1992) that because divorce has become more common in recent years, the effects are not as negative as in earlier years. Looking at the effects of when the study was conducted will help to test this notion. Table 4 reveals that significant trends over time ex-

TABLE 4. Differences in Effect Sizes Between Studies Conducted in 1950-70s and 1980s

Domain of Interpersonal Relationship	N	X̄ Effect Size	Q–Between	Q–Within
All relationships			16***	
1950-70s	11	.09		72***
1980s	71	−.15		701***
Mother-child relationship			.07	
1950-70s	01	−.13		0
1980s	15	−.08		99***
Father-child relationship			.70	
1950-70s	01	−.16		0
1980s	10	−.33		108***
Family relationship			6*	
1950-70s	04	.27		50***
1980s	17	−.04		128***
Peer relationship			15***	
1950-70s	05	.10		16**
1980s	26	−.22		249***

Note: N refers to the number of effect sizes based on independent samples. A negative effect size indicates that the divorced group scores lower than the intact group in interpersonal relationships. Q is the Hedges and Olkin (1985) measure of heterogeneity.
*p < .05   **p < .01   ***p < .001

isted for all, family and peer relationships domains. We predicted that results of studies published earlier will have more negative effects of divorce on children's interpersonal relationships when compared to older children from divorced homes. However, effect sizes for studies conducted in the 1980s were more negative than those carried out in earlier decades. Overall, this table demonstrates that the effects of studies of divorce were more positive in earlier decades and have become more negative over time.

Table 5 presents comparisons of effect sizes based on the type of sample used: clinical, convenience, or random. The heterogeneity-between values reveal that all five interpersonal relationship domains were significantly related to effect sizes. We predicted that results of

TABLE 5. Differences in Effect Sizes Between Clinical, Convenience, and Random Samples

Domain of Interpersonal Relationship	N	X̄ Effect Size	Q–Between	Q–Within
All relationships			70***	
Clinical	11	.18		75***
Convenience	65	−.19		596***
Random	06	−.17		50***
Mother-child relationship			10**	
Clinical	02	−.26		5*
Convenience	13	−.08		84***
Random	01	.39		0
Father-child relationship			75***	
Clinical	01	.32		0
Convenience	09	−.45		34***
Random	01	.71		0
Family relationship			50***	
Clinical	05	.26		40***
Convenience	17	−.06		101***
Random	01	−.37		0
Peer relationship			12**	
Clinical	03	.21		5
Convenience	26	−.21		263***
Random	03	−.20		8*

Note: *N* refers to the number of effect sizes based on independent samples. A negative effect size indicates that the divorced group scores are lower than the intact group in interpersonal relationships. *Q* is the Hedges and Olkin (1985) measure of heterogeneity.
*$p < .05$ **$p < .01$ ***$p < .001$

studies concerning interpersonal relationships will be more positive among children in clinical samples. Effect sizes for clinical samples in the all relationship, father-child, family, and peer relationship domains agreed with our prediction. However, clinical samples in the mother-child domain did not agree with our prediction. Findings concerning clinical samples for father-child and random samples for both mother-child and family relationships should also be viewed with caution because they are based on only one independent sample. The overall pattern suggests that results of studies that use convenience and random samples report more negative interpersonal relationships for children from divorced homes when compared to results of studies that use clinical samples of children from divorced homes.

The next study characteristic analyzed was sample size. Table 6

TABLE 6. Differences in Effect Size by Size of Sample

Domain of Interpersonal Relationship	N	X̄ Effect Size	Q–Between	Q–Within
All relationships			6*	
14-99	30	− .02		131***
100-499	35	− .14		455***
500 +	17	− .16		198***
Mother-child relationship			24***	
14-99	06	.04		22**
100-499	07	− .25		31***
500 +	03	.12		21***
Father-child relationship			15***	
14-99	01	.53		0
100-499	07	− .22		91***
500 +	03	− .45		2
Family relationship			17***	
14-99	09	.05		59***
100-499	08	.10		75***
500 +	04	− .16		39***
Peer relationship			4	
14-99	14	− .10		45***
100-499	12	− .14		192***
500 +	05	− .23		47***

Note: N refers to the number of effect sizes based on independent samples. A negative effect size indicates that the divorced group scores lower than the intact group in interpersonal relationships. Q is the Hedges and Olkin (1985) measure of heterogeneity.
**$p < .01$ ***$p < .001$

reveals that sample size was significantly related to effect sizes in four domains of interpersonal relationships. Sample size was not significantly related to peer relationships. Our sixth prediction was that children included in larger samples will experience more negative interpersonal relationships when compared to children included in smaller samples. The prediction was supported for all relationships, father-child, and family relationship domains. These results suggest that the negative impact of divorce on children's interpersonal relationships is greater for results of studies that use large samples when compared to studies that use small and medium sized samples.

Table 7 contains the mean effect size according to the type of measure used in the study. Significant differences emerged only for the domains of peer relationships and all relationships when compared on type of measures used. Finally, we predicted that results of studies that used attitude scale measures would have more negative consequences for children's interpersonal relationships when compared to those that used other types of measurement techniques. None of the effect sizes supported this prediction. The overall pattern suggests that

TABLE 7. Measurement Differences in Effect Size

Domain of Interpersonal Relationship	N	X̄ Effect Size	Q–Between	Q–Within
All relationships			25***	
Attitude scale	55	−.08		492***
Other	27	−.26		272***
Mother-child relationship			3	
Attitude scale	11	−.05		82***
Other	05	−.19		14*
Father-child relationship			2	
Attitude scale	08	−.36		74***
Other	03	−.25		32***
Family relationship			1	
Attitude scale	19	−.03		138***
Other	04	.02		53***
Peer relationship			32***	
Attitude scale	17	−.01		99***
Other	15	−.33		157***

Note: *N* refers to the number of effect sizes based on independent samples. A negative effect size indicates that the divorced group scores lower than the intact group in interpersonal relationships. *Q* is the Hedges and Olkin (1985) measure of heterogeneity.
*$p < .05$ ***$p < .001$

results of studies that do not use attitude scales to measure interpersonal relationships reveal more positive interpersonal relationships for children from divorced homes when compared to the results of studies that use non-attitude instruments.

DISCUSSION

The purpose of this paper is to explore the difference in interpersonal relationships (e.g., peer relations, relationships with siblings and parents) between children whose parents divorced and children from intact families. Further, we did not seek to disprove what researchers had already demonstrated, but rather to expound upon previous research through a systematic evaluation of study characteristics. Thus, the second objective was to study specific characteristics that account for variation in effect sizes (e.g., ethnicity or race, age of child, year studies were conducted, type of sample, size of sample, type of measure used).

Meta-analysis included variables found to be important in previous research (Kunz, 1992, 1995; Amato & Keith, 1991a, 1991b). Effect size expressed the results of the study in a common metric which made it possible to synthesize results across studies and to identify general conclusions about interpersonal relationships and to ask why some studies showed larger effects than others.

Fifty-three studies in our sample reported data on 116 independent samples. For each sample, effect sizes were computed comparing children in the "divorced" group and those in the "intact" groups on interpersonal relationships with mother-child, father-child, family, sibling, peer, and dating relationships. The overall pattern of our analysis suggests that divorce has negative consequences for children's interpersonal relationships. As predicted, Table 1 demonstrates that children who have experienced divorce have less positive interpersonal relationships with mother-child, father-child, family, peer, and dating relationships than children in intact, two-parent families. However, contrary to our prediction, children who were from divorced homes had more positive sibling relationships than children from intact homes. Our data led to the conclusion that parental divorce has a negative impact on children's interpersonal relationships. These findings can be explained through parental absence and economic disadvantage perspectives.

Parental absence perspective suggests that for children's socialization and overall development, two parents are better than one. When parents divorce, children often have less involvement with the noncustodial parent. Consequently, the children from divorced homes often experience a decrease in parental attention, assistance, direction, and supervision (Amato & Keith, 1991a; Kunz, 1995). This also supports the notion of Rollins and Thomas (1979) who said that a decrease in parental support and supervision might contribute to problems, such as less satisfying interpersonal relationships. However, why would the quality of sibling relationships be higher for children from divorced homes than those children from intact homes? One explanation from the parental absence argument is that because divorce is often accompanied by a decrease in parental attention, assistance, direction, and supervision, children might turn to their siblings for the support they need.

The economic disadvantage argument assumes that it is the economic deprivation, and not the family structure per se, that affects the overall quality of well-being of children in divorced families (Amato & Keith, 1991a; Kunz, 1995). Then, in turn, economic stress may affect the development of children (Kunz, 1992). Children living in poverty might be negatively labeled by society and their peer group. Labeling theory suggests that these children might join deviant subcultures (Jones, Gallegher, and McFalls, 1995) which may have an impact on their interpersonal relationships with others.

Although we conclude that parental divorce has a negative impact on children's interpersonal relationships, there are several factors that we need to take into consideration when making such a bold statement. First, most of the differences in interpersonal relationships between children whose parents have experienced a divorce compared with those children whose parents were continuously married were rather small.

Second, what about the impact of clinical research? Is it reliable? Previous research has consistently demonstrated that clinical research results in painting a more optimistic portrait of divorce than community, convenience or random samples (Amato & Keith, 1991b; Kunz, 1995). Children from divorced homes in clinical samples do exhibit a higher quality of interpersonal relationships when compared with children included in random and convenience samples. But this can be explained partially by the fact that children who enter a clinical setting are more likely to have received help or counseling on how to get along with their parents and peers.

The issue of time must also be taken into consideration. Some researchers argue that because divorce has become more common in recent decades, the effects are more negative than in earlier years. Amato and Keith (1991a) concluded that for some domains, more recent studies displayed weaker effect sizes than did studies carried out in earlier decades. However, the data in Table 4 do not support this prediction. In reality, the quality of divorced children's interpersonal relationships was higher in studies conducted during the 1950-70s when compared to studies conducted during the 1980s. This suggests that in earlier years, the effects of divorce were not as serious to children's interpersonal relationships as they were during the 1980s. This result is partially consistent with Kunz' (1995) finding. She concluded that there is an inverted curvilinear relationship between divorce and time. For example, academic achievement, math ability, and IQ test's effect sizes for studies conducted in the 1980s were larger than those carried out in earlier and later decades (Kunz, 1995).

Although we have stated some things that need to be taken into consideration, there are some important conclusions that can be made from this analysis. First, the age of the child. In this analysis, age was significantly associated with all interpersonal relationships domains. One thing that is rather interesting is that age has a different impact depending upon which domain of interpersonal relationship you are discussing. Table 3 demonstrates that younger children experience a lower quality of interpersonal relationship with their mothers than the other age categories. This could be partially explained by the fact that a majority of mothers work outside of the home and consequently, don't have time to spend with their younger children. This is the opposite of mother-child relationships where the older children have a positive effect size. On the other hand, parental divorce is more negative on older children's father and peer relationships when compared to younger children. This could partially be explained by who has custody of the children following divorce. The majority of children live with their mothers following divorce.

The second issue concerns one's racial or ethnic background. Table 2 shows that overall, there are racial difference when comparing mixed-race samples of children to white samples of children. Divorce is more detrimental for mixed-race samples when compared to white samples of children. This finding is consistent with Kunz (1995) who found that consequences of divorce were more detrimental for mixed-race samples than white samples of children in intellectual functioning. However, this finding contradicts one conclusion of Amato and Keith (1991b) who found that effect sizes tended to be stronger for white adults than for black adults. Their analysis was based on 15 dependent variables and did not specifically focus on interpersonal relationships.

In conclusion, this meta-analysis focused on the inconsistencies that exist in the literature concerning the impact of parental divorce on the quality of children's interpersonal relationships, compared with those children whose parents were continuously married. Further, it specifically revealed that parental divorce was negatively associated with mother-child, father-child, family, peer, and dating relationships. It was also revealed that parental divorce is positively associated with sibling relationships. However, the differences between the two groups were rather small. For all domains of interpersonal relationships, mixed-race samples of children had more negative interpersonal relationships. Younger children from divorced homes experience more negative mother-child relationships. The quality of relationships are lower for studies conducted more recently when compared with those conducted previously. Larger samples and studies utilizing attitude measures yielded strongest evidence for lower levels of interpersonal relationships. Effect sizes were stronger in clinical samples than in studies based on convenience or random samples.

REFERENCES

Ackerman, N.W. 1958. *The Psychodamics of Family Life.* New York: Basic Books.

Amato, P.R., and Keith, B. 1991a. "Parental divorce and the well-being of children: A meta-analysis." *Psychological Bulletin, 110,* 26-46.

Amato, P.R., and Keith, B. 1991b. "Parental divorce and adult well-being: A meta-analysis." *Journal of Marriage and the Family, 53,* 43-58.

Atkinson, B.R. and Ogston, D.G. 1974. "The effect of father absence on male children in the home and school." *Journal of School Psychology, 12,* 213-221.

Bernard, J.M., and Nesbitt, S. 1981. "Divorce: An unreliable predictor of children's emotional predispositions." *Journal of Divorce, 4,* 31-42.

Booth, A., Brinkerhoff, D.B., and White, L.K. 1984. "The impact of parental divorce on courtship." *Journal of Marriage and the Family, 46,* 85-94.

Bowlby, J. 1969. *Attachment and Loss, Volume 1: Attachment.* New York: Basic Books.

Bowlby, J. 1973. *Attachment and Loss, Volume 2: Separation-anxiety and Anger.* New York: Basic Books.

Brady, C.P., Ray, J.H., and Zeeb, L. 1986. "Behavior problems of clinic children: Relation to parental marital status, age and sex of child." *American Journal of Orthopsychiatry, 56*, 399-412.

Burchinal, L.G. 1964. "Characteristics of adolescents from unbroken, broken, and reconstituted families." *Journal of Marriage and the Family, 26*, 44-51.

Compas, B.E. and Williams, R.A. 1990. "Stress, coping, and adjustment in mothers and young adolescents in single-and two-parent families." *American Journal of Community Psychology, 18*, 525-545.

Crain, A.J., and Stamm, C.S. 1965. "Intermittent absence of fathers and children's perceptions of parents." *Journal of Marriage and the Family, 27*, 344-347.

Demo, D.H., and Acock, A. 1988. "The impact of divorce on children." *Journal of Marriage and the Family, 50*, 619-648.

Deutsch, F. 1983. "Classroom social participation of preschoolers in single-parent families." *The Journal of Social Psychology, 119*, 77-84.

Devall, E., Stoneman, Z., and Brody, G. 1986. "The impact of divorce and maternal employment on pre-adolescent children." *Family Relations, 35*, 153-159.

Dornbusch, S.M., Carlsmith, J.M., Bushwall, S.J., Riter, P.L. Leiderman, H., Hastory, A.H., and Gross, R.T. 1985. "Single parents, extended households, and the control of adolescents." *Child Development, 56*, 326-341.

Edwards, J.N. 1987. "Changing family structure and youthful well-being: Assessing the future." *Journal of Family Issues, 8*, 355-372.

Emery, R.E. 1982. "Interparental conflict and the children of discord and divorce." *Psychological Bulletin, 92*, 310-330.

Emery, R.E., and O'Leary, D. 1982. "Children's perceptions of marital discord and behavior problems of boys and girls." *Journal of Abnormal Child Psychology, 10*, 11-24.

Enos, D.M. and Handal, P.J. 1986. "The relation of parental marital status and perceived family conflict to adjustment in white adolescents." *Journal of Consulting and Clinical Psychology, 54*, 820-824.

Falbo, T. 1980. "Some consequences of growing up in a non-intact family." Paper presented at the Annual Convention of the American Psychological Association, September 1-5, 1980.

Falk, C. 1987. "Gifted children's perception of divorce." *Journal for the Education of the Gifted, 11*, 29-44.

Felner, R.D., Farber, S.S., Ginter, M.A., Boike, M.F., and Cowen, E.L. 1980. "Family stress and organization following parental divorce or death." *Journal of Divorce, 4*, 67-76.

Felner, R.D., Ginter, M., Bulke, M., and Cowen, E. 1981. "Parental death or divorce and the school adjustment of young children." *American Journal of Community Psychology, 9*, 181-191.

Fine, M.A., Moreland, J.R., and Schwebel, A.I. 1983. "Long-term effects of divorce on parent-child relationships." *Developmental Psychology, 19*, 703-713.

Forehand, R., McCombs, A., and Long, N. 1988. "Early adolescent adjustment to recent parental divorce: The role of interparental conflict and adolescent sex as mediating variables." *Journal of Consulting and Clinical Psychology, 56,* 624-627.

Forehand, R., Middleton, K., and Long, N. 1987. "Adolescent functioning as a consequence of recent parental divorce and the parent-adolescent relationship." *Journal of Applied Development Psychology, 8,* 305-315.

Furstenberg, F.F. and Seltzer, J.A. 1986. *Sociological studies of child development, 1,* 137-160.

Furstenberg, F.F., Jr. 1983. "Divorce and Child Development." Paper presented at the annual meeting of the American Orthopsychiatric Association, Boston.

Glass, G.V., McGaw, B., and Smith, M.L. 1981. *Meta-analysis in Social Research.* Beverly Hills, CA: Sage.

Glenn, N.D., and Kramer, K. 1987. "The marriages and divorces of the children of divorce." *Journal of Marriage and the Family, 44,* 335-347.

Green-Bailey, P. and McCluskey-Fawcett,K. 1991. "The role of familial stress in personality development of older adolescents from divorced and non-divorced families." Paper presented at the Biennial meeting of the Society for Research in Child Development, April, 1991.

Greenberg, E.F. and Nay, W.R. 1982. "The intergenerational transmission of marital instability reconsidered." *Journal of Marriage and the Family, 44,* 335-347.

Guidubaldi, J., and Perry, J. 1984. "Divorce, socioeconomic status, and children's cognitive-social competence at school entry." *American Journal of Orthopsychology, 54,* 59-68.

Guidubaldi, J., and Perry, J. 1985. "Divorce and mental health sequelae for children: A two year follow-up of a nationwide sample." *Journal of the American Academy of Child Psychiatry, 24,* 531-537.

Guttmann, J., Hertz-Lazarowitz, R.L., and Rosenberg, M. 1989. "Children of divorce and their intimate relationships with parents and peers." *Youth & Society, 21,* 85-104.

Hammond, J.M. 1979. "Children of divorce: A study of self-concept, academic achievement, and attitudes." *Elementary School Journal, 80,* 55-62.

Hedges, L.V., and Olkin, I. 1985. *Statistical Methods for Meta-Analysis.* New York: Academic Press.

Hertz-Lazarowitz, R.L., Rosenberg, M. and Guttmann, J. 1989. "Children of divorce and their intimate relationships with parents and peers." *Youth and Society,* 21 (1), 85-104.

Hess, R.D. and Camara, K.A. 1979. "Post-divorce family relationships as mediating factors in the consequences of divorce for children." *Journal of Social Issues, 35,* 79-96.

Hetherington, E.M., Camara, K., and Featherman, D.L. 1983. "Achievement and intellectual functioning of children in one-parent households." *Child Relations,* 205-284. Washington D.C.: National Association for the Education of Young Children.

Hetherington, E.M., Cox, M., and Cox, R. 1976. "Divorced fathers." *The Family Coordinator, 25,* 417-427.

Hetherington, E.M., Cox, M., and Cox, R. 1978. "The aftermath of divorce," in J.H.

Stevens and M. Mathews (eds.), *Mother-Child, Father-Child Relations*. Washington, DC: National Association for the Education of Young Children.

Hetherington, E.M., Cox, M., and Cox, R. 1979. "Play and social interaction in children following divorce." *Journal of Social Issues, 35,* 26-49.

Hetherington, E.M., Cox, M., and Cox, R. 1982. "Effects of divorce on parents and young children." In M. Lamb, ed., *Nontraditional Families: Parenting and Child Development.* New Jersey: Erlbaum.

Hetherington, E.M., Cox, M., and Cox, R. 1985. "Long-term effects of divorce and remarriage on the adjustment of children." *Journal of the American Academy of Child Psychiatry, 24,* 518-530.

Hetherington, E.M. et al. 1978. "Family interaction and the social, emotional and cognitive development of children following divorce." Paper presented at the Symposium on The Family: Setting Priorities, sponsored by the Institute for Pediatric Service of the Johnson & Johnson Baby Company (May 17-20, 1978).

Hodges, W.F., London, J., and Colwell, J.B. 1990. "Stress in parents and late elementary age children in divorced and intact families and child adjustment." *Journal of Divorce & Remarriage, 14,* 63-79.

Hodges, W.F., Wechsler, R.C., and Ballantine, C. 1979. "Divorce and the preschool child: Cumulative stress." *Journal of Divorce, 3,* 55-67.

Horns, V. and Abbott, G. 1985. "A comparison of concepts of self and parents among elementary school children in intact, single parent, and blended families." Paper presented at the Mid-South Education Researcher's Association, November, 1985.

Hutchinson, T., French, S., Scherman, A., Walker, P., and Doan, R. 1988. "Relationship between family structure and heterosexual activity in college aged women." Paper presented at the Annual Meeting of the Association for Counselor Education and Supervision, St. Louis, MO, October 6-9, 1988.

Jacobs, N.L., Guidubaldi, J., and Natasi, B. 1986. "Adjustment of divorced-family day care children." *Early Childhood Research Quarterly, 1,* 361-378.

Jenkins, J.E., Hedlund, D.E., and Ripple, R.E. 1988. "Marital status and child outcomes in a rural school population." Paper presented at the 80th Annual Conference of the National Rural Education Association, Bismarck, North Dakota, September, 1988.

Johnson, B.T. 1989. *DSTAT: Software for the Meta-Analytic Review of Research Literatures.* Hillsdale, NJ: Lawrence Erlbaum Associates Publishers.

Jones, B.J., Gallagher III, B.J. and McFalls, J.A. 1995. *Sociology Micro, Macro, Mega Structures.* Fort Worth, TX: Harcourt Brace College Publishers.

Kinard, E.M., and Reinherz, H. 1986. "Effects of marital disruption on children's school aptitude and achievement." *Journal of Marriage and the Family, 48,* 283-293.

Kinard, E.M. and Reinherz, H. 1984. "Marital disruption–effects on behavioral and emotional functioning in children." *Journal of Family Issues, 5,* 90-115.

Kinnaird, K.L. and Gerrard, M. 1986. "Premarital sexual behavior and attitudes toward marriage and divorce among young women as a function of their mothers' marital status." *Journal of Marriage and the Family, 48,* 757-765.

Koch, M.B. 1961. "Anxiety in preschool children from broken homes." *Merrill-Palmer Quarterly, 7,* 225-231.

Kunz, J. 1992. "The effects of divorce on children," In Stephen J. Bahr (ed). *Family Research: A Sixty Year Review, 1930-1990*, 2, 325-376.

Kunz, J. 1995. "The impact of divorce on children's intellectual functioning: A meta-analysis." *Family Perspective, 29*, 1: 75-101.

Kurdek, L.A. 1983. (ed.) *Children and Divorce*. San Francisco: Jossey-Bass.

Kurdek, L.A., and Siskiyou, A.J., Jr. 1980. "Sex-role self-concepts of single divorced parent and their children." *Journal of Divorce, 3*, 249-261.

Lands, J.R. 1956. "The pattern of divorce in three generations." *Social Forces, 34*, 213-216.

Loers, D.L. and Prentice, D.G. 1988. "Children of divorce: Group treatment in a school setting." Paper presented at American Psychological Association meeting, August, 13, 1988.

Lopez, F.G., Campbell V.L., and Watkins C.E. 1988. "The relation of parental divorce to college student development." *Journal of Divorce, 12*, 83-98.

Lowenstein, J.S., and Koopman, J. 1978. "A comparison of the self-esteem between boys living with single-parent mothers and single-parent fathers." *Journal of Divorce, 2*, 195-208.

Lussen, L.B. 1988. "The female adolescents unconscious experience of parental divorce." *Smith College Studies in Social Work, 58*, 101-121.

MacKinnon, C.E. 1989a. "Sibling interactions in married and divorced families: Influence on ordinal position, socioeconomic status, and play context." *Journal of Divorce, 9*, 65-78.

MacKinnon, C.E. 1989b. "An observational investigation of sibling interactions in married and divorced families." *Developmental Psychology, 25*, 36-44.

MacKinnon, C.E., Brody, G.H., and Stoneman, Z. 1986. "The longitudinal effects of divorce and maternal employment on the home environments of preschool children." *Journal of Divorce, 9*, 65-78.

McNemar, Q. 1962. *Psychological Statistics* (3rd ed.). New York: Wiley. Mechanic, D. and Hansell, S. 1989. "Divorce, family conflict, and adolescents' well-being." *Journal of Health and Social Behavior, 30*, 105-116.

Mowrer, E.R. 1938. "The trend and ecology of family disintegration in Chicago." *American Sociological Review, 3*, 344-353.

Mueller, C.W., and Hallowell, P. 1977. "Marital instability: A study of its transmission between generations." *Journal of Marriage and the Family, 39*, 83-93.

National Center for Health Statistics. 1990. Advance Report of Final Divorce Statistics, 1987. *Monthly Vital Statistics Report, 38*, (12):2. Maryland: Public Health Service.

Nelson, G. 1982. "Coping with the loss of father, family reaction to death or divorce." *Journal of Family Issues, 3*, 41-60.

Newcomer, S., and Udry, J.R. 1987. "Parental marital status effects on adolescent sexual behavior." *Journal of Marriage and the Family, 49*, 235-240.

Nunn, G.D., Parish, T.S., and Worthing, R.J. 1983. "Perceptions of personal and familial adjustment by children from intact, single-parent, and reconstituted families." *Psychology in the Schools, 20*, 166-174.

Nye, I.F. 1957. "Child adjustment in broken and in unhappy, unbroken homes." *Marriage and Family Living, 19*, 356-361.

Parish, T.S. 1981. "The impacts of divorce on the family." *Adolescence, 16,* 577-580.

Parish, T.S., and Dostal, J.W. 1981. "Evaluations of self and parent figures by children from intact, divorced, and reconstituted families." *Journal of Youth and Adolescence, 9,* 347-351.

Partridge, S. and Kotler, T. 1987. "Self-esteem and adjustment in adolescents from bereaved, divorced, and intact families: Family type versus family environment." *Australian Journal of Psychology, 39,* 223-234.

Pasternack, R. and Peres, Y. 1991. "To what extent can the school reduce the gaps between children raised by divorced and intact families?" *Journal of Divorce & Remarriage, 15,* 143-159.

Porter, B., and O'Leary, K.D. 1980. "Marital discord and childhood behavior problems." *Journal of Abnormal Child Psychology, 8,* 287-295.

Rickel, A.U., and Langner, T. 1985. "Short-term and long-term effects of marital disruption on children." *American Journal of Community Psychology, 13,* 599-611.

Rollins, B.C. and Thomas, D.L. 1979. "Parental support, power, and control techniques in the socialization of children." Pp. 317-364 in W.R. Burr, R. Hill, F. I. Nye, and I. L. Reiss (eds.), *Contemporary Theories About the Family* (Vol. 1). New York: The Free Press.

Rosenthal, D., Leigh, G.K., and Elardo, R. 1985. "Home environment of three-to six-year-old children from father-absent and two-parent families." *Journal of Divorce, 9,* 41-48.

Sable, P. 1989. "Attachment, anxiety, and loss of a husband." *American Journal of Orthopsychiatry,* 59(4), October, 550-556.

Santrock, J.W. 1979. "Father custody and social development in boys and girls." *Journal of Social Issues, 35,* 112-125.

Santrock, J.W., Warshak, R., Lindbergh, C., and Meadows, L. 1982. "Childrens' and parents' observed social behavior in stepfather families." *Child Development, 53,* 472-480.

Shapiro, E.K. and Wallace, D.B. 1987. "Siblings and parents in one-parent families." *Journal of Children in Contemporary Society, 19,* 91-114.

Sharabany, R. 1984. "The development of capacity for altruism as a function of object relations development and vicissitudes," in E. Staub, D. Bar-Tal, J. Karylowski, and J. Rewylowki (eds.), *Development and Maintenance of Prosocial Behavior.* New York: Plenum.

Shybunko, D.E. 1989. "Effects of post-divorce relationships on child adjustment." *Children of Divorce: Development and Clinical Issues,* 299-314.

Slater, E.J., and Haber, J.D. 1984. "Adolescent adjustment following divorce as a function of familial conflict." *Journal of Consulting and Clinical Psychology, 52,* 920-921.

Slater, E.J., Stewart, K.J., and Linn, M.W. 1983. "The effects of family disruption on adolescent males and females." *Adolescence, 18,* 931-942.

Stolberg, A.L., Camplair, C., Currier, K., and Wells, M.J. "Individual, familial and environmental determinants of children's post-divorce adjustment and maladjustment." *Journal of Divorce, 11,* 51-70.

Springer, C., and Wallerstien, J. 1984. "Young adolescents' responses to their parents' divorce." In L.A. Kurdek (ed.), *Children of Divorce: New Directions in Child Development*. San Francisco: Jossey-Bass.

Svanum, S., Bringle, R., and McLaughlin, J. 1982. "Absence and cognitive performance in a large sample of six-to-eleven-year-old children." *Child Development, 53*, 136-143.

U.S. Bureau of the Census. 1992. *Current Population Reports*, series P-20. No. 461. Washington DC: United States Government Printing Office.

Wallen, P. 1954. "Marital happiness of parents and their children's attitude to marriage." *American Sociological Review, 19*, 20-23.

Wallerstein, J.S. 1985. "The overburdened child: Some long-term consequences of divorce." *Social Work, 30*, 116-123.

Wallerstein, J.S., and Corbin, S.B. 1986. "Father-child relationships after divorce: Child support and educational opportunities." *Family Law Quarterly, 20*, 109-128.

Wallerstein, J.S., and Kelly, J.B. 1980. "Children and divorce: A review." *Social Work, 24*, 468-475.

Wallerstein, J.S., and Kelly, J.B.1980. *Surviving the Breakup: How Children and Parents Cope with Divorce*. New York: Basic Books.

Wallerstein, J.S. and Kelly, J.B. 1975. "The effects of parental divorce: Experiences of the preschool child." *American Academy of Child Psychiatry Journal, 14*, 600-616.

Webster-Stratton, C. 1989. "The relationship of marital support, conflict, and divorce to parent perceptions, behaviors, and childhood conduct problems." *Journal of Marriage and the Family, 51*, 417-430.

Weinraub, M. and Wolf, B.M. 1983. "Effects of stress and social supports on mother-child interactions in single-and two-parent families." *Child Development, 54*, 1297-1311.

Werner, E.E., and Smith, R.S. 1982. *Vulnerable but Invisible: A Study of Resilient Children*. New York: McGraw-Hill.

White, L.K., Brinkerhoff, D.B., and Booth, A. 1985. "The effect of marital disruption on child's attachment to parents." *Journal of Family Issues, 6*, 5-22.

Wiehe, V.R. 1985. "Self-esteem, attitude toward parents, and locus of control in children of divorced and non-divorced families." *Journal of Social Service Research, 8*, 17-27.

Winch, R.F. 1949. "The relation between the loss of a parent and progress in courtship." *Journal of Social Psychology, 29*, 51-56.

Wojciechowska, L. 1981. "Maternal rearing and social adaptation of children from broken homes." *Polish Psychological Bulletin, 12*, 213-218.

Wyman, P.A., Cowan, E.L., Hightower, A.D., and Pedro-Carrol, J.L. 1985. "Perceived competence, self-esteem, and anxiety in latency-aged children of divorce." *Journal of Clinical Child Psychology, 14*, 20-26.

Wynn, R.L. and Bowering, J. 1990. "Homemaking practices and evening meals in married and separated families with young children." *Journal of Divorce & Remarriage, 14*, 107-123.

Young, T.S. and Parish, E.R. 1972. "Impact of father absence during childhood on college age females' psychological adjustment."

APPENDIX

Studies Used in the Meta-Analysis

Amato, 1987

Atkinson and Ogston, 1974

Bernard and Nesbitt, 1981

Booth, Brinkerhoff, and White, 1984

Borduin and Henggeler, 1987

Brady, Ray, and Zeeb, 1986

Burchinal, 1964

Compas and Williams, 1990

Devall, Stoneman, and Brody, 1986

Falbo, 1980

Felner, Farber, Ginter, Boike, and Cowen, 1980

Fine, Moreland, and Schwebel, 1983

Forehand, McCombs, and Long, 1988

Furstenberg and Seltzer, 1986

Greenberg and Nay, 1982

Hammond, 1979

Hertz-Lazarowitz, Rosenberg, and Guttman, 1989

Hess and Camara, 1979

Hetherington, Cox, and Cox, 1976

Hodges, Wechsler, and Ballantine, 1979

Hodges, London, and Colwell, 1990

Horns and Abbott, 1985

Hutchinson, French, Scherman, Walker, and Doan, 1988

Jacobs, Guidubaldi, and Natasi, 1986

Jenkins, Hedlund, and Ripple, 1988

Kinard and Reinherz, 1984

Kinnaird and Gerrard, 1986

Koch, 1961

Loers and Prentice, 1988

Lopez, Campbell, and Watkins, 1988

MacKinnon, 1989

MacKinnon, Brody, and Stoneman, 1986

Mechanic and Hansell, 1989

Nelson, 1982

Nunn, Parish, and Worthing, 1983

Nye, 1957

Parish, 1981

Parish and Dostal, 1980

Partridge and Kotler, 1987

Peres and Pasternack, 1991

Rosenthal, Leigh, and Elardo, 1985

Santrock, Warshak, Lindbergh, and Meadows, 1982

Shapiro and Wallace, 1987

Shybunko, 1989

Slater, Stewart, and Linn, 1983

Stolberg, Camplair, Currier, and Wells, 1987

Southworth and Schwarz, 1987

Wallen, 1954

Webster-Stratton, 1989

Weinraub and Wolf, 1983

Wiehe, 1985

Wynn and Bowering, 1990

Young and Parish, 1972

RELATIONSHIP ISSUES

Family Conflict
and Young Adults' Attitudes
Toward Intimacy

Elise T. Toomey
Eileen S. Nelson

SUMMARY. The purpose of this study was to explore the relationship between parental conflict and young adults' levels of intimacy. The participants were 317 college students. The hypotheses that offspring from high-conflict families would have less favorable attitudes toward intimacy and more sexual partners than those from low-conflict families were not supported. Also not supported was the prediction that females who had experienced high family conflict would have more positive attitudes toward dating relationships than males who had had similar family experiences. However, a predicted significant relationship between relationship dependency and high family conflict was upheld. *[Article copies available for a fee from The Haworth Document*

Elise T. Toomey is a graduate student in Clinical-Counseling Psychology Program, LaSalle University. Eileen S. Nelson, EdD, is Professor, Department of Psychology, James Madison University, Harrisonburg, VA 22807.

[Haworth co-indexing entry note]: "Family Conflict and Young Adults' Attitudes Toward Intimacy." Toomey, Elise T., and Eileen S. Nelson. Co-published simultaneously in *Journal of Divorce & Remarriage* (The Haworth Clinical Practice Press, an imprint of The Haworth Press, Inc.) Vol. 34, No. 3/4, 2001, pp. 49-69; and: *Divorce and the Next Generation: Perspectives for Young Adults in the New Millennium* (ed: Craig A. Everett) The Haworth Clinical Practice Press, an imprint of The Haworth Press, Inc., 2001, pp. 49-69. Single or multiple copies of this article are available for a fee from The Haworth Document Delivery Service [1-800-342-9678, 9:00 a.m. - 5:00 p.m. (EST). E-mail address: getinfo@haworthpressinc. com].

KEYWORDS. Family conflict, young adults, intimacy

The rate of divorce is not waning; as such, it is a topic that has stimulated research efforts. Consequently, researchers have begun to examine its distinguishing factors and causes. However, according to Amato, Loomis, and Booth (1995), it is not necessarily the divorce itself that is psychologically damaging to children, but the amount of parental conflict that occurs prior to and during the divorce that may negatively impact the children.

The literature on marital dissolution and discord form two major bodies of thought: physical wholeness and psychological wholeness perspectives. First, the physical wholeness perspective holds that "the divorce itself is the salient variable that adversely affects children via the physical dissolution of the family" (Dancy & Handal, 1984, p. 222). According to this position, with the breakdown of the two-parent household, divorce is the primary cause of detrimental effects on children. The main support for this position emerges from early research which focused on children living with only one parent due to divorce (Hetherington, 1966). These children tended to have more emotional and behavioral problems than control children from two-parent homes.

However, more current research has supported the psychological wholeness perspective which holds that it is not the physical event of the divorce but the conflict and crisis that surrounds the marital dissolution that is damaging to the children. The main support for the psychological wholeness perspective is found in research that reveals parental discord to be the deciding influence in offspring adjustment (Borrine, Handal, Brown, & Searight, 1991; Dancy & Handal, 1984; Enos & Handal, 1986; Jaycox & Repetti, 1993). In fact, one study, Markland and Nelson (1993), produced results which indicated that conflict is the key variable that impacts future identity.

There is still much debate among professionals in the field about the different aspects of divorce, parental conflict, and children's adjustment. If children are in an extremely harsh, combative environment while their parents are married, divorce may come as a relief, since conflict may be reduced. The divorce might increase stress temporarily but reduce family conflict in the long run (Wiener, Harlow, Adams, & Grebstein, 1995). Kozuch and Cooney (1995) have reported that offspring attitudes and beliefs are greatly affected by parental conflict and that divorce can, in some cases, provide children with comfort.

Children in high-conflict two-parent homes and divorced families exhibit more behavioral and emotional problems than do children from low-conflict two-parent families (Amato et al., 1995). Amato and Keith (1991) ranked the levels of behavior problems displayed by children according to familial arrangements. First in the hierarchy, with the most problems, are children in high-discord, two-parent families. Second are children of divorce who indicate moderate adjustment. Third are children in low-discord two-parent families who have the least problems. These results indicate a need to examine more closely the psychological effects of conflict and hostility in lieu of parents' physical separation.

That parental conflict may have a more significant effect on children than parental divorce is exemplified by the study of Amato et al. (1995), who found that if conflict between parents is relatively high, offspring fared better in adulthood if their parents divorced than if they did not. These researchers concluded that the consequences of divorce might depend on the level of conflict that occurred before the divorce. Amato et al. indicated that if parental conflict was relatively low prior to the divorce, children were negatively affected by the divorce itself. Their data disclosed an interesting pattern. The children who experienced the least amount of parental conflict and whose parents divorced were the least well adjusted in early adulthood. Other studies have found corresponding results with regard to intact high-conflict families. For example, Wiener et al. (1995) in their study of intact versus divorced, high-conflict families, reported that parental conflict was the strongest predictor of child adjustment although divorced families reported significantly more conflict. This data reinforces the supposition that parental separation may actually benefit the children in high-conflict homes.

There is an apparent need to gain a greater understanding of parental discord and its effects upon children with regard to conflict. It has been empirically demonstrated by researchers that divorce and parental discord have detrimental effects on offspring (Camara & Resnick,1988; Stone & Hutchinson, 1992). By studying young adults' perceptions of their parents' marriages, young people's courtship, sexual, and marital behaviors might be better understood. Family counselors might be able to serve the needs of parents and offspring more effectively if they have access to more information about the effects of parental conflict. Through education on this topic, young people may be helped to avoid such rancorous conflict in their own marriages and to develop effective skills for coping with marital discord.

PARENTAL CONFLICT

While a great deal of research has been done on the effects of family structure, it has become apparent that adjustment problems are due to more than the physical properties of divorce. Examination of divorce alone provides insufficient evidence to explain offspring attitudes, behaviors, and development. Many studies have supported parental conflict as an essential variable in the adjustment of children (Dancy & Handal, 1984; Enos & Handal, 1986; Markland & Nelson, 1993; Slater & Haber, 1984). In a landmark review of the literature, Grych and Fincham (1990) found that 15 out of 19 studies supported the relationship between parental conflict and children's adjustment, regardless of family structure. This research supports the psychological wholeness perspective rather than the physical wholeness position. Accordingly, individual adjustment should be viewed as a process influenced by parental and familial conflict.

Social Learning Theory

One salient explanation for the effect of parental conflict on child adjustment may be inherent in social learning theory. This theory proposes that it is through parental modeling that children learn strategies for dealing with interpersonal conflict (Bandura, 1989). According to Bandura, modeling has two stages; it is not a simple replication of the behavior of another individual. The first stage, *acquisition*, occurs when a child witnesses parental conflict. Thus, the child in a divorced situation learns that aggression and hostility are acceptable means of dealing with conflict (Slater & Calhoun, 1988). The second stage, *internalization*, identified by Bandura, occurs as the child internalizes the behavior and then may replicate what he learned from his parents.

Behavioral outcomes may vary with the strategies children employ for coping with parental conflict. O'Brien, Margolin, and John (1995) proposed that children who cope with parental discord by distancing themselves seem to be less likely to become aggressive when involved in conflict than the children who involve themselves in parental conflict. Cummings and Cummings (1988) responded to children's tendency to become violent when witnessing violence by describing the *contagion theory*. This theory suggests that children who are close to intense expressions of hostility may become hostile themselves. Children who are living in an openly hostile home environment often become more hostile at school with peers and teachers. When children witness aggression and hostility between their parents, they come to view these behaviors as suitable (O'Brien et al.). Additionally, Grych and Fincham (1990) proposed that these children might have learned coercion techniques from parental modeling, which also will lead these children to exhibit behavior problems. Modeling of aggression may also occur when the child's role model, the parent, is using aggression to cope with a conflict.

Children's Perceptions of Conflict

While some researchers have focused on the actual amount of parental conflict, others have begun to examine children's perceptions of parental conflict. Perhaps not all problems that occur in a marriage may affect the children, especially if the children are unaware that there is marital distress. In a cross-sectional study, O'Brien et al. (1995) found that the quantity and quality of marital conflict that children report witnessing is predictive of child adjustment. Some children may attempt to involve themselves in parental conflict while others try to distance themselves from the stress of interparental hostility. Regardless of whether or not the parents try to conceal the conflict, the child is often aware that there is conflict and distress in the home environment. One research question has been whether parental conflict can be hidden from offspring. Data from a study by Landis (1960) showed that 62% of children who were old enough to remember the home situation prior to parental divorce described it as either "very happy" or "happy." Similarly, Grych and Fincham (1990) found that conflict, which was concealed from children, was not detrimental to their adjustment. David, Steele, Forehand, and Armistead (1996) contend that conflict would have to be openly exposed to the children for detrimental effects to occur. Therefore, these researchers concluded that it might be advisable for parents to shield children from excessive exposure to marital problems.

YOUNG ADULTS' RELATIONSHIPS

A relationship between parental discord and negative offspring attitudes toward romantic relationships has been indicated by several researchers (Jennings Salts, & Smith, 1991; Kozuch & Cooney, 1995; & Long, 1987). This relationship has been studied in order to analyze the components that cause negative attitudes. The direction (negative or positive) of these attitudes has also been analyzed as to determine which specific aspects of romantic relationships cause wariness among young adults' who have experienced high levels of parental conflict. The reality of parental discord for these young adults may have influenced them to believe that even the most well-intentioned couples can become dissatisfied in marriage (Kozuch & Cooney).These young adults were more likely to believe that divorce should be an easy process for unhappy couples. Remaining single throughout life was more acceptable to youth from high discord families. The component pieces of this research are important to understanding young people's reasoning, and therefore essential to educating parents and children about transgenerational effects.

Modeling

A firm relationship between negative attitudes toward divorce among young adults and parental marital status has yet to be established by most studies (Jones & Nelson, 1996; Stone & Hutchinson, 1992). However, research has indicated that parental conflict may be an important factor in young adults' perceptions of marriage (Gabardi & Rosen, 1991; Jennings et al., 1991). These findings support the psychological wholeness perspective. What exactly is it that ties these two variables together? Some researchers have begun to investigate the connection between modeling and marital expectations. Teenaged daughters of divorced parents have been found to be more involved in dating and have higher levels of sexual activity than other girls of the same age group (Booth, Brinkerhoff, & White, 1984). Wallerstein and Kelly (1980) also reported finding that latency-aged girls who have experienced divorce often show a sophisticated knowledge about and eagerness to become sexually active. Glenn and Kramer (1987) proposed that these findings may be due to an "emotional neediness" which is created by a hostile home environment or this may be due to the modeling of the parents. Parents who are separated and beginning to date again may be exhibiting new intimacy patterns. It may be due to the change in these behaviors, witnessed by the children, which leads them to feel that it is acceptable to date more often and to be more sexually active (Hetherington, 1972). In a somewhat contradictory study, Kozuch and Cooney (1995) found that young people often develop negative feelings toward the idea of romantic relationships and marriage due to their bad experiences. While these young adults may seek more partners, they seem to be less interested in long-term intimate relationships.

Gender

Another important factor that has been found to affect children's attitudes is gender. For example, a study by Cummings, Davies, and Simpson (1994) noted gender differences in children aged nine to twelve, in relation to high parental conflict. They found similarity between sons' and mothers' perceptions of conflict while daughters had little similarity with their mothers. Cummings et al. hypothesized that boys are less shielded from parental conflict than girls and are, therefore, more realistic in their perceptions. If children are beginning to demonstrate gender differences toward parental conflict at the young age of nine, young adults' attitudes toward marriage and conflict may have been shaping since early childhood.

Both sexes of young adults from high-conflict homes appear to be more cautious about entering a marital state than young adults from low-conflict homes. One result is that youth from high-conflict and recently divorced families generally want to cohabitate prior to marriage (Kozuch & Cooney, 1995). The young adults in this study were less likely to agree with the statement, "Unless a couple is prepared to stay together for life they should not get married" (Kozuch & Cooney, p. 53). Jennings et al. (1992) found that males have less favorable attitudes toward matrimony than females. It was reported by Jaycox and Repetti (1993) that a family environment encompassed by anger had a greater impact on girls', rather than boys', emotional development. Further, Long (1987) found that young girls from high-discord, separated families reported a later expected age of marriage. These girls were also found to go on fewer dates and become less serious in relationships. Long found that the girls' attitudes toward marriage were affected by parental discord and that these girls had reported greater anxiety in relationships than did girls from happy parental situations. Furthermore, emotionally distant mother-child relationships seem to have a more negative impact on offspring dating relationships than do emotionally distant father-child relationships (Tasker, 1996).

In summary, recent research has begun to establish connections between parental conflict and young adults' attitudes toward intimacy. Some researchers have found that child adjustment is negatively affected by high levels of parental conflict (Davies & Cummings, 1994; Grych & Fincham, 1990). It has also been found that young adults who have experienced high levels of parental conflict have more negative attitudes toward dating and romantic relationships (Jaycox & Repetti, 1993; Jennings et al., 1992).

PURPOSES AND HYPOTHESES OF THE STUDY

Researchers are just beginning to examine the link between parental conflict and the attitudes of young adults toward intimate relationships. Although there are relatively few studies that directly associate high parental conflict with young adults' levels of intimacy, logical associations between the bodies of knowledge can be deduced, with the understanding that more research must be completed in order to draw more definitive conclusions.

In order to define clearly the variables to be examined in this study, operational definitions are provided. Intimacy, in this study is defined as, "sustained love between partners, mutual trust, and partner cohesiveness" (Prager, 1995). Intimacy levels were measured using the Miller Social Intimacy Scale, a valid and reliable instrument used to assess intimacy. Mature relationships, as defined in the current study, have a need for self-acceptance and individual autonomy. Mature relationships are conceptualized as opposite of dependent relationships by the author of the Love Relationships Questionnaire which was used to assess relationship dependency (Nelson, 1986).

We divided participants into four groups according to the level of conflict in the parental relationship, high or low, and gender, male or female. Conflict was measured using the Family Environment Scale, Conflict Subscale and the scores were used to divide the participants into two groups according to their reported level of family conflict. The groups were compared to one another.

There were five dependent variables assessed in this study. The first variable, intimacy level, chosen because of the previous link that literature had established between parental discord offspring intimacy difficulties, and was assessed using the Miller Social Intimacy Scale. The second variable, number of sexual partners, was chosen in order to examine the sexual activity of young adults in an operational way. The third variable, overall pleasantness experienced in dating, was used to derive a notion of the young adults' general attitude toward the experience of dating. Many studies have examined attitudes toward marriage, however none has closely examined dating pleasantness. Fourth, current relationship satisfaction, was chosen to determine the relationship between intimacy, dependency, and satisfaction. Fifth, relationship dependency, as measured by the Love Relationships Questionnaire, was used to assess the degree of dependency that young adults experience in their relationships.

Four hypotheses were derived:

1. Young adults from high-conflict homes will report less intimacy in their relationships than young adults from low-conflict homes.
2. Young adults who report higher parental conflict scores will report a significantly higher number of sexual partners than young adults from low-conflict families.
3. Females who have experienced high levels of parental conflict will rate dating as a more pleasant experience overall than males who are also from high-conflict families.
4. Young adults from high parental conflict situations will indicate significantly higher levels of relationship dependency than young adults from low-conflict homes.

METHOD

Participants

Three hundred and thirty-five students enrolled at a mid-sized southeastern university participated in this study. Data from 18 students were not used in the data analysis because they had not been in an intimate relationship for three or more months. Thus, the sample was comprised of 317 students, 78 males and 234 females. The participants were volunteers from the School of Psychology participant pool, and received credit for participating. Of the participants, 34.9% were 17 to 18, 24% of participants were age 19, 18.9% of participants were age 20, 14.1% of participants were age 21, and 8% of participants were age 22 or older. The study strictly adhered to the American Psychological Association guidelines concerning the use of human participants and was approved by the university Institutional Review Board.

Questionnaires

An informed consent form described the extent of the confidentiality and participant rights. In order to obtain information regarding participants' number of sexual partners, gender, current relationship satisfaction, and overall degree of pleasantness experienced in dating, a demographic questionnaire was completed.

The conflict subscale of the *Family Environment Scale* (FES) (Moos, 1974) was used to measure the independent variable, perceived parental conflict. This instrument was chosen because of its ability to measure offspring's perceived conflict in the parental relationship rather than parental report of actual conflict. Participants answered nine questions with either "true" or "false" responses. Scores could range from 9 to 18 on this scale with lower scores being indicative of greater perceived parental conflict. The internal consistency coefficient was reported to be .75 and the test-retest reliability was reported to be .85 (Moos).

The *Miller Social Intimacy Scale* (MSIS) was used to measure the maximum level of intimacy that the participants experienced (Miller & Lefcourt, 1982). There are seventeen questions that are answered using a 10-point Likert-type scale. An example of an item would be "How often do you show him/her affection?" which would be rated from "not much" to a "great deal." This scale may have scores ranging from 38 to 114 with high scores indicating a high level of intimacy. The internal consistency as estimated by Cronbach alpha coefficient (alpha = .91 and .86) indicates the scale items assess a single construct (Miller & Lefcourt). The authors also reported high

convergent, discriminant, and construct validity. The test-retest relia-
bilities were measured as $r = .84$ and $r = .96$ at one and two month
intervals. This instrument was selected for use in this study because of
its consistency with the desired construct and its psychometric characteristics.

The *Love Relationship Questionnaire* (LRQ) (Nelson, 1986), an
instrument designed to assess the level of dependency in intimate
relationships, was used. The questionnaire consists of 39 items. The
first 38 items have response choices of "agree," "disagree," or "un-
certain," while the last item is an overall measure of relationship
satisfaction on a 10-point Likert-type scale with responses ranging
from "very unsatisfied" to "very satisfied." An example of a question
from the LRQ is, "I often feel uneasy as to my partner's whereabouts
when we are not together." Its use in a study by Nelson, Hill-Barlow,
and Benedict (1994) indicated that the scale has moderately high
reliability and validity using the internal consistency method (Cronbach's alpha) to acquire an alpha coefficient of .84 for reliability.
Scores on the LRQ range from 38 to 119 with lower scores being
associated with lower levels of dependency in relationships. The measure was chosen to assess relationship dependency because of its
unique purpose of distinguishing between dependent, immature and
independent, mature relationships.

Procedure

After reading the informed consent forms, the participants completed paper and pencil questionnaires. Participants were asked to
think of their most meaningful dating relationship and to refer to this
relationship when answering all questionnaires dealing with a romantic relationship.

The participants were assured of their confidentiality and anonym-
ity prior to their participation. Participants who requested a summary
of the results signed a separate list after turning in their questionnaires,
and were debriefed at the end of the session.

Scores on the FES were used to divide participants into low and
high family conflict groups. The scores were divided at the mid-point
of the scale. High-conflict participants had scores on the FES ranging
from 9 to 13 and low-conflict participants had scores ranging from 14
to 18. There were 65 participants in the high-conflict group: 19 males

and 46 females. There were 233 participants in the low-conflict group: 56 males and 177 females.

RESULTS

There were five dependent variables examined in this study: number of sexual partners, level of intimacy, amount of relationship dependency, current relationship satisfaction, and overall pleasantness experienced in dating overall. The independent variables were parental conflict level, and gender.

The first hypothesis predicted that offspring from high-conflict families would report less intimacy in their relationships than offspring from low-conflict families. A 2 (Level of conflict) × 2 (Gender) analysis of variance was performed. There was no main effect found for conflict level $F(1, 296) = 1.02$, $p > .05$. No conflict by gender interaction effect was found, $F(1, 296) = .018$, $p > .05$. However, there was a main effect found for gender, $F(1, 296) = 9.27$, $p < .05$. (Male $M = 131.91$, female $M = 139.65$).

The second hypothesis suggested that young adults from high-conflict families would have more sexual partners than young adults from low-conflict families. The demographic question gave participants the following choices for the number of sexual partners that they had experienced: none, 1, 2 to 4, 5 to 7, and 8 or more. There were 310 participants who answered the question; 24.8% of the respondents replied no sexual partners, 27.7% answered one partner, 30.3% answered 2 to 4 partner, 6.8% answered 5 to 7 partners, and 10.3% answered 8 or more partners. A chi square test compared people from high and low familial conflict groups to see if they differed in the number of sexual partners, $\chi^2(4, N = 310) = 6.321$, $p > .05$. The two groups did not differ significantly.

The third hypothesis predicted that females who have experienced high parental conflict would report more overall pleasant experiences with dating relationships than males who have had similar family experiences. To test this hypothesis, a 2 (Level of Conflict) × 2 (Gender) analysis of variance was performed on the overall pleasantness experienced in dating. There was no main effect found for gender, $F(1, 294) = .322$, $p > .05$, or for conflict, $F(1, 294) = .259$. Also, there was no significant interaction effect for conflict and gender, $F(1, 294) =$

.107, $p > .05$. In general, all participants reported a high level of pleasantness in their dating relationships. (All means $= > 4.0$.)

The final hypothesis was that high parental conflict would be related to a more dependent attitude toward relationships. In order to determine the relationship between family conflict and dependency in relationships in these participants, a 2 (Level of conflict) × 2 (Gender) analysis of variance was performed (see Table 1). There was no interaction effect found, $F(1, 306) = .094, p > .05$. There was no main effect found for gender, $F(1, 306) = 3.314, p > .05$, however there was a main effect found for conflict level, $F(1, 306) = 13.097, p < .05$. The high-conflict level group ($M = 59.26$) reported significantly more dependency than the low-conflict group ($M = 57.46$).

A correlational analysis was used to assess the relationships of variables with one another (see Table 2). The scores on the MSIS were negatively correlated with the scores on the LRQ, indicating that the greater intimacy the less the relationship dependency. The MSIS scores were positively correlated with current relationship satisfaction, indicating that the greater the intimacy, the more satisfying the current relationship. The MSIS scores were also positively correlated with overall pleasantness experienced in dating, where the greater the intimacy, the more pleasant the experience of dating. The LRQ scores were negatively correlated with current relationship satisfaction, indicating that less dependency is related to more relationship satisfaction. The LRQ scores were also negatively correlated with overall dating pleasantness, which indicates that less dependency is related to a more pleasant dating experience. Finally, current relationship satisfaction

TABLE 1. Means for LRQ

	High Conflict	Low Conflict	Column Means
Males	61.21	55.32	56.76
	(N = 19)	(N = 59)	(N = 78)
Females	58.52	51.54	53.04
	(N = 50)	(N = 182)	(N = 232)
Row Means	59.26	52.46	53.98
	(N = 69)	(N = 241)	(N = 310)

Note. Scores on the LRQ range from 38 to 114, with high scores being indicative of greater dependency.

TABLE 2. Correlations for MSIS, LRQ, Current Satisfaction, and Dating Pleasantness

		LRQ	Satisfaction	Pleasantness
MSIS	Pearson	−.556	.621	.472
	Sig.	.000	.000	.000
	N	305	293	291
LRQ	Pearson		−.668	−.316
	Sig.		.000	.000
	N		303	300
Satisfaction	Pearson			.365
	Sig.			.000
	N			290

was positively correlated with overall dating pleasantness, indicating that the more current satisfaction, the more pleasant were the dating experiences.

DISCUSSION

This study compared young adults from high-conflict families to young adults from low-conflict families in order to gain a better understanding of the relationship between intimacy and family conflict. While most of the hypotheses were not supported, there are still important implications for the findings of this study.

The first hypothesis, predicting that offspring from high-conflict families would have less intimacy in their relationships than offspring from low-conflict families, was not supported by the data. These results are inconsistent with the findings reported by Jennings et al. (1991) and Kozuch and Cooney (1995), which suggested that offspring from high-conflict families have negative attitudes toward intimacy and romantic relationships. Response bias may be one explanation for the lack of difference between the two groups in the study. The nature of the questions on the MSIS could cause participants to want to present themselves in a socially desirable way. This could explain the reason why the participants reported relatively high mean scores of intimacy on the MSIS, well above the mid-point of the scale. The questions were of a sensitive and personal nature, which could influence respondents to reflect themselves in a more positive way. If the participants were aware of the construct being measured, the participants may have been trying to respond to the questions in a favorable manner.

Another possible explanation is that the effects of parental conflict might fade over time. If the conflict occurred early in the participants' lives, intervening events or the presence of more positive models may lessen the impact of the conflict. The results could also be attributed to the scale used to assess parental conflict, the FES. The instrument was designed to measure family conflict and not specifically parental conflict.

There might not be an effect on intimacy because of the ceiling effect that is apparent in the respondents' scores. All groups scored very high on the MSIS, in the top 25% of the scale, which makes it difficult to detect differences.

There was a significant effect found for gender on intimacy. This may be expected due to the socialization process of women and men. It is more socially acceptable for women to report high levels of intimacy than it is for men. There exists a gender stereotype of women that they are more intimate beings than men are, the participants in this study may have been adjusting their answers to respond in a desirable way.

According to the results, parental conflict is not a significant element in young adults' levels of intimacy. It may be that other variables, such as parental marital status and parent-child relationship quality, are more notable in young adults' development of intimacy. However, it is important to consider that parental conflict has been linked to many other factors that affect offspring adjustment. These collective variables have not been teased apart, making the analysis of individual effects difficult.

The second hypothesis, young adults from high-conflict families would have more sexual partners than young adults from low-conflict families, was not supported. These results contradicted findings by Booth et al. (1984) and Wallerstein and Kelly (1980) who found young adults from high-conflict, divorced families tended to have accelerated sexual patterns. The number of participants who were from divorced families was not known, so the effects of divorce and family conflict on the number of sexual partners are not clear.

Some previous literature has shown that offspring from conflicted home environments may be less involved in romantic relationships. Long (1987) found that daughters of high discord, separated families had fewer dates than daughters of low discord, intact families. While this study examined parental marital status, it may be in accordance with the research on parental conflict. If the participants who reported high-conflict families went on fewer dates than participants from low-conflict, than it would be expected that the high-conflict group would have a lesser numbers of sexual partners. The results from the findings on the effects of family conflict on offspring number of sexual partners are mixed, so conclusions are difficult to deduce.

An interesting characteristic of this sample was that the participants who reported higher intimacy levels, also reported more dependency in relationships. This finding is discussed later in the paper. The lack of significant differences in number of sexual partners may also be due to the dependency of the high-conflict group on their partners. Relationship-dependent individuals often do not have many relationships because they remain in relationships even when they are unsatisfied (Charkow & Nelson, 1999). Therefore, participants who reported high conflict may choose to remain in long-term relationships, and may not experience many partners.

The third hypothesis predicted that females who experienced high parental conflict would report more pleasant dating experiences than males who have had similar family experiences. No significant differences were found. The measure of dating pleasantness was meant to assess a broad construct of dating attitudes. The measure may not have been an accurate measure of the construct. Previous research had shown that young adults from divorced families had a more negative attitude toward marriage (Kozuch & Cooney, 1995; Long, 1987). However, the term "pleasantness" may have been too vague and not sufficient to differentiate the complex qualities that comprises dating relationships. A more sensitive instrument may be better able to evaluate the construct. It is also possible that the participants did not clearly understand the terminology of the question. A definition of the term "pleasant" in the particular context could have contributed to the comprehension of the question and a more accurate assessment.

The final hypothesis, high parental conflict would be related to a more dependent relationship, was supported by the data. Participants in the high-conflict group did report significantly more dependency in their relationships than participants in the low-conflict group. The results may also be attributed to young adults' insecurity or low self-efficacy in intimate relationships, due to the high amount of conflict experienced in the family environment. There were no gender main effects and no interaction between gender and parental conflict on dependency in relationships. Males and females in this sample apparently experience the same amounts of dependency in their relationships.

Evans (1987) indicated that children who are neglected sometimes fear intimacy and abandonment. These children learn to be independent of others for their emotional needs because their needs are often not met. However, when relationships do develop for these individuals, they tend to adhere to their partner even if the situation is emotionally detrimental in order to avoid being alone. Parental conflict may have a similar effect on children as neglect. For example, Sinclair and Nelson (1998, p. 126) reported that "parents who model a significant amount of disagreement create a feeling of instability within a child which leads him or her to believe that any discord within the relationship may be harmful." Thus, individuals from high-conflict homes may become dependent on their partners to provide a feeling of security about their relationships and about themselves. These individuals may settle for any relationship, positive or negative, to avoid being alone.

Some additional analyses revealed more information about the role of intimacy in young adults' lives. Intimacy was found to be is negatively correlated with dependency in relationships. It may be that higher levels of intimacy help to increase maturity in relationships or vice versa. We also found relationship dependency to be negatively correlated with current relationship satisfaction, as would be expected. However, it is interesting that intimacy was not found to be related to parental conflict while high relationship dependency was related to conflict. This may be due to the nature of the questions on the FES. The questions were in reference to general family conflict that may influence dependency. It is possible that intimacy is more closely related to parental conflict because of the romantic nature of the parental relationship.

Since the FES measured family conflict rather than parental conflict, this may explain why the dependency scores differed between the high and low conflict groups but the intimacy scores did not.

In order to further understand the relationships among the constructs, further analysis was warranted. Current relationship satisfaction, while unrelated to parental conflict, was positively correlated to the level of intimacy that the individual reported. This may be because higher levels of intimacy indicate more mature, committed relationships, which may provide young adults with security and happiness. This finding is in line with the result that high current relationship satisfaction is correlated with less dependency in relationships. This could be due to the notion that dependent relationships are not mature, therefore those individuals involved in dependent relationships tend to be less satisfied.

CONCLUSIONS

There are many limitations to this study which restrict the generalizability of the findings. The age of the participants was a very narrow range, the majority of the participants were between 17 and 22. Due to the relative young age of the sample, the participants may not have much experience in dating and intimate relationships. There were 78 males and 238 females included in most of the analyses, so the analyses may have been gender-biased. All the participants were from the same university so the findings may not represent other university settings, non-academic settings, or regions of the country.

While there has been a great deal of research already conducted, there is still little known about the effects of familial conflict on young adults. Any study that is concerned with intimate relationships will be very complex because of the multitude of interdependent factors that influences the nature of relationship. The findings of this research are important to the broad understanding of family conflict and young adult intimacy, but also for the more narrow distinctions between aspects and roles of intimacy in understanding young adults' intimate behaviors.

The findings may be used in the education of parents and young people for better comprehension about intimacy and the effects of family conflict. The findings may be useful to middle and high school teachers and counselors who are in direct contact with adolescents who are exploring intimacy and relationships. Adolescents are also exploring independence from their families and friends. Education of this age group could prevent some relationship dependency and unhealthy intimacy. College counseling centers may be able to use this information to assist students with dependency and intimacy issues in their relationships. There may also be implications for parents. Ideally, if parents are aware of the consequences of a hostile home environment, they may be more apt to resolve their discord more efficiently and discuss the conflict with their children. In this way, children can understand that the discord is within the parental relationship and does not interfere with the parent-child relationship. Parents may also make a concerted effort to teach their adolescents about intimacy and healthy relationships.

Future research may be conducted with different populations of young people such as high school students and adults over the age of twenty-five. High school students because they are exploring their intimacy for the first time and adults because they have more experience with dating and relationships. Research in the different areas of intimacy, such as communication patterns, relationship patterns, loving styles, and expectations for intimate relationships, is needed to more clearly understand the interaction of intimacy and parental conflict.

REFERENCES

Amato, P. R., & Keith, B. (1991). Parental divorce and adult well-being: A meta-analysis. *Journal of Marriage and the Family, 53*, 43-58.

Amato, P. R., Loomis, L. S., & Booth, A. (1995). Parental divorce, marital conflict, and offspring well-being during early adulthood. *Social Forces, 73*(3), 895-915.

Bandura, A. (1989). Social cognitive theory. In R. Vasta (Ed.), *Annals of Child Development* (Vol. 6, pp. 1-60). Greenwich, CT: JAI Press.

Booth, A., Brinkerhoff, D. B., & White, L. K. (1984). The impact of parental divorce on courtship. *Journal of Marriage and the Family, 48*, 85-94.

Borrine, M. L., Handal, P. J., Brown, N. Y., & Searight, H. R. (1991). Family conflict and adolescent adjustment in intact, divorced, and blended families. *Journal of Clinical and Consulting Psychology, 59*, 753-755.

Camara, K. A., & Resnick, G. (1988). Interparental conflict and cooperation: Factors moderating children's post-divorce adjustment. In E. M. Hetherington and J. D. Arasteh (Eds.), *Impact of Divorce, Single Parenting, and Stepparenting on Children* (pp. 169-195). Hillsdale, New Jersey: Erlbaum.

Charkow, W. B., & Nelson, E. S. (1999). A study of relationship dependency dating abuse and scripts of female college students. *Journal of College Counseling*. (In press.)

Cummings, E. M., & Cummings, J. L. (1988). A process-oriented approach to children's coping with adults' angry behavior. *Developmental Review, 8*, 296-321.

Cummings, E. M., Davies, P., & Simpson, K. (1994). Special section: Mediators of child adjustment. *Journal of Family Psychology, 8*(2), 141-149.

Dancy, B. L., & Handal, P. J. (1984). Perceived family climate, psychological adjustment, and peer relationships of black adolescents: A function of parental marital status or perceived family conflict. *Journal of Community Psychology, 12*, 222-231.

David, C., Steele, R., Forehand, R., & Armistead, L. (1996). The role of family conflict and marital conflict in adolescent functioning. *Journal of Family Violence, 11*(1), 81-91.

Davies, P. T., & Cummings, E. M. (1994). Marital conflict and child adjustment: An emotional security hypothesis. *Psychological Bulletin, 116*(3), 387-411.

Enos, D. M., & Handal, P. J. (1986). The relation of parental marital status and perceived family conflict to adjustment in white adolescents. *Journal of Consulting and Clinical Psychology, 54*(6), 820-824.

Evans, S. (1987). Shame, boundaries, and dissociation in chemically dependent, abusive, and incestuous families. *Alcoholic Treatment Quarterly, 4*, 155.

Garbardi, L., & Rosen, L. A. (1991). Differences between college students from divorced and intact families. *Journal of Divorce & Remarriage, 15*, 175-191.

Glenn, N. D., & Kramer, K. B. (1987). The marriages and divorces of the children of divorce. *Journal of Marriage and the Family, 49*, 811-825.

Grych, J. H., & Fincham, F. D. (1990). Marital conflict and children's adjustment: A cognitive-contextual framework. *Psychological Bulletin, 108*(2), 267-290.

Hetherington, E. M. (1966). Effects of parental absence on sex-typed behavior in negro and white preadolescence males. *Journal of Personality and Social Psychology, 4*, 87-91.

Hetherington, E. M. (1972). Effects of father-absence on personality development in adolescent daughters. *Developmental Psychology, 7*, 313-326.

Jaycox, L. H., & Repetti, R. L. (1993). Conflict in families and the psychological adjustment of preadolescent children. *Journal of Family Psychology, 7*(3), 344-355.

Jennings, A. M., Salts, C. J., & Smith, T. A. (1991). Attitudes toward marriage: Effects of parental conflict, family structure, and gender. *Journal of Divorce & Remarriage, 17*(1/2), 67-79.

Jones, G. D., & Nelson, E. S. (1996). Expectations of marriage among college students from intact and non-intact homes. *Journal of Divorce & Remarriage, 26*(1/2), 171-189.

Kozuch, P., & Cooney, T. M. (1995). Young adults' marital and family attitudes: The role of recent parental divorce, and family and parental conflict. *Journal of Divorce & Remarriage, 23*(3/4), 45-62.

Landis, J. (1960). The trauma of children when parents divorce. *Marriage and Family Living, 22*, 7-13.

Long, B. H. (1987). Perceptions of parental discord and parental separations in the United States: Effects on daughters' attitudes toward marriage and courtship progress. *Journal of Social Psychology, 127*(6), 573-582.

Markland, S. R., & Nelson, E. S. (1993). The relationship between familial conflict and the identity of young adults. *Journal of Divorce & Remarriage, 20*(3/4), 193-209.

Miller, R. S., & Lefcourt, H. M. (1982). The assessment of social intimacy. *Journal of Personality Assessment, 46*, 514-518.

Moos, R. H. (1974). *Family Environment Scale.* Palo Alto, CA: Consulting Psychologists Press.

Nelson, E. S. (1986). Love Relationships Questionnaire. Harrisonburg, VA: James Madison University.

Nelson, E. S., Hill-Barlow, D., & Benedict, J. O. (1994). Addiction versus intimacy as related to sexual involvement in a relationship. *Journal of Sex and Marital Therapy, 20*, 35-45.

O'Brien, M., Margolin, G., & John, R. S. (1995). Relation among marital conflict, child coping, and child adjustment. *Journal of Clinical Child Psychology, 24*(3), 346-361.

Prager, K. J. (1995). *The Psychology of Intimacy.* New York: Guilford Press.

Sinclair, S. L., & Nelson, E. S. (1998). The impact of parental divorce on college students' intimate relationships and relationship beliefs. *Journal of Divorce & Remarriage, 29(1/2)*, 103-130.

Slater, E. J., & Calhoun, K. S. (1988). Familial conflict and marital dissolution: Effects on the social functioning of college students. *Journal of Social and Clinical Psychology, 6*, 118-126.

Slater, E. J., & Haber, J. D. (1984). Adolescent adjustment following divorce as a function of familial conflict. *Journal of Consulting and Clinical Psychology, 52*, 920-921.

Stone, M. K., & Hutchinson, R. L. (1992). Familial conflict and attitudes toward marriage: A psychological wholeness perspective. *Journal of Divorce & Remarriage, 18*(3/4), 79-81.

Tasker, F. L. (1996). Parent-child relationships postdivorce and adolescents' involvement in heterosexual relationships. *Journal of Divorce & Remarriage, 25*(3/4), 137-149.

Wallerstein, J. S., & Kelly, J. B. (1980). *Surviving the break-up.* New York: Basic Books.

Weiner, J., Harlow, L., Adams, J., & Grebstein, L. (1995). Psychological adjustment of college students from families of divorce. *Journal of Divorce & Remarriage, 23*(3/4), 75-95.

Students' Expectations and Optimism Toward Marriage as a Function of Parental Divorce

Michelle E. Boyer-Pennington
John Pennington
Camille Spink

SUMMARY. Two hundred seventy-three single college students from intact, single-divorce, and multiple-divorce homes answered questions concerning their optimism and perceptions of control regarding a future marriage. Students from intact homes had more favorable expectations about the quality of their future marriage than students from single- and multiple-divorce homes. However, all three groups were (1) equally optimistic about their likelihood of getting married and (2) more optimistic about the success of their own future marriage than about the marital success of similar and dissimilar comparison others. Interestingly, students from multiple-divorce homes reported significantly higher amounts of relationship control than students from other back-

Michelle E. Boyer-Pennington, PhD, is with the Department of Psychology, John Pennington, PhD, is with the Department of Psychology, and Camille Spink, is with the Department of Psychology, all at Middle Tennessee State University.

Address correspondence to: Michelle E. Boyer-Pennington, Department of Psychology, P. O. Box 87, Middle Tennessee State University, Murfreesboro, TN 37132 (E-mail: mboyer@mtsu.edu).

Portions of this data were presented as "Examining the role of unrealistic optimism on students' attitudes about marriage," at the 11th Annual Convention of the American Psychological Society, Denver, CO, June 1999.

[Haworth co-indexing entry note]: "Students' Expectations and Optimism Toward Marriage as a Function of Parental Divorce." Boyer-Pennington, Michelle E., John Pennington, and Camille Spink. Co-published simultaneously in *Journal of Divorce & Remarriage* (The Haworth Clinical Practice Press, an imprint of The Haworth Press, Inc.) Vol. 34, No. 3/4, 2001, pp. 71-87; and: *Divorce and the Next Generation: Perspectives for Young Adults in the New Millennium* (ed: Craig A. Everett) The Haworth Clinical Practice Press, an imprint of The Haworth Press, Inc., 2001, pp. 71-87. Single or multiple copies of this article are available for a fee from The Haworth Document Delivery Service [1-800-342-9678, 9:00 a.m. - 5:00 p.m. (EST). E-mail address: getinfo@haworthpressinc.com].

KEYWORDS. Parental divorce, multiple divorce, marriage, unrealistic optimism, attitudes

The present study examined marital expectations, marital optimism, and perceptions of marital control among single college students whose parents were either still married, divorced once, or divorced more than once. According to Berk (1997), more than one million American children experience parental separation and divorce each year. The Monthly Vital Statistics Report (National Center for Health Statistics, 1998) placed the number of people who divorced in 1997 at 1,163,000, up from 1,150,000 in 1996. Some research suggests that the divorce rate is even higher for remarriages than for first marriages (see Hetherington, Bridges, & Insabella, 1998). Given these divorce rate trends in the United States, it is likely that an increasing number of children will experience multiple parental divorces. Although considerable research in the past 20 years has investigated the effects of parental divorce on children, little research has directly compared the effects of single divorce to that of multiple divorce. As a consequence, we do not know what impact multiple parental divorces have on adult children's expectations and optimism about marriage.

THE EFFECTS OF SINGLE
AND MULTIPLE PARENTAL DIVORCE

Numerous studies have found a negative impact of parental divorce on adult children's marital attitudes, expectations, and outcomes. For example, those who have witnessed parental divorce report (a) more negative attitudes about marriage (Gabardi & Rosen, 1991; Jennings, Salts, & Smith, 1991; Long, 1987); (b) more favorable attitudes toward divorce (Franklin, Janoff-Bulman, & Roberts, 1990; Greenberg & Nay, 1982); (c) less optimism about having a successful future marriage (Franklin et al., 1990; Wallerstein, 1987); and (d) less trust of current and future partners (Duran-Aydintug, 1997; Franklin et al.,

1990; Johnston & Thomas, 1996). Further, children of divorced parents exhibit both a reluctance to commit fully to marriage (Glenn & Kramer, 1987) and a fear of repeating their parents' mistakes (Franklin et al., 1990; Gabardi & Rosen, 1991; Glenn & Kramer, 1987; Kalter, Riemer, Brickman, & Chen, 1985; Wallerstein, 1987; Wallerstein & Kelly, 1980). Given these findings, it is not surprising that divorce rates and other incidences of marital instability are higher among children of divorce (Amato & Booth, 1991; Black & Sprenkle, 1991; Greenberg & Nay, 1982; Kulka & Weingarten, 1979; Mueller & Pope, 1977; Webster, Orbuch, & House, 1995).

It should be noted, however, that Wallerstein (1984) claims many negative effects of divorce diminish over time. In her study, adolescents whose parents had been divorced for at least 10 years were optimistic about having an enduring marriage, and most believed that their parents' divorce would not affect the likelihood that they would divorce. Still other researchers find that the divorce of one's parents has little impact on one's marital attitudes and expectations (Carson & Pauly, 1990; Jones & Nelson, 1996; Landis-Kleine, Foley, Nall, Padgett, & Walters-Palmer, 1995; Stone & Hutchinson, 1992). For example, Landis-Kleine et al. (1995) found most college students from intact and divorce homes report a strong desire for and commitment to marriage, and similar attitudes toward marriage and divorce. Similarly, students from intact and divorce homes have reported comparable expectations for marriage (Jones & Nelson, 1996) and children of divorce have expressed significant optimism about getting married and avoiding parental mistakes (Wallerstein, 1984). In summary, previous research indicates parental divorce is often, but not always, associated with lowered marital expectations and optimism.

Within the substantial body of research examining the effects of parental divorce, few studies have distinguished between children from single- and multiple-divorce homes. The few that have suggest parental divorce has additive (negative) effects on children's marital outcomes. For example, Amato and Booth (1991) found that married persons who had experienced multiple parental divorces had less maternal contact, more marital problems, greater marital instability, and higher divorce rates than persons who had experienced a single parental divorce. Further, the more parental divorces a person experienced, the more severe and prolonged his or her adjustment difficulties. In other research, Duran-Aydintug (1997) found that most students from divorced homes expressed a fear of commitment; of these students, half had parents who changed partners frequently or remarried more than once. Finally, Spink and Boyer-Pennington (in press) asked college students from intact, single- and multiple-divorce homes to report their expectations regarding the quality of their future marriage. Although the differences were not statistically significant, participants' marital expectations tended to worsen with each parental divorce.

The small number of studies on this topic generally indicate that multiple parental divorces have more negative consequences for marriage outcomes than a single parental divorce. Given this finding and the prevalence of divorce in the U.S., it is important to examine whether multiple parental divorces affect the marital expectations of those who witness them. Specifically, do single adult children from multiple-divorce homes hold less positive expectations regarding the quality of their own (possible) future marriage (as hinted at by Spink & Boyer-Pennington, in press)? If so, are such individuals less optimistic about their chances of getting and staying married? Further, to what extent do single adults from multiple-divorce homes recognize or acknowledge parental divorce as a risk factor in others' marital outcomes? Finally, how do these expectations compare to those of single students from intact and single-divorce homes? To answer these questions, in the present study, unmarried college students from intact, single-divorce, and multiple-divorce homes were asked questions about their expectations for future marriage, their own expectations for divorce, as well as their expectations that others would divorce, and their perceptions of control over their own future marriage.

PREDICTIONS OF THE PRESENT STUDY

Based on previous findings by Franklin et al. (1990), Spink and Boyer-Pennington (in press), Kalter et al. (1985), and Wallerstein (1987), unmarried students from intact homes were expected to have more positive expectations about the quality of their future marriage than those from single-divorce homes. We expected that the former would view their (never divorced) parents as positive marital role models whose positive marriage experience reflects the typical state of affairs in marriage (see Wallerstein, 1991). For the same reason, those from intact homes were also expected to be more optimistic than students from single-divorce homes regarding their likelihood of marrying and avoiding divorce.

Two different patterns of results were considered possible regarding the marital expectations and optimism expressed by participants from multiple-divorce homes. On the one hand, each parental divorce witnessed by an individual may adversely color or shape his or her view of marriage and the likelihood of its success. If this is the case, participants from multiple-divorce homes should hold the most negative marital expectations and should be least optimistic about getting married and avoiding divorce. On the other hand, observing the divorce of one's parents may motivate individuals to avoid making the same mistakes (Wallerstein, 1984), increasing the sense of control over one's future marriage outcomes. Witnessing multiple parental divorces may lead individuals to believe that they can learn from their parents' mistakes, recognize serious marital troubles when they arise, avoid such troubles, and ultimately to believe that they have more control over whether their marriage succeeds or fails (although see Carson & Pauly, 1990). Research indicates that people are very optimistic about events that they believe they can control (Higgins, St. Amand, & Poole, 1997; Hoorens, 1995; Tennen & Affleck, 1987; Weinstein, 1980, 1984), especially events perceived as threatening to one's self-worth or well-being (Taylor & Armor, 1996; Taylor & Brown, 1988). Thus, if unmarried children from multiple-divorce homes express a strong sense of marital control, they may also express relatively positive marital expectations and optimism.

Predictions regarding whether unmarried students acknowledge parental divorce as a risk factor for others were based on findings from the significant body of research on "unrealistic optimism," that indicates that people consider themselves at less risk for various negative events than comparable others (see Armor & Taylor, 1998, for a comprehensive review). For example, people often believe they are less likely than others to (a) be involved in automobile accidents (Robertson, 1977); (b) have an unwanted pregnancy (Burger & Burns, 1988); and (c) develop illnesses such as cancer and hypertension (Perloff & Fetzer, 1986). Although individuals recognize "at risk" groups and estimate those groups' risk accordingly, most still see themselves as invulnerable (even when they are a member of the at-risk group) (McKenna, Warburton, & Winwood, 1993; McMaster & Lee, 1991; Pennington, Crecelius, & Ray, 1997, Pennington & Tate, 1998; Strecher, Kreuter, & Krobin, 1995). Based on these findings, we expected that participants would view parental divorce as a risk factor for other unmarried students, but not for themselves. As a result, they should report being less likely to divorce than other students, regardless of the parental marital status of themselves or the comparison student.

METHOD

Participants

Two hundred and seventy-three single students (196 women, 95 men; M Age = 20.2 years, range = 17-36 years) from a medium-size southern university volunteered to participate. One hundred five students were from intact homes, 124 students were from single-divorce homes, and 44 students were from multiple-divorce homes. Of the 44 participants from multiple-divorce homes, 37 had parents who had divorced twice, 5 had parents who had divorced 3 times, 1 had parents who had divorced 4 times, and 1 had parents who had divorced 5 times. Most participants were Caucasian, traditional college-age students from lower- to upper-middle income backgrounds.

Procedure

Participants were recruited through their general psychology courses and completed a four-part survey. This survey consisted of (a) the Attitudes Toward Marriage Scale (ATMS) (Kinnaird & Gerrard, 1986; Wallin, 1954); (b) a demographic questionnaire; (c) questions regarding participants' views of their own and comparison others' likelihood of getting divorced; and (d) questions that assessed participants' perceptions of control regarding future marriage. The majority of surveys were group administered, and all participants were informed that their responses would be anonymous. The entire survey took approximately 20 minutes to complete.

Survey Instruments

Demographic questionnaire. Participants reported their age, gender, marital status, and biological parents' marital status. Participants from divorced homes also reported the number of times their parents had been divorced, their own age when the divorce(s) occurred, and with whom they lived after the divorce.

Marriage expectations. Participants' marriage expectations were assessed using the ATMS, a self-report questionnaire that measures one's expectations about the quality of one's own future marriage. The questionnaire used in the present study contained nine items from Wallin's (1954) ATMS scale (e.g., "Do you ever have doubts as to whether you will enjoy living exclusively in marriage with one person after marriage?" and "How happy do you think you will be if you marry?") and two items from Kinnaird and Gerrard's (1986) modification of Wallin's (1954) scale (e.g., "Do you ever worry that the person you marry won't fulfill his or her responsibilities in the marriage?") (see Touliatos, Perlmutter, & Strauss, 1990, for a description of the differences between the two scales). Most items were scored using a 6-point Likert-type scale (0 = not at all or very unhappy, 5 = very much or very happy). Higher totals indicated more favorable marriage expectations; the maximum score possible was 43.

Optimism questionnaire. First, all participants estimated their own likelihood of getting married in the future (0 = definitely will not get married, 5 = definitely will get married). Then participants estimated the likelihood that their marriage would end in divorce. They also considered typical college students from their university whose parents had never divorced, divorced once, and divorced more than once, and reported the likelihood that the marriage of each individual would end in divorce. Divorce likelihood estimates were made using a 7-point Likert-type scale (1 = definitely will not get divorced, 7 = definitely will get divorced). Lower scores indicated greater optimism about avoiding divorce.

Perceptions of control. Participants answered six questions developed by the second author to assess how much control they perceived having over the success of their own future marriage. Three of the items were worded such that agreement indicated greater perceived control (e.g., "If I work at my marriage hard enough, it will not end in divorce"), and three were worded such that agreement indicated less perceived control (e.g., "If my marriage is successful, it will probably be a matter of luck"). Responses to the six items were made using a 5-point Likert-type scale (1 = strongly disagree, 5 = strongly agree).

The three low control items were reverse scored. Higher total scores reflected greater perceived control.

RESULTS

A series of 2 (Participant Sex) $\times$ 3 (Parent Marital Status: intact marriage, single-divorce, multiple-divorce) analyses of variance (ANOVAs) were conducted on participants' (a) overall expectations regarding their own future marriage (as assessed by the ATMS); (b) estimated likelihood of getting married; (c) estimated likelihood of getting divorced; and (d) perceptions of relationship control. Analyses revealed sex main effects on several dependent measures; generally, females expressed more positive expectations and were more optimistic than males. However, these sex effects did not qualify any of the effects of parental status described below and are conceptually uninteresting. For these reasons they will not be discussed further.

Marriage Expectations

Analyses revealed a main effect of parent marital status for participants' overall expectations for marriage, F (2, 270) = 4.41, $p < .05$. Simple effects tests indicated that students from intact homes had more positive expectations for their future marriage ($M = 31.94$, $SD = 7.38$) than students from single-divorce homes ($M = 29.23$, $SD = 7.75$), t (227) = 2.70, and multiple-divorce homes ($M = 29.05$, $SD = 6.99$), t (147) = 2.22, $ps < .05$. Marriage expectations did not differ between participants from single- and multiple-divorce homes, $p > .05$.

Marital Optimism

Students from all three parent marital status groups were equally optimistic about marrying in the future (M Intact Marriage = 4.41, $SD = 1.01$; M Single-Divorce = 4.30, $SD = 1.00$; M Multiple-Divorce = 4.25, $SD = 1.01$), $p > .05$. A 3 (Parent Marital Status) $\times$ 4 (Individual Rated: self, intact other, single-divorce other, multiple-divorce other) mixed model analysis of variance (ANOVA) was conducted to examine participants' divorce likelihood estimates. A main effect of individual rated was found, F (3, 214) = 169.22, $p < .05$. Simple effects tests revealed significant differences among all four groups, $ts > 9.91$, $ps < .05$. Specifically, participants rated themselves as least likely to get divorced ($M = 2.13$, $SD = 0.98$), followed by typical college students from intact homes ($M = 2.93$, $SD = 1.06$), single-divorce homes ($M = 3.87$, $SD = 1.12$), and multiple-divorce homes ($M = 4.59$, $SD = 1.29$).

Analyses indicated that this pattern was qualified by parent marital status, F (6, 430) = 5.78, $p < .05$. Subsequent Tukey post-hoc simple effects tests were conducted to decompose the two-way interaction. As shown in Figure 1, individuals from intact homes were more optimistic about avoiding divorce ($M = 1.88$, $SD = 0.84$) than individuals from single-divorce homes ($M = 2.31$, $SD = 1.02$), t (213) = -3.30, $p < .05$, but not multiple-divorce homes ($M = 2.17$, $SD = 1.03$), t (134) = -1.69, $p = .09$. Further, participants from intact homes rated someone from an intact home as less likely to get divorced ($M = 2.48$, $SD = 1.02$) than did participants from single-divorce homes ($M = 3.21$, $SD = 0.91$), t (208) = -5.51, and multiple-divorce homes ($M = 3.41$, $SD = 1.12$), t (140) = -4.65, $ps < .05$. The latter two groups provided similar divorce risk estimates for a comparison other from an intact home, $p > .05$.

In contrast, participants from single-divorce homes rated someone from a single-divorce home as less likely to get divorced ($M = 3.63$,

FIGURE 1. Optimism ratings as a function of parental marital status.

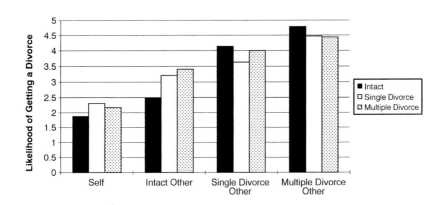

SD = 1.18) than did participants from intact homes (M = 4.14, SD = 0.98), t (213) = 3.38, p < .05. Finally, all three parent marital status groups provided comparably high divorce likelihood ratings for individuals from multiple-divorce homes (M Intact Marriage = 4.79, SD = 1.28; M Single-Divorce = 4.47, SD = 1.27; M Multiple-Divorce = 4.44, SD = 1.35), ps > .05.

Thus, participants (especially those from intact homes) were optimistic about avoiding divorce. All participants rated themselves as less likely to get divorced than each of the other three comparison persons. Further, participants from intact and single-divorce homes exhibited in-group favoritism by providing relatively lower divorce risk estimates for another whose parents had the same marital status. All participants were equally pessimistic about the marriage of someone from a multiple-divorce home.

Perceptions of Relationship Control

Analyses conducted on participants' perceptions of marital control revealed a main effect of parent marital status, F (2, 268) = 8.40, p < .05. Simple effects tests indicated that participants from multiple-divorce homes reported higher levels of relationship control (M = 21.00, SD = 3.52) than did participants from intact homes (M = 18.96, SD = 2.11), t (147) = −4.36, and single-divorce homes (M = 19.32, SD = .28), t (164) = −3.01, ps < .05. The latter two groups did not differ from one another on perceptions of control, p > .05.

DISCUSSION

In the present study, participants from intact homes held more positive expectations for their future marriage than did participants from single- and multiple-divorce homes. This finding is consistent with prior research findings that children of divorced parents hold less positive attitudes and lower expectations about marriage (Gabardi & Rosen, 1991; Jennings et al., 1991; Long, 1987; Wallerstein, 1987). Thus, our results echo the general finding that, in some ways, parental divorce adversely affects those who experience it. Further, the present study extends this general finding to include children of multiple-divorce.[1] However, divorce effects on marriage quality expectations do not appear to be additive. The level of marriage expectation positivity expressed by single- and multiple-divorce participants was virtually identical (see also Spink and Boyer-Pennington, in press).

Upon initial consideration, one might conclude that those individuals from intact homes are especially fortunate. Research examining the "self-fulfilling prophecy" has demonstrated that an individual's expectations may create conditions that result in his or her beliefs coming true (see Hilton, Darley, and Fleming, 1989; Rosenthal & Rubin, 1978). For example, Murray and Holmes (1997) found that optimism about the future of an intimate relationship (and perceptions of relationship control) predicted greater relationship satisfaction, love, and trust up to 12 months later in dating couples. Once married, those holding positive expectations about marriage may act in ways that lead to the confirmation of such expectations. In the absence of unforeseen, uncontrollable impediments (e.g., extreme financial problems, life-threatening illness or injury), acting in ways that promote the quality of one's marriage should lead to happier, more stable marriages. Further, holding negative expectations or fearing rejection might be self-defeating and detrimental to one's marriage to the extent that those expectations and fears cause one to elicit otherwise unlikely or avoidable relationship conflicts and problems (see Downey, Freitas, Michaelis, & Khouri, 1998; Hilton et al., 1989).

However, careful examination of the marital expectation scores observed in the present study suggests a difference of degree rather than kind. That is, all three groups of participants had average ATMS scores above the midpoint of the scale. Thus, although those from intact homes held more favorable expectations about marriage than those who had experienced parental divorce from divorce homes, all participants held somewhat positive marital expectations. In light of this, it is possible that those with divorced parents (single or multiple divorce) also benefit (to a lesser extent) from the effects of the self-fulfilling prophecy. The role of marriage expectations on actual marital success should be examined more closely by future research.

In the present study, differences in marriage expectations associated with parental divorce were not accompanied by lowered marriage likelihood estimates. Participants from intact, single-divorce, and multiple-divorce homes rated themselves as equally likely to get married in the future (see Long, 1987, for similar findings). Results regarding the likelihood of avoiding divorce are somewhat less straightforward.

On the one hand, participants from single-divorce homes did rate themselves as more likely to get divorced than did those from intact homes (with participants from multiple-divorce homes scoring in-between). However, mean scores suggest that all three groups generally expected to avoid divorce. On average, each group rated its own likelihood of getting divorced as approximately "2" on a 7-point scale (corresponding to "very unlikely to get divorced"). The fact that all participants in the present study expected to get and stay married, despite their parents' marital status, suggests that individuals who experienced parental divorce were not "turned off" from the prospects of marriage by their parents' divorces.

Participants were also optimistic when comparing themselves with others. Each group viewed itself as significantly less likely to get divorced than each of the other three comparison targets. That is, students from all three groups rated themselves as less likely to get divorced than any of the three similar/dissimilar comparison others they rated. It is interesting that even participants from multiple-divorce homes saw themselves as less likely to divorce than a typical college student from an intact home. The degree of marital optimism expressed by participants in the present study resembles that found in Wallerstein's (1991) 10 year follow-up in which children of divorce seemed eager to avoid divorce for themselves and for the sake of their future children. This is also consistent with the level of optimism expressed in optimism studies involving high school students (Hoorens, 1995), college students (Higgins et al., 1997; Weinstein, 1980, 1984; Weinstein & Lachendro, 1982), and dating and married couples (Baker & Emery, 1993; Murray & Holmes, 1997) (but see Franklin et al., 1990; Wallerstein, 1987, for different findings).

In general, participants did acknowledge the potential adverse impact of parental divorce for others (although not for themselves). They saw parental divorce as contributing, in an additive fashion, to another person's likelihood of getting divorced. For instance, they rated peers from intact homes as less likely to get divorced than peers from single-divorce homes. Further, peers from multiple-divorce homes were judged by all three groups as most likely to have their future marriage end in divorce. Unexpectedly and interestingly, this effect was tempered by the degree of similarity between the participant and comparison other. Participants whose parents were still married rated a similar comparison other as less likely to divorce than did the other two groups of participants. Similarly, participants whose parents had divorced once rated a similar comparison other as less likely to divorce than did participants with never-divorced parents. Thus, when considering risk estimate differences across the three groups of participants, it appears that those with never-divorced and those with single-divorce parents expressed favoritism toward the comparison person most similar to them. Perhaps this represents a specific example of the more general "in group bias"–the tendency for individuals to be more positive toward members of their own group than toward members of other groups (see Tajfel & Turner, 1986). This phenomenon is also consistent with prior research that finds that people generally view close, similar others (e.g., friends, family members) as almost as invulnerable to negative events as themselves (Pennington et al., 1997; Pennington & Tate, 1998; Perloff & Fetzer, 1986).

It should be noted that marital optimism was especially striking among participants from multiple-divorce homes. First, as previously mentioned, such individuals' own divorce risk estimates resembled those of participants from intact homes. Second, this occurred even though multiple-divorce participants regarded a typical same-university student from a multiple-divorce home as having a rather large chance of getting divorced (as reflected by an average rating of 4.44 on a scale of 1 to 7). Clearly, participants whose parents divorced multiple times did not regard parental divorce as a relevant "risk factor" for their own marital outcomes. Why? Single students from multiple-divorce homes may have regarded the multiple unsuccessful marital experiences of their parents as instructive of how (not) to interact with one's spouse, thereby leading them to believe they possess significant control over their own marital success. This explanation is consistent with the fact that, in the present study, participants from multiple-divorce homes reported having more control over a future marriage than did students from intact and single-divorce homes. This is also consistent with Taylor and Armor's (1996) findings that those who experience a negative event often have exaggerated perceptions of the future, in general, and a distorted sense of control about the future, in specific. Additionally, prior research showing that people are especially optimistic about events over which they feel they have control (Weinstein, 1980, 1984) supports the possibility that multiple-divorce participants' optimism arises from increased perceptions of control. Interestingly, it is not clear why those with divorced parents do not view others from a similar background as benefitting from such experience. Future research should examine this question.

In summary, although participants from divorced homes had less favorable expectations for their own future marriage than participants from intact homes, all participants held generally positive expectations, and were equally optimistic about getting married. Also, participants from single- and multiple-divorce homes were relatively optimistic that they would not get divorced. Thus they did not consider their own likelihood of divorce to be affected by their parents' marital history, even though they recognized the divorce risk for others from divorced homes (by rating individuals from intact homes as less likely to divorce than individuals from single- and multiple-divorce homes). Participants from intact and single-divorce homes also showed in-group favoritism for comparison others described as similar to them; both groups rated similar comparison others as less likely to divorce than dissimilar comparison others. Finally, participants from multiple-divorce homes saw themselves as having more control over their future marriage than did participants from the other two groups, perhaps accounting for their optimistic beliefs regarding avoiding divorce. These findings, coupled with more general findings regarding optimism and control, have important implications for individuals from divorced homes because they suggest that a reasonable degree of relationship illusion can be beneficial, whereas unrealistic expectations about marriage may increase the likelihood that individuals will experience marital instability or failure in the future.

NOTE

1. Participants who had witnessed two or more parental divorces had nearly identical scores on the ATMS as those who had witnessed one parental divorce. This finding should be encouraging for those who have experienced successive parental divorces. We should note that 82% of participants in the multiple-divorce condition had parents who had only divorced twice. Consequently, conclusions made about individuals from multiple-divorce homes can most safely be generalized to those individuals who have experienced two parental divorces. However, an examination of the means of participants who had experienced more than two parental divorces suggests that their expectations for marriage are similar to those who had experienced two parental divorces.

REFERENCES

Amato, P. R., & Booth, A. (1991). Consequences of parental divorce and marital unhappiness for adult well-being. *Social Forces, 69*, 895-914.

Armor, D. A., & Taylor, S. E. (1998). Situated optimism: Specific outcome expectancies and self-regulation. In M. P. Zanna (Ed.), *Advances in experimental social psychology* (Vol. 30, pp. 309-379). New York: Academic Press.

Baker, L. A., & Emery, R. E. (1993). When every relationship is above average: Perceptions and expectations of divorce at the time of marriage. *Law and Human Behavior, 17*, 439-450.

Berk, L. E. (1997). *Child development* (4th ed.). Needham Heights, MA: Allyn and Bacon.

Black, L. E., & Sprenkle, D. H. (1991). Gender differences in college students' attitudes toward divorce and their willingness to marry. *Journal of Divorce & Remarriage, 14*, 47-60.

Burger, J. M., & Burns, L. (1988). The illusion of unique invulnerability and the use of effective contraception. *Personality and Social Psychology Bulletin, 14*(2), 264-270.

Carson, D. K., & Pauly, K. M. (1990). Perceptions of marriage and family life of young adults with and without histories of parental divorce. *Psychological Reports, 66*, 33-34.

Downey, G., Freitas, A. L., Michaelis, B., & Khouri, J. (1998). The self-fulfilling prophecy in close relationships: Rejection sensitivity and rejection by romantic partners. *Journal of Personality and Social Psychology, 75*, 545-560.

Duran-Aydintug, C. (1997). Adult children of divorce revisited: When they speak up. *Journal of Divorce & Remarriage, 27*, 71-83.

Franklin, K. M., Janoff-Bulman, R., & Roberts, J. E. (1990). Long-term impact of parental divorce on optimism and trust: Changes in general assumptions or narrow beliefs? *Journal of Personality and Social Psychology, 59*, 743-755.

Gabardi, L., & Rosen, L. A. (1991). Differences between college students from divorced and intact families. *Journal of Divorce & Remarriage, 15*, 175-191.

Glenn, N. D., & Kramer, K. B. (1987). The psychological well-being of adult children of divorce. *Journal of Marriage and the Family, 49*, 811-825.

Greenberg, E., & Nay, R. (1982). The intergenerational transmission of marital instability reconsidered. *Journal of Marriage and the Family, 44*, 335-347.

Hetherington, E. M., Bridges, M., & Insabella, G. M. (1998, February). What matters? What does not? Five perspectives on the association between marital transitions and children's adjustment. *American Psychologist*, 167-184.

Higgins, N. C., St. Amand, M. D., & Poole, G. D. (1997). The controllability of negative life experiences mediates unrealistic optimism. *Social Indicators Research, 42*, 299-323.

Hilton, J. L., Darley, J. M., & Fleming, J. H. (1989). Self-fulfilling prophecies and self-defeating behavior. In R. C. Curtis (Ed.), *Self-defeating behaviors: Experimental research, clinical impressions, and practical implications* (pp. 41-65). New York: Plenum Press.

Hoorens, V. (1995). Self-favoring biases, self-presentation, and the self-other asymmetry in social comparison. *Journal of Personality, 63*, 793-817.

Jennings, A. M., Salts, C. J., & Smith, T. A. (1991). Attitudes toward marriage: Effects of parental conflict, family structure, and gender. *Journal of Divorce & Remarriage, 17,* 67-79.

Johnston, S. G., & Thomas, A. M. (1996). Divorce versus intact parental marriage and perceived risk and dyadic trust in present heterosexual relationships. *Psychological Reports, 78,* 387-390.

Jones, G. D., & Nelson, E. S. (1996). Expectations of marriage among college students from intact and non-intact homes. *Journal of Divorce & Remarriage, 26,* 171-189.

Kalter, N., Riemer, B., Brickman, A., & Chen, J. W. (1985). Implications of parental divorce for female development. *Journal of the American Academy of Child Psychiatry, 24,* 538-544.

Kinnaird, K., & Gerrard, M. (1986). Premarital sexual behavior and attitudes toward marriage and divorce among young women as a function of their mothers' marital status. *Journal of Marriage and Family, 48,* 757-765.

Kulka, R. A., & Weingarten, H. (1979). The long term effects of parental divorce in childhood on adult adjustment. *Journal of Social Issues, 35,* 50-78.

Landis-Kleine, C., Foley, L. A., Nall, L., Padgett, P., & Walters-Palmer, L. (1995). Attitudes toward marriage and divorce held by young adults. *Journal of Divorce & Remarriage, 23,* 63-73.

Long, B. (1987). Perceptions of parental discord and parental separations in the U. S.: Effects on daughters' attitudes toward marriage and courtship progress. *Journal of Social Psychology, 127,* 573-582.

McKenna, F. P., Warburton, D. M., & Winwood, M. (1993). Exploring the limits of optimism: The case of smokers' decision making. *British Journal of Psychology, 84,* 389-394.

McMaster, C., & Lee, C. (1991). Cognitive dissonance in tobacco smokers. *Addictive Behaviors, 16,* 349-353.

Mueller, C., & Pope, H. (1977). Marital instability: A study of its transmission between generations. *Journal of Marriage and Family, 39,* 83-93.

Murray, S. L., & Holmes, J. G. (1997). A leap of faith? Positive illusions in romantic relationships. *Personality and Social Psychology Bulletin, 23,* 586-604.

National Center for Health Statistics. (1998). Births, marriages, divorces, and deaths for 1997. *Monthly Vital Statistics Report (Vol. 46, No. 12).* National Center for Health Statistics: Hyattsville, MD.

Pennington, J., Crecelius, M., & Ray, J. A. (1997, June). *The extension of optimism bias to close others who smoke.* Paper presented at the meeting of the Society for Research on Nicotine and Tobacco. Nashville, TN.

Pennington, J., & Tate, J. C. (1998, June). *Why is unrealistic optimism extended to close others who smoke?* Paper presented at the meeting of the Society for Research on Nicotine and Tobacco. Houston, TX.

Perloff, L. S., & Fetzer, B. K. (1986). Self-other judgments and perceived vulnerability to victimization. *Journal of Personality and Social Psychology, 50,* 502-510.

Robertson, L. S. (1977). Car crashes: Perceived vulnerability and willingness to pay for crash protection. *Journal of Community Health, 3,* 136-141.

Rosenthal, R., & Rubin, D. B. (1978). Interpersonal expectancy effects: The first 345 studies. *Behavioral and Brain Sciences*, *3*, 377-386.

Spink, C., & Boyer-Pennington, M. E. (in press). An examination of the impact of parental divorce on students' attitudes about marriage. *Psi Chi Journal of Undergraduate Research*.

Strecher, V. J., Kreuter, M. W., & Krobin, S. C. (1995). Do cigarette smokers have unrealistic perceptions of their heart attack, cancer, and stroke risks? *Journal of Behavioral Medicine*, *18*(1), 45-54.

Stone, M. K., & Hutchinson, R. L. (1992). Familial conflict and attitudes toward marriage: A psychological wholeness perspective. *Journal of Divorce & Remarriage*, *18*, 79-91.

Tajfel, H., & Turner, J. C. (1986). The social identity theory of intergroup behavior. In W. Worchel & W. G. Austin (Eds.), *Psychology of Intergroup Relations* (2nd ed., pp. 7-24). Chicago: Nelson-Hall.

Taylor, S. E., & Armor, D. A. (1996). Positive illusions and coping with adversity. *Journal of Personality*, *64*, 873-898.

Taylor, S. E., & Brown, J. D. (1988). Illusion and well-being: A social psychological perspective on mental health. *Psychological Bulletin*, *103*, 193-210.

Tennen, H., & Affleck, G. (1987). The costs and benefits of optimistic explanations and dispositional optimism. *Journal of Personality*, *55*, 377-393.

Touliatos, J., Perlmutter, B. F., & Strauss, M. A. (Eds.) (1990). Intimacy. *Handbook of Family Measurement Techniques* (pp. 203). Newsbury Park, CA: Sage.

Wallerstein, J. S. (1984). Children of divorce: Preliminary report of a ten year follow-up of young children. *American Journal of Orthopsychiatry*, *54*, 444-458.

Wallerstein, J. S. (1987). Children of divorce: Report of a ten year follow-up of early latency-age children. *American Journal of Orthopsychiatry*, *57*, 199-211.

Wallerstein, J. S. (1991). The long-term effects of divorce on children: A review. *Journal of the American Academy of Child and Adolescent Psychiatry*, *30*, 349-360.

Wallerstein, J. S., & Kelly, J. B. (1980). *Surviving the breakup: How children and parents cope with divorce.* Grant McIntyre.

Wallin, P. (1954). Marital happiness of parents and their children's attitude toward marriage. *American Sociological Review*, *19*, 20-23.

Webster, P. S., Orbuch, T. L., & House, J. S. (1995). Effects of childhood family background on adult marital quality and perceived stability. *American Journal of Sociology*, *101*, 404-432.

Weinstein, N. D. (1980). Unrealistic optimism about future life events. *Journal of Personality and Social Psychology*, *39*, 806-820.

Weinstein, N. D. (1984). Why it won't happen to me: Perceptions of risk factors and susceptibility. *Health Psychology*, *3*, 431-457.

Weinstein, N. D., & Lachendro, E. (1982). Egocentrism as a source of unrealistic optimism. *Personality and Social Psychology Bulletin*, *8*, 195-200.

The Influence of Parental Divorce
on the Romantic Relationship Beliefs
of Young Adults

David Mahl

SUMMARY. A qualitative study was conducted, in which 28 college students were interviewed about their romantic relationships and the experiences associated with their parents' divorce. Variability was found to exist in the nature of the participants' divorce-related experiences. This variability is captured by categories representing the pre-divorce context and post-divorce changes surrounding parental divorce. A number of categories also emerged which characterize the participants' beliefs about and behaviors in romantic relationships. A model was developed to describe the apparent influence of parental divorce and individual characteristics on the participants' romantic relationships. Results demonstrate that parental divorce should not be simply viewed as a negative event. Rather, many situations exist in which parental divorce results in improved family relationships.

KEYWORDS. Parental divorce and the romantic relationships of young adults

Divorce has become a significant feature of the American family landscape. For the past twenty years the divorce rate has remained

Address correspondence to: David Mahl, PhD, P. O. Box C, New Rochelle, NY 10804.

This study was completed as a doctoral dissertation, School of Psychology, University of Texas at Austin.

[Haworth co-indexing entry note]: "The Influence of Parental Divorce on the Romantic Relationship Beliefs of Young Adults." Mahl, David. Co-published simultaneously in *Journal of Divorce & Remarriage* (The Haworth Clinical Practice Press, an imprint of The Haworth Press, Inc.) Vol. 34, No. 3/4, 2001, pp. 89-118; and: *Divorce and the Next Generation: Perspectives for Young Adults in the New Millennium* (ed: Craig A. Everett) The Haworth Clinical Practice Press, an imprint of The Haworth Press, Inc., 2001, pp. 89-118. Single or multiple copies of this article are available for a fee from The Haworth Document Delivery Service [1-800-342-9678, 9:00 a.m. - 5:00 p.m. (EST). E-mail address: getinfo@haworthpressinc. com].

stable. Half of all recent marriages will end in divorce, 60% of these involving children (Klee, Schmidt & Johnson, 1989). This results in more than one-third of children experiencing the divorce of their parents before the age of 16 (Walsh, 1993). Assumptions about "normal" or "traditional" family structures which were held in the past do not apply to the realities of many modern families. The prevalence of divorce in the lives of children provides the impetus for exploring the ways in which it alters their experiences and beliefs.

A perusal of the research literature concerning the impact of divorce on children reveals that the following topics have been of particular interest: children's understanding of and response to divorce; the long- and short-term effects of divorce on children's adjustment; and exploration of the aspects of divorce which affect this adjustment. In tracking the impact of divorce on children's development some researchers have only investigated children whose parents have separated (Wallerstein & Kelly, 1980; Wallerstein & Blakeslee, 1989; Shaw & Emery, 1987). Yet such studies do not have the benefit of a control group to which the adjustment of the divorced group can be compared. In order to adjust for this, some researchers have compared the development of children from divorced families to those from intact families (Kulka & Weingarten, 1979; Stolberg & Anker, 1983; Amato & Keith, 1991a; Warren et al., 1985; Block et al., 1986), whereas others have differentiated between divorced, low-conflict and high-conflict intact families (Birnbach & Hyman, 1996).

Research on children's adjustment following parental separation has produced results that can be organized into two broad categories. Some studies have concluded that exposure to marital dissolution has deleterious consequences for the development of children (Amato & Keith, 1991a; Wallerstein, 1991). Other researchers have explained the negative effects of parental separation using other factors that are positively correlated with divorce, specifically parental conflict, lower socioeconomic status and inconsistent parenting (Block, Block & Gjerde, 1986; Emery, 1982; Emery & O'Leary, 1982).

As children mature and encounter new developmental tasks, it has been found that they reconceptualize the divorce in relation to new experiences. Numerous authors have presented results that indicate that divorce affects the beliefs that adult offspring hold about romantic relationships (Garbardi & Rosen, 1992; Tayler, Parker & Roy, 1995; Westervelt & Vandenberg, 1997), the marital success of these offspring (Hetherington, Bridges & Insabella, 1998; Guttmann, 1989), and their desire to start their own families (Booth & Edwards, 1990). In considering these long-term effects of divorce, it is important to remember that most adults adjust well to their parents' divorce, so that the differences between adults from divorced versus intact families is relatively small (Amato & Booth, 1991).

The ability to sustain successful social and intimate relationships is an essential component of human functioning. Children who come from a background of marital disharmony often develop cautious expectations of future relations. Chronic exposure to parental conflict can leave children with a negative view of the world and how people relate to each other (Franklin et al., 1990). Their prior experiences are borne out in the new relationships they develop as adults. Wallerstein and Kelly (1980) found that some adult children of divorce, due to their early exposure to independence and their reliance upon peers' support during the acute stage of adjustment, had a mature understanding of social relationships. In a later documentation of their longitudinal study, Wallerstein and Blakeslee (1989) found children of divorce to be tentative about intimate relations and love.

Although the differences are small in many studies, researchers have found that adults from divorced families differ significantly from peers who were raised by continuously married parents on a number of relationship behaviors. Offspring of divorced parents begin their relationship careers earlier, become sexually active at an earlier age, have a greater number of sexual partners, have shorter relationships, and have a more negative opinion of their romantic relationships (Gabardi & Rosen, 1992; Hetherington et al., 1998; Spruijt, 1995). These negative adjustment markers are reflected in the beliefs and conceptions that many adult children of divorce hold about relationships. For example, Westervelt and Vanderberg (1997) found that adult children of divorced families reported less intimate relationships than peers from intact families. These researchers suggested that the marital relationship is the prototype for all intimate relationships and that children from divorced families are likely exposed to a parental relationship marked by conflict, distance, and less intimacy. In addition, Gabardi and Rosen (1992) explain the finding that offspring from divorced families have a greater number of sexual partners by stating that these individuals may view sex as a means of achieving intimacy, demonstrating commitment, and avoiding conflict. They also found that young adults from divorced families desire greater sexual involvement in their relationships. Gabardi and Rosen hypothesized that children may observe their parents engaging in sexual relationships as a way to establish intimate relationships following divorce and that, as adults, these offspring view sex as a way to create a better relationship for themselves.

Fear of betrayal and rejection, similar to their experiences with the noncustodial parent, impinges on the ability of adults from divorced families to depend on others, particularly in intimate relationships. Compared to adults from intact families, young adults from divorce backgrounds have been found to be "less trusting of their partners and more hesitant to get involved [in intimate relationships] on a deeper emotional level as they fear being rejected and hurt" (Johnston & Thomas, 1996, p. 390). Franklin and her colleagues (1990) explored the issue of trust, which they defined as the belief in the integrity and dependability of others, in connection with relationships. They found that adult children of divorce were pessimistic about the ability to trust intimate partners, but did not differ from adults from intact families on measures of general trust in others. Therefore adult children of divorce may be more cautious about getting involved in intimate relationships, but will not be affected in their ability to trust others with whom they engage in social relations. Franklin and her colleagues (1990) concluded that many adults may have reshaped their schemata about romantic relationships in response to the experiences associated with their parents' divorce. Yet, they found that these adults apply these theories, specifically, to marriage and intimate relationships, rather than allowing it to impact their ability to trust in all social relationships.

Conflict resolution is an important skill in sustaining harmonious relationships of all kinds. Social learning theories can be used to understand how exposure to parental conflict and divorce affects adults' schemata, specifically regarding conflict resolution techniques. Guttmann (1989) found that children learn from parental divorce to resolve differences by withdrawing from the situation. Jenkins, Smith and Graham (1989), on the other hand, proposed that adult children of divorce have improved conflict resolution skills. These children likely had greater opportunities to develop empathic, consoling skills, perhaps through helping siblings or parents adjust during the divorce process. Gabardi and Rosen (1992) present still a different view. They suggest that young adults from divorced families may view conflict as detrimental to a relationship, a sign that the relationship is not "healthy," and therefore disagreements are to be avoided.

This study is an exploration of the intimate relationship schemata of young adults from divorced families. These individuals were recruited and asked to share their beliefs and ideas about romantic relationships. A primary area of interest for this study is the connection between these beliefs and the perceptions that adults hold of their family background.

METHODOLOGY

As mentioned above, ambiguities exist in the research literature concerning the effects of parental divorce on children's adjustment, with some researchers finding differences between adult offspring from divorced and intact families and others finding no such differences. When contradictions such as these are present, a qualitative methodology is recommended (Strauss & Corbin, 1990). A grounded theory approach can be used to facilitate the development of a theory that will integrate the ambiguities present in previous research studies.

Participants

The participants for this study were college students (ages 19-26) at the University of Texas. This age group was sampled because, according to Erikson (1962), it is the stage in life during which developing romantic relationships is a primary task. In order to identify potential participants, the researcher distributed a pre-test questionnaire, consisting of a brief demographic section and a 15-item self-report measure (see instruments), to three undergraduate classes. The demographic information requests the participants' age, their parents' marital status, and if their parents' are divorced, their age at the time of the divorce and whether each biological parent remarried. The self-report measure is composed of a 15-item Likert scale which assesses people's beliefs about themselves and their romantic relationships. This instrument has been used in previous studies measuring the relationship schemata of young adults and is described in more detail below (Hazan & Shaver, 1987).

A total of 166 undergraduate students completed the pre-test measure. One hundred fourteen were from intact families, five came from families disrupted by the death of one parent, and 46 experienced parental divorce. The prevalence of parental divorce within this sample is similar to the national rate, where approximately 33% of children experience their parents' divorce before the age of 16 (Walsh, 1993). For the students from divorced families, 34 lived with their mothers following the divorce, three lived with their fathers, seven spent time in both parents' homes, and two lived with neither biological parent. Twenty-one of the young adults from divorced families experienced at least one remarriage of their custodial parent(s). Once again, this is consistent with the national rate of remarriage, which is cited as 50% (Hetherington et al., 1993).

Information from the demographic questionnaire was used to guide sampling. Participants were chosen to represent a range of divorce-related demographic variations. Gender, participants' age at the time of their parents' divorce, which parent the participant lived with following the divorce, and whether the participants' custodial parent(s) remarried were chosen as the variables upon which sampling was based. These variables were selected because they have been found to impact children's long-term adjustment to parental divorce (Amato & Keith, 1991b; Wallerstein & Blakeslee, 1989).

Procedure

As was described above, the researcher distributed a pre-test measure to students in three undergraduate classes. Potential participants were then identified and subsequently contacted by phone to schedule an interview time convenient for the participant. All appointments were held in interview rooms to ensure privacy. Once participants arrived, they were provided with a consent form which describes the nature and purpose of the study, as well as insures the confidentiality of the information which they share with the researcher. Following this, participants completed the second part of the self-report measure, the Adult Attachment Typology, and then the interview was conducted.

Interview

Unstructured interviews are often used in a grounded theory study to learn how the participants interpret particular aspects of their experiences (Bogdan & Biklen, 1992). The goal of unstructured interviews is to understand the participants' way of life in their own language (Fontana & Frey, 1995). It is important to start with general questions and move to more specific areas as the interview progresses so that the participant is allowed to guide the content of the interview.

In the present study, the interview questions were initially based on the categories which emerged from a Pilot Study. The interviews, which usually lasted approximately 1 1/2 hours, had two parts. In the first part, participants were asked to reflect on their past romantic relationships in order to gather information about the participants' belief systems about and behaviors within these relationships. Specific topics that were addressed included participants' conceptions of intimacy, sex, communication, trust, and the role that they and their partners play in creating successful and unsuccessful relationships. The second part of the interview included questions about the participants' perception of their parents' relationship, the changes resulting from the divorce, and the nature of their relationships with each parent. In addition, participants were asked to describe any connections they saw between the experiences associated with their parents' divorce and their approach to romantic relationships. Finally, one-fifth of the participants were asked to return for a follow-up interview. This interview provided the researcher with an opportunity to verify his interpretations with the participants' intended meanings.

Although a continuous process of data collection and analysis was conducted, three phases of data collection can be demarcated. During the first phase, fourteen interviews were administered. These interviews focused on encouraging participants to describe critical incidents from past and/or current romantic relationships, thus allowing the researcher to identify the key characteristics of the participants' conceptualizations of romantic relationships and of the experiences associated with their parents' divorce. The second wave of data collection, which was comprised of four interviews, expanded the focus of the interviews, as the connections between participants' conceptualizations of romantic relationships and their family experiences were explored in more detail during the interview. As analyses continued, an initial theory emerged and then three test cases were added during the third phase of data collection. These three cases served to support the initial theory and provided the basis for the researcher to conclude that theoretical saturation had been obtained.

Self-Report Measure

The majority of the information gathered in this study was obtained through the interviews. Yet, two questionnaires were used to provide supplemental information regarding the participants' views of romantic relationships and their behaviors in them. The self-report measure consists of two instruments which have been used extensively in previous studies on intimate relationships among young adults:

Adult Attachment Typology (Hazan & Shaver, 1987). This three-item questionnaire was originally developed to provide a method for classifying adults according to their self-reported attachment style. There are three paragraphs, each of which reflect the relationship style of one attachment style (secure, anxious/ambivalent, avoidant). Participants were asked to rate each of the three relationship descriptions on a five-point scale: not at all like me (1) to exactly like me (5). The attachment style paragraphs reflect a holistic description of three romantic relationship styles.

Love Experiences Measure (Hazan & Shaver, 1987). This 15-item questionnaire was developed to measure adults' working mental models of romantic relationships. The basis for design of the items was "that conscious beliefs about romantic love are colored by underlying, and perhaps not fully conscious, mental models" (p. 513, Hazan & Shaver, 1987). The items were intended to assess various aspects of the participants' mental models. In the original design, participants were asked to indicate whether or not each statement describes their views of romantic love. For this study, a five-point Likert-type scale was used: strongly disagree (1) to neutral (3) to strongly agree (5).

Analysis

Data analysis is the process of arranging the data that is collected to increase the researcher's understanding of and ability to present the material. It involves breaking down the data into manageable units and then re-organizing it in the patterns that are present within the data (Bogdan & Biklen, 1992). As data collection progressed, categories and concepts emerged through a process called open coding. The interview was analyzed to reveal the content of the participants' romantic relationship conceptualizations. Axial and selective coding were then utilized to organize the relationships among these categories. Although the three types of coding procedures are discussed separately, they were often performed simultaneously. The theory that results from the grounded theory methodology is a representation of the relationships among the concepts and the patterns present within the data (Strauss & Corbin, 1990). In this way, the categories and subcategories of the participants were examined to address the research questions delineated above and to develop a theory explaining the connections between people's experiences within their family of origin and their romantic relationship conceptualizations.

RESULTS

Over the course of this study, twenty-eight college students shared their experiences and insights about romantic relationships and the experiences associated with their parents' divorce. A large volume of data (exceeding 600 pages of transcribed interviews) was collected and analyzed using a grounded theory methodology. The primary outcome of these analyses is a model describing the impact of parental divorce on the romantic relationship beliefs and behaviors of young adults.

Figure 1 presents a graphical representation of the model emerged throughout the course of this study. The left side of the model contains two sets of factors which seem to influence the participants' romantic relationships. The *Perceptions of Their Family Background* refers to the participants' current conception of their parents' divorce and the experiences associated with that event. Yet, not all people are affected by this event in the same manner. Analyses revealed that the way individuals *React to their Parents' Relationship* impacts both their perception of their family and their own romantic relationships. The *Intervening Conditions* are the third set of factors found to influence the participants' relationships. Finally, the model depicts the two pertinent aspects of the participants' romantic relationships which emerged: their beliefs and behaviors. Although inter-related, the *Beliefs* refer to the abstract ideas and views people hold regarding what it takes to maintain a successful romantic relationship, while the *Behaviors* are the actions participants take within their relationships.

Perception of Family Background

Although all the people chosen to participate in this study have experienced the divorce of their biological parents, it was apparent

FIGURE 1. The Influence of Parental Divorce on the Beliefs About and Behaviors Within Romantic Relationships

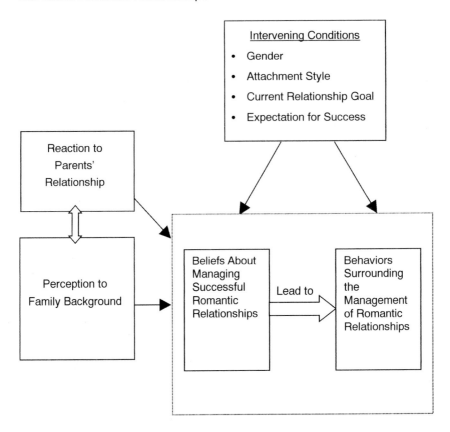

that there exists great variability in the nature of these experiences and in the way these young adults currently perceive the relationships that existed within their family. Seven categories emerged from the analyses which can be used to characterize the divorce-related experiences of the young adults in this study. Two of these categories, reason for divorce and amount of pre-divorce conflict, represent a description of their families prior to the divorce. The most salient aspect of this description is their explanation of why their parents sought a divorce. The reasons, as described by the participants, can be classified into four categories: communicating poorly; being incompatible; incidents of cheating; and growing apart.

Three other categories capture the nature of the participants' experiences following their parents' divorce. One category is the participants' perceptions of their parents' post-divorce relationship, characterized as friendly, hostile or avoidant. In addition to discussing their parents' relationship, participants frequently describe changes in their own relationships with their parents. The participants' relationships with their custodial parents tend to be either close or distant. Differences also exist in the amount of support these offspring felt they received during the post-divorce adjustment process.

The last two categories which emerged constitute the young adults' perception of the family changes which followed their parents' divorce: evaluation of changes and evaluation of remarriages. The former category refers to the participants' overall sense of their family's functioning before and after the divorce and is a way to capture whether they feel the divorce was beneficial or detrimental to themselves and/or their family. That is, in some instances, especially when there is a lot of conflict, divorce may be a positive change for the family, reducing the amount of hostility to which parents and children are exposed. Yet, when there is little overt conflict, divorce may seem like a negative event, resulting in what the child perceives to be primarily negative changes, including fewer family resources and less time spent with parents. Many participants also seem to learn about romantic relationships by viewing their parents' remarriages. For some, the remarriage is seen as a positive event, where parents are happier and the participants enjoy spending time with both their parent and stepparent. For others, though, the remarriage or re-partnering has a negative impact on the family. These parents were described as not being happier than they were in the original marriage or as engaging in a series of unstable relationships/marriages.

Reaction to Parents' Relationship

During the interviews, many participants spontaneously identified connections between the experiences surrounding their parents' divorce and their *Beliefs* about romantic relationships, while others drew such connections when asked how their family experiences influenced their views of romantic relationships. Additional connections were discovered through analyses of the patterns that existed within the family and romantic relationships of individual participants.

Overall, these connections can be classified into three categories: modeling, struggling, and reconciling. Modelers are distinguished from the other participants as a result of their apparently direct patterning within their own relationships of what they observed in their parents' relationship. This patterning often leads to difficulties in their romantic relationships, even leading to the end of their relationships, just as it had in their parents' marriage. An important note is that even though four of the six modelers experienced the remarriage of their custodial parents, these individuals barely spoke about their step-parents or these remarriages. This is in sharp contrast to most of the participants from the other two categories (strugglers and reconcilers) who spoke at length about their parents' remarriages.

Individuals classified as struggling are differentiated from others by the overtly stated difficulties which they are experiencing in their romantic relationships. For many, these difficulties are directly related to the observations they made of their parents' relationships, particularly the perceived reason for parental divorce. Another defining feature of this category is the inconsistency that exists between their stated beliefs and behaviors. These inconsistencies are particularly prevalent with regard to communication, where the participants indicate that it is important to have open, direct communication with their partners, but the behaviors they describe indicate that they do not "practice what they preach." The inconsistencies evident in their romantic relationship conceptualizations are likely influenced by their parents' relationship, as well as by the subsequent remarriages that took place within their families. In fact, many of the participants seem to be struggling with how to negotiate the multiple models of how to manage romantic relationships to which they were exposed as a result of these numerous parental relationships.

Reconcilers are actively trying to view their parents' relationship as a learning experience. In order to do so, most of these young adults are cognizant of "warning signs" which point to potential problems they might experience in their romantic relationships. These warning signs are likely drawn from their perceptions of their parents' relationship. Reconcilers whose parents remarried view these changes as having a positive effect on their lives, as well as the lives of their parents. This apparently facilitates their ability to use these new relationships as positive models with which to contrast the "things that went wrong in their parents' marriage." Thus, unlike the modelers and strugglers, reconcilers have reconciled the potentially competing models of relationships and have identified characteristics that they associate with successful romantic relationships. In addition, reconcilers do not exhibit inconsistencies between the beliefs they hold about successful romantic relationships and the behaviors they enact in their relationships. This is the defining feature of this group: that they are most able to develop relationships which possess the characteristics that define successful romantic relationships, as laid out in their conceptualizations.

Intervening Conditions

Another set of conditions exist which seem to affect the *Beliefs* individuals hold about romantic relationships. Three of these conditions (expectation for success, attachment style and current relationship goal) are a product, at least in part, of the participants' experiences surrounding their parents' divorce. The fourth condition is gender. What do these conditions have in common? While gender and expectation for success have a larger impact on the participants' romantic relationship conceptualization, attachment style and current relationship goal seem to have more minor effects.

Optimism and pessimism are attribution tendencies that pervade people's view of the world and their experiences. When it comes to romantic relationships, the participants in this study display such prediction biases that it is possible to classify them as being either optimistic, pessimistic or moderate with regard to their expectation for success in their romantic relationships. This disposition was found to be related to the amount of effort individuals expend to manage their relationships, with pessimists doing little to prolong their romantic relationships. Consequently, pessimists tended to indicate that they adjusted easily to the end of their relationships, whereas optimists tend to be hurt when relationships end, even if they are the ones to initiate the break-ups.

Gender also impacts the participants' conceptualizations. Although gender differences do not exist with regard to the experiences surrounding their parents' divorces, men and women react to these experiences differently. That is, gender differences exist in terms of the participants' conceptualizations of successful romantic relationships.

In particular, women strive to develop their relationships gradually and put forth more effort to sustain their relationships than male participants.

Approximately two-thirds of the participants in this study identified themselves as possessing a secure attachment style, a proportion which is consistent with results from previous studies (Hazan & Shaver, 1987). Secure individuals tend to come from families in which parents established a friendly relationship after the divorce and the children received support from their parents. These individuals tend to trust others rather easily and indicated that it is relatively easy to find romantic partners. Participants classified as insecure, on the other hand, have parents who fought a lot before and after the divorce. These individuals also indicated that they received little parental support and subsequently are reluctant to trust others and have difficulty finding potential partners.

Although all the participants hold a conceptualization of what it means to have a successful relationship, not everyone was interested in attaining such a long-term relationship. Rather, some individuals expressed a desire not to enter into a committed relationship, wanting, instead, to date or remain single. Although this current goal does not impact any particular aspect of their romantic relationship conceptualizations, it does affect the behaviors they described with regard to romantic relationships.

Relationship Beliefs

When asked what it takes to have a successful romantic relationship, most participants cited the same components: trust, communication, arguments, intimacy, and compatibility. The descriptions were usually an integration of these concepts, set within the context of their current and/or previous romantic relationships. Although all participants wanted to have these characteristics within their relationships, there exists variability in the definitions people gave of these components.

Analyses conducted throughout this study revealed connections between these beliefs and the divorce-related experiences of the participants. For instance, the reason individuals cite as resulting in their parents' divorce seems to have a significant influence on their ideas about managing successful relationships. The nature of this influence, though, is dependent on the individual's reaction type. Modelers tend to break up with their partners as a result of problems which are similar to the difficulties that led to their parents' divorce. Chachi, a 23 year-old male, for example, perceives that his parents grew apart and attributes a similar explanation for the end of his relationships.

> Chachi: I think not arguing is the most important thing in a relationship and waiting to get married until you are ready, until you at least finish growing up. A lot of people, especially I'm from a small town, are getting married 18, 17 and I have to say that at least 75% of those end in divorce. People grow and change so much, I think most divorces happen because people grow apart–kind of like what happened with Charlotte and I. I think we just grew apart and if we had gotten married when we were 18, I think we'd be divorced today. My mom and father got divorced because they grew apart. When two people change and don't change together, then you're going to have some irreconcilable differences and if you can't work with those, that's going to lead to divorce.

Like the modelers, some strugglers described relationships which ended as a result of problems similar to their perceived reason for their parents' divorce. The differences between these strugglers and the modelers, though, is that the modelers are not aware of the influence of their parents' relationship on their own romantic relationships. The strugglers, on the other hand, speak directly about the difficulties they are having in their relationships and relate it back to their parents' relationship. For instance, Tootie noted the similarities between her father and her first boyfriend:

> Tootie: I had a relationship in high school and I just worshipped this guy and he totally screwed around on me the whole time . . . And so I'm real leery of getting into a relationship–I'd rather just have fun right now. I say that and I hate dating because I hate uncomfortableness. . . . My dad was an alcoholic before and did his own thing. . . . I'm sure that's another reason [my parents] got divorced and my mom says that is the reason. . . . And I have so many alcoholics in my family, but that guy I dated in high school was a bad alcoholic–he would wake up and pop open a beer, it was ridiculous. That is a turn-off to me now because I like to go out and party, but it doesn't need to be the center of someone's

life because I know it can develop into alcoholism so easily without you even knowing it.

Reconcilers strive to create in their own relationships what was not present in their family. For instance, Marsha said her parents did not communicate and were never affectionate. In response to these observations, Marsha stresses communication as a key to resolving problems that arise in relationships. In addition, Marsha indicated that she was not able to express her ideas and opinions within her family, so she defines a successful relationship as one in which there is direct communication and her partner respects and wants to listen to her opinions.

> Marsha: I was brought up not to ask questions, but somehow in this relationship I feel I have more control or like the confrontation or am comfortable with confrontation maybe because I didn't have that when I was growing up. I was brought up–the oriental girl, no opinions, can't say anything–In this relationship, it's completely reversed, so it's kind of strange. . . . We were talking about the open communication thing. Maybe I just missed someone always there to talk to and to depend on. Maybe I haven't been able to express my ideas or how I feel about certain things all my life. . . . Security is a big thing, very important. My family wasn't all that–we don't really communicate that much so I didn't really feel that sense of security growing up, so now that I have [my boyfriend], he has become my family–I depend on him for everything, we share everything, we act like this old married couple. Security is a big issue for me.

Management of Trust and Intimacy

Connections emerged linking the participants' romantic relationship conceptualizations and the parent-child relationships that developed following their parents' divorce. Of particular importance is the nature of the participants' relationships with their custodial parent. Many of the young adults in this study maintained a close relationship with their custodial parent following the divorce. For some of the participants, though, the changes resulting from the divorce included a diminished relationship with their parents, including decreased parental monitoring and nurturing.

Participants who had close relationships with their parents seek to develop romantic relationships which stress characteristics found in their relationships with their custodial parents, such as *intimacy*, open *communication* and nurturing. For example, throughout the interview, Daisy drew many connections between her relationship with her mother and her romantic relationships. In particular, Daisy said she is very close to her mother and can just be herself, characteristics which she feels are also important in her romantic relationships.

> Daisy: With my partner, you have the intimacy and sometimes have a different personality with him–you talk a little bit cute and the gestures you do with him, I'm a little bit more spoiled with him, I'll complain to him. But with my friends I don't do that as much, I'm a stronger person.

> I: You were saying intimate, so I am wondering what you mean by intimate?

> Daisy: Close. From everything you say to everything you do. We are not hesitant to express something–Like feelings or "I need to go to the bathroom." So we openly express everything.

Individuals who had distant relationships with their parents following the divorce tend to have a difficult time becoming attached or feeling connected to their partners. Cindy's comments illustrate the impact that a disrupted relationship with one's parents can have on an individual's romantic relationships. Cindy indicated that following her parents' divorce, her mother was no longer involved in her life, focusing, instead, on her own dating relationships. This left Cindy without an attentive parent, as her father moved away and had little contact with Cindy and her brother.

> I: You talked about how you are not really in contact with your mom–that relationship got . . .

> Cindy: I mean this was my mom, the person you're supposed to trust the most in life and for her to go–I was used to something for ten years, my mom was always there. My mom was soccer coach and all this stuff. Was always concerned about what was going on at school, gave me rides to dance class, gave me rides to

soccer practice, and then she was a completely different person–I had to take the bus everywhere, I had to bum rides. In high school–track, cross country, soccer–she never came to a track meet, never came to a soccer game or anything like that. For my mom to go from this person to a completely different person within a year, this isn't right–what the hell is going on. It was hard to know that my mom could do something like that. And if my mother, the person who gave birth to me can do that, then it makes me wonder about anyone else. If my mom could do it, anyone can.

In describing the difficulties she experienced in her first romantic relationship, Cindy revealed the impact that her mother's "betrayal" had on her ability to trust her first boyfriend and feel secure in the relationship. In fact, Cindy indicated that she "didn't really connect with anyone emotionally until [her] first boyfriend" after her "attachment to her mother had been disrupted" following the divorce.

I: Generally it seemed like trust is a big thing for you.

Cindy: Absolutely.

I: It looked like building up trust took a while with your previous boyfriend.

Cindy: Definitely with my first boyfriend, even though, I guess I trusted him, I still looked for reassurance at all times and maybe deep down–I have a hard time trusting anyone, so even after a three year relationship, I still find it hard to trust people. I have trust in him, but this whole 'complete trust' is far away. I tried, I tried to trust him, but deep down it's hard . . . I was always afraid that he just wouldn't like me all of a sudden. He could go from liking me to not liking me quickly. For a long, long time, I thought he could dump me at any second. Even when things were going well and even when he told me he loved me, I still thought–like the next day–it could be over and he would just walk away and be like 'see ya'.

The difficulty Cindy had trusting her boyfriend may be based on two factors: (1) she feared that she would be rejected by her boyfriend if he did not feel the same way she did, just as she felt rejected by her mother; and (2) since her emotional attachment to her mother had been disrupted, she possessed no model of how to feel secure in her romantic relationships. Cindy's fear of being rejected by her boyfriend is also reflected in her need for frequent reassurance and the difficulty she had feeling secure in her relationship.

Management of Conflict

Although a common perception is that children from divorced families have been exposed to a lot of conflict, the results of this and other studies (Amato and Keith, 1991b) indicate that many offspring feel their parents did not fight much prior to the divorce. In fact, some participants described divorces which were amicable and free from conflict. There are others, though, whose parents fought a lot and who describe childhood memories marked by such conflict. According to the results of this study, though, individuals from low-conflict divorced families are not necessarily better off than those from high-conflict divorced families, at least when it comes to their ability to resolve conflicts within their own relationships.

For many participants in this study, managing conflict in their romantic relationships is an issue that was discussed at length. Three aspects of this category emerged: expectation of arguments, conflict resolution approach, and outcome of argument. All three of these components seem to be influenced by the participants' experiences within their family of origin. For instance, individuals from low-conflict families tend to avoid arguments and strive to remain calm when arguments arise. For participants from high-conflict families, differences exist according to the manner with which they *React to their Parents' Relationship*. People who display a modeling or struggling response tend to avoid arguments, perhaps because they feel conflicts have a negative impact on romantic relationships. Reconcilers, though, expect arguments to arise in their relationships and attempt to utilize more of a compromising approach to conflict resolution. This is an effort to achieve a positive outcome from fights, which is precisely what their parents did not do. In this way, they view arguments as a chance to improve their romantic relationships.

Behaviors in Relationships

In the previous sections, people's beliefs about managing romantic relationships were examined. Now it is important to ask the following question: What is the consequence of having a certain set of beliefs? For the participants in this study, their beliefs strongly influence the characteristics they seek in partners, the manner in which they feel commitment develops, and the way they react to the ending of their romantic relationships.

According to responses to survey items, most of the young adults in this study think it is difficult to find someone with whom you can fall in love, while others find it easy to fall in love. People in the former category often discuss their desire to find "Mr./Ms. Right." This phrase implies a sense of searching for partners with particular characteristics or a certain personality. Most people base these discussions on the characteristics of current and/or previous romantic partners. Some of the young adults in the study also base their choice of partners on their family experiences.

Commitment, which is commonly defined as dedication to one's relationship, is another aspect of the approach participants take to their romantic relationships which is guided by their conceptualizations and affected by the experiences surrounding their parents' divorce. For the young adults in this study, commitment develops as a result of mutual experiences with one's partner, through verbal and behavioral signs of devotion, and when partners share intimate aspects of each other's lives. Previous literature has differentiated between two models of commitment: positive-pull and barrier (Berscheid & Lopes, 1997; Lund, 1985). These two types also emerged from the data in the present study, although the latter type has been termed "investment" in this study.

Although much of the interviews centered on the participants' conceptions of successful romantic relationships, each person also spoke about what can and does go wrong in relationships. Such comments concerned break-ups and actions that are required to sustain relationships when problems arise. A wide variety of reasons was cited as causing problems in relationships or leading to break-ups, including cheating, poor communication, arguments, growing apart, no longer compatible, and not enjoying each other's company.

Participants also cited efforts that can be made to address these problems, such as having special evenings out together and helping to make their partners happier so that the relationship would improve.

Differences exist, though, in the effort put forth by the participants. Some people, especially women, put forth a great deal of effort to make their relationships work, whereas others, particularly men, are quick to end their relationships when problems arise.

Despite differences in the amount of effort put forth by participants to sustain their relationships, most of the participants indicated that they are usually the ones to initiate break-ups in their relationships. A difference exists, though, in the way the participants react to the end of their relationships. A number of people, especially those who are pessimistic about relationships, are able to detach themselves emotionally from their former partners rather easily and quickly seek new partners. Participants who are optimistic, though, said that they retain feelings for their ex-partner and can be "set emotionally adrift" when a relationship ends.

DISCUSSION

To depict the connections which emerged between the young adults' experiences surrounding parental divorce and their romantic relationship beliefs, a model was constructed. This model, depicted in Figure 1, illustrates that three sets of factors were found to impact the way young adults from divorced families manage romantic relationships: (1) their perception of their family background; (2) their reaction to their parents' relationship; and (3) a set of intervening conditions which comprise other factors, such as gender, which are considered to be separate from the experiences with their families. The components of the first set represent the variation that exists in the participants' divorce-related experiences, while the second factor reflects the observation that different people may respond differently to the same set of experiences. Since this study was primarily concerned with the impact of parental divorce on young adults' romantic relationship beliefs, these two sets of factors were the focus of the analyses and are emphasized in the present discussion.

The results of this study demonstrate the importance of the post-divorce contextual factors, particularly the parent-child relationship and remarriages, on the long-term adjustment of children. Unlike the pre-divorce factors, especially parental conflict, post-divorce factors have not been the focus of previous research studies (Amato & Rezac, 1994; Emery, 1988; Kline et al., 1991). The evaluation of changes category exemplifies the conclusion that adjustment to divorce should not be treated as a homogenous situation because the effects of divorce depend on the nature of the changes this event sparks. Finally, the intervening conditions demonstrate that individual personality factors also affect the adjustment to parental divorce and the development of people's beliefs about romantic relationships.

In this study, participants were classified as modelers, strugglers or reconcilers depending on the way they were responding, at the time of the interview, to their parents' relationship. Although individual disposition (optimism/pessimism) certainly plays a role in determining the type of reaction a person exhibits, divorce-related factors are also a source of influence. For example, the participants' evaluations of the changes resulting from their parents' divorce affects whether someone is a modeler, struggler or reconciler. A perception that the divorce brought about negative changes in one's family tends to place someone within one of the first two categories. Individuals who view their parents' divorce as resulting in positive changes, though, are more likely to consciously judge their parents' relationship as a bad example of a romantic relationship and thus attempt to create relationships which do not possess the negative qualities present within their parents' relationship. A positive evaluation of the changes resulting from parental divorce is likely when offspring feel that remarriages had a positive effect on their own and their parents' lives. A happy remarriage also emphasizes children's perception that their parents' relationship was bad and, at the same time, provides a positive model upon which reconcilers base healthy relationship behaviors. Strugglers, on the other hand, spoke about the confusion caused by having multiple parent-relationship models. By reconciling the often conflicting views represented in these different models, strugglers can solidify their romantic relationships beliefs and be more likely to develop satisfying relationships.

The final source of influence that emerged from the analyses is the participants' own romantic relationship experiences. Individuals with more experience tend to be reconcilers. Many of the young adults in this study indicated that their conceptions of romantic relationships have been strongly formed through incidents within their relationships. Sinclair and Nelson (1998) described a similar finding and stated that through dating experiences people "gain valuable insight into what it means to engage in and maintain healthy and satisfying relationships" (p. 123).

Examining the various factors which influence people's reaction to their parents' relationship, it is clear that gaining romantic relationship experience and analyzing the problems within their parents' relationships allows people to improve upon their parents' relationships and thus progress along this "reaction process." This process of development is consistent with schema theory and the notion that schemata are continuously revised in response to new experiences (Fiske & Linville, 1980). Additionally, the romantic relationship conceptualization also influences the inferences and interpretations made during interaction with romantic partners. In this sense, romantic relationship conceptualizations have properties similar to those of schemata (Rumelhart, 1984).

Numerous studies have investigated the long-term effects of parental divorce on the romantic relationships of offspring from such families. Some studies have found children from divorced families have a greater understanding of romantic relationships than people from intact families (Jenkins et al., 1989; Wallerstein & Kelly, 1980). Through comparisons to peers from intact families, many studies have also concluded that young adults from divorced backgrounds are less trusting, are less intimate, and have a greater fear of betrayal or rejection by their romantic partners (Gabardi & Rosen, 1992; Johnston & Thomas, 1996; Sprague & Kinney, 1997; Walker & Ehrenberg, 1998; Westervelt & Vanderberg, 1997). Yet, the analyses conducted during the current study revealed that such findings do not accurately portray the effects of parental divorce for many young adults.

Trust and intimacy are considered to be the cornerstones of close romantic relationships (Barnes & Sternberg, 1997; Rempel et al., 1985). As Duck (1988) noted, partners must make themselves vulnerable in order to create trust and intimacy. During the interviews conducted over the course of this study, many participants indicated that while they feel cautious about marriage, they do not sense such caution with regard to their dating relationships. In fact, reconcilers and other optimistic people believe that their relationships will be successful and are not hesitant about entering into dating relationships. However, many strugglers and modelers are cautious about becoming emotionally close to romantic partners. They attribute their caution and reluctance to engage in relationships to two primary reasons: (1) they fear they will make the same mistakes in their relationships that their parents made and (2) they worry about the feelings of rejection that would result if their partner were to betray them. This latter fear is particularly salient for individuals who described having a distant relationship with and receiving little support from their parents following the divorce.

During the initial stages of adjustment following divorce, parents may become disengaged from their children's lives, which often leaves children feeling rejected and abandoned (Amato & Keith, 1991a; Wallerstein et al., 1989). Many of the participants in this study indicated that they were forced to become independent as a result of their parents' unresponsiveness. Some of these individuals seem to have had their attachment to their parents disrupted by the divorce and the lack of support they received following the divorce. This disrupted attachment is a phenomenon noted by Walker and Ehrenberg (1998): "major life events, such as parental divorce, may alter relationships with caregivers sufficiently to produce changes in individuals' attachment patterns" (p. 323).

On the other hand, individuals who retained close relationships with at least one of their parents following the divorce are more comfortable with trust and intimacy. They tend to allow trust to develop gradually through interactions with their romantic partners. This finding is consistent with Sprague and Kinney's (1997) conclusion that young adults from more cohesive families have higher levels of trust in their romantic relationships. In addition, the parent-child relationship has also been found to be a resiliency factor within the post-divorce adjustment process (Emery & Forehand, 1996).

These results can be explained through the application of attachment theory, which holds that an individual's attachment to their caregiver provides a model for his/her beliefs in the trustworthiness and availability of romantic partners (Hazan & Shaver, 1987; Kobak & Sceery, 1988). Individuals who received support from and retained a close relationship with at least one parent have a "working model" which enables them to trust their romantic partners, thus allowing them to become emotionally close in and more committed to relationships. Yet, when the caregiver attachment is disrupted, people are likely to struggle with creating trust and intimacy in their romantic relationships. Thus, the nature of the post-divorce parent-child relationship and parental support have a significant influence on the adjustment of young adults who have experienced parental divorce.

Limitations

Although a myriad of procedures were undertaken to ensure the scientific rigor of this study, limitations exist which likely had an impact on the results obtained. In particular, the trustworthiness of the results may be threatened by the nature of the methods employed. First, the data collected over the course of this study was primarily gathered with the interview, although the questionnaires were used to provide supplemental information. However, the information shared by most of the participants in this study appears to be honest and complete, despite the personal nature of the topic investigated.

Additionally, many steps were taken to address the effects of researcher bias: meeting with a fellow doctoral student experienced with qualitative researcher, regular meetings with an advisor to review data collection and analysis procedures, maintaining consistent notes throughout the analysis process, and conducting follow-up interviews with 20% of the participants.

Conducting studies with a limited number of participants is an inherent feature of the grounded theory methodology, particularly when an interview is the primary data collection instrument. In such studies, numbers are sacrificed to capture the participants' experiences, although theoretical sampling is used to access a range of experiences (Guba, 1981; Bogdan & Biklen, 1992). For the current study, the participants were chosen to represent the myriad of divorce-related experiences in order to investigate the consequence of these experiences on romantic relationship beliefs.

Finally, the focus of this study also acts as a limitation, in that divorce-related experiences were investigated to examine their impact on romantic relationship beliefs. The participants indicated that other factors, including the media and observation of friends' relationships, also affect such beliefs. This is an observation cited in previous studies and highlights the idea that the results which emerged during this study must be viewed as a partial model of the development of romantic relationship beliefs (Fletcher & Kininmonth, 1992).

Implications for Research

One of the initial goals of this study was to address the limitations inherent in the comparison studies which treat children of divorce as a distinct group. Results from this study highlight these limitations and the need to take a more individualistic, contextual approach to investigating the short- and long-term affects of parental divorce on children, adults and families. That is, research studies should account for the variability that exists in the divorce-related experiences. This variability can be captured by the following factors: amount of parental conflict, reason for divorce, parental support, parent-child relationship, evaluation of remarriages, evaluation of the changes resulting from divorce, and the type of reaction exhibited by individuals.

One factor absent from this list, as well as from the list of family background categories, is the age of the participant at the time of the divorce. This factor has been found to significantly influence children's short-term adjustment to parental divorce and was therefore used as part of the criteria guiding the sampling in this study (Wallerstein & Blakeslee, 1989). Yet, the results of this study found no differences in the participants' romantic relationship beliefs due to the age at the time of their parents' divorce. Given the contradiction between these findings, additional studies should be conducted to determine if age at the time of divorce affects offspring's long-term adjustment.

The primary result of the current study is the creation of a model depicting the effects of parental divorce on the romantic relationship beliefs of young adults. A myriad of family background and relationship belief categories emerged from the analyses. Given these factors, a study is warranted to determine the relative influence of these various factors. Such a study requires the operationalization of these categories, so that they could be assessed using self-report questionnaires, thus enabling researchers to sample a large number of participants.

Implications for Clinical Practice

Given the prevalence of divorce within American families, mental health practitioners will continue to be asked to assist children and families with the adjustment to divorce. Although many people are likely to seek such assistance during the earlier stages of the adjustment process, the long-term impact of parental divorce has been found to be a significant influence for many young adults (Kulka & Weingarten, 1979; Wallerstein & Blakeslee, 1989). The results of this study can inform the approach practitioners take to working with such issues. In particular, it is crucial that practitioners consider the variability of the divorce-related experiences and the way offspring respond to parental divorce. This variability is represented by the seven categories which characterize children's perceptions of their family backgrounds and the three reaction types (modelers, strugglers and reconcilers).

A critical aspect of working with families contemplating or adjusting to divorce is for practitioners to be aware of their own biases towards divorce and marriage. In particular, people should understand that divorce is not necessarily a negative event for children and their families. Additionally, the notion that "parents should stay together for the sake of the children" may be a mistake, particularly if it results in children remaining in families marked by conflict and a lack of warmth. In fact, as the results of this and other studies demonstrate, parental divorce can result in positive changes for parents and children, particularly when close family relationships are retained and when parents engage in stable, satisfying relationships after the divorce.

The development of satisfying relationships is a task with which some adults from divorced families, represented by the modelers and strugglers, have difficulty. Mental health practitioners working with people from such families should identify the connections between the clients' relationship difficulties and the experiences surrounding their parents' divorce. Then, in an effort to promote the development of satisfying relationships, clients should be encouraged to analyze the apparent influence of their parents' divorce on their romantic relationships, as well as any disparities that may exist between their stated relationship beliefs and behaviors. As is evident in the difference between the three reaction types, such insight, along with increased relationship experiences, provides people with opportunities to revise their perceptions of their divorce experiences and to effect more control over the way these experiences influence their own romantic relationships. In effect, this would promote people's ability to progress from the modeler or struggler stage to the reconciler stage, leaving them better able to develop satisfying romantic relationships.

REFERENCES

Allen, K. R. (1993). The dispassionate discourse of children's adjustment to divorce. *Journal of Marriage and the Family, 55*, 46-50.

Amato, P. R. (1993). Children's adjustment to divorce: Theories, hypotheses, and empirical support. *Journal of Marriage and the Family, 55*, 23-38.

Amato, P. R. & Booth, A. (1991). Consequences of parental divorce and marital unhappiness for adult well-being. *Social Forces, 69*, 895-914.

Amato, P. R. & Keith, B. (1991a). Parental divorce and the well-being of children: A meta-analysis. *Psychological Bulletin, 110(1)*, 26-46.

Amato, P. R. & Keith, B. (1991b). Parental divorce and adult well-being: A meta-analysis. *Journal of Marriage and the Family, 53,* 43-58.

Amato, P. R. & Rezac, S. J. (1994). Contact with nonresident parents, interparental conflict, and children's behavior. *Journal of Family Issues 15(2),* 191-207.

Amato, P. R., Loomis, L. S., & Booth, A. (1995). Parental divorce, marital conflict, and offspring well-being during early adulthood. *Social Forces, 73,* 895-915.

Barnes, M. L. & Sternberg, R. J. (1997). A hierarchical model of love and its prediction of satisfaction in close relationships. In R. J. Sternberg & M. Hojjat (Eds.), *Satisfaction in Close Relationships* (pp.79-101). New York: The Guilford Press.

Berscheid, E. & Lopes, J. (1997). A temporal model of relationship satisfaction and stability. In R. J. Sternberg & M. Hojjat (Eds.), *Satisfaction in Close Relationships* (pp.129-159). New York: The Guilford Press.

Birnbach, L. & Hyman, B. (1996). *Divorce in America: Growing through divorce.* Manuscript submitted for publication.

Block, J. H., Block, J., & Gjerde, P. F. (1986). The personality of children prior to divorce: A prospective study. *Child Development, 57,* 827-840.

Bogdan, R. C. & Biklen, S. K. (1992). *Qualitative Research for Education.* Boston, MA: Allyn and Bacon.

Duck, S. (1991). *Relating to Others.* Milton Keynes: Open University Press.

Emery, R. E. (1982). Interparental conflict and the children of discord and divorce. *Psychological Bulletin, 92(2),* 310-330.

Emery, R. E. (1988). *Marriage, Divorce and Children's Adjustment.* Newbury Park, Ca.: Sage Publications, Inc.

Emery, R. E. & Forehand, R. (1996). Parental divorce and children's well-being: A focus on resilience. In R. J. Haggerty & L. R. Sherrod (Eds.), *Stress, Risk, and Resilience in Children and Adolescents: Processes, mechanisms, and intervention* (pp. 64-99). New York: Cambridge University Press.

Emery, R. E. & O'Leary, D. (1982). Children's perceptions of marital discord and behavior problems of boys and girls. *Journal of Abnormal Child Psychology, 10(1),* 11-24.

Erikson, E. H. (1963). *Childhood and Society, Second Edition.* New York: W. W. Norton & Company.

Fiske, S. T. & Linville, P. W. (1980). What does the schema concept buy us? *Personality and Social Psychology Bulletin, 6,* 543-557.

Fletcher, G. J. O. & Fincham, F. D. (1991). Attribution processes in close relationships. In G. J. O. Fletcher & Fincham, F. D. (Eds.), *Cognition in Close Relationships* (pp. 7-36). Hillsdale, N.J.: Lawrence Erlbaum Associates, Publishers.

Fletcher, G. J. O. & Kininmonth, L. A. (1992). Measuring relationship beliefs: An individual differences scale. *Journal of Research in Personality, 26,* 371-397.

Fletcher, G. J. O. & Kininmonth, L. A. (1991). Interaction in close relationships and social cognition. In G. J. O. Fletcher & Fincham, F. D. (Eds.), *Cognition in Close Relationships* (pp. 235-256). Hillsdale, N.J.: Lawrence Erlbaum Associates, Publishers.

Fletcher, G. J. O., Rosanowski, J., & Fitness, J. (1994). Automatic processing in intimate contexts: The role of close-relationship beliefs. *Journal of Personality and Social Psychology, 67,* 888-897.

Fontana, A. & Frey, J. H. (1994). Interviewing. In N. K. Denzin & Y. S. Lincoln

(Eds.), *Handbook of Qualitative Research* (pp. 361-377). Thousand Oaks, CA: Sage Publications.

Franklin, K. M., Janoff-Bulman, R., & Roberts, J. E. (1990). Long-term impact of parental divorce on optimism and trust: Changes in general assumptions or narrow beliefs? *Journal of Personality and Social Psychology, 59(4)*, 743-755.

Gabardi, L. & Rosen, L. A. (1992). Intimate relationships: College students from divorced and intact families. *Journal of Divorce & Remarriage, 18*, 25-56.

Guba, E. G. (1981). Criteria for assessing the trustworthiness of naturalistic inquiries. *Educational Communication and Technology Journal, 29*, 75-91.

Guba, E. G. & Lincoln, Y. S. (1994). Competing paradigms in qualitative research. In N. K. Denzin & Y. S. Lincoln (Eds.), *Handbook of Qualitative Research* (pp. 105-117). Thousand Oaks, CA: Sage Publications.

Guttmann, J. (1989). Intimacy in young adult males' relationships as a function of divorced and non-divorced family of origin structure. *Journal of Divorce, 12*, 253-261.

Hazan, C. & Shaver, P. (1987). Romantic love conceptualized as an attachment process. *Journal of Personality and Social Psychology, 52*, 511-524.

Hetherington, E. M. (1989). Coping with family transitions: Winners, losers, and survivors. *Child Development, 60*, 1-14.

Hetherington, E. M., Bridges, M., & Insabella, G. M. (1998). What matters? What does not? Five perspectives on the association between marital transitions and children's adjustment. *American Psychologist, 53*, 167-184.

Hetherington, E. M., Cox, M. & Cox, R. (1982). Effects of divorce on parents and children. In M. E. Lamb (Ed.), *Nontraditional Families: Parenting and child development.* (pp. 233-288). Hillsdale, N. J.: L. Erlbaum Associates.

Hetherington, E. M., Law, T. C., & O'Connor, T. G. (1993). Divorce: Challenges, changes, and new chances. In F. Walsh (Ed.), *Normal Family Processes* (pp. 208-234). New York: The Guilford Press.

Jenkins, J. M., Smith, M. A. & Graham, P. J. (1989). Coping with parental quarrels. *Journal of the American Academy of Child and Adolescent Psychiatry, 28*, 182-189.

Johnston, S. G. & Thomas, A. M. (1996). Divorce versus intact parental marriage and perceived risk and dyadic trust in present heterosexual relationships. *Psychological Reports, 78*, 387-390.

Klee, L., Schmidt, C., & Johnson, C. (1989). Children's definitions of family following divorce of their parents. *Journal of Divorce, 12*, 109-127.

Kline, M., Johnston, J. R., & Tschann, J. M. (1991). The long shadow of marital conflict: A model of children's post-divorce adjustment. *Journal of Marriage and the Family 53*, 297-309.

Kobak, R. R. & Sceery, A. (1988). Attachment in late adolescence: Working models, affect regulation, and representations of self and others. *Child Development, 59*, 135-146.

Kulka, R. A. & Weingarten, H. (1979). The long-term effects of parental divorce in childhood on adult adjustment. *Journal of Social Issues, 35(4)*, 50-78.

Lund, M. (1985). The development of investment and commitment scales for predicting continuity of personal relationships. *Journal of Social and Personal Relationships, 2*, 3-23.

Rempel, J. K., Holmes, J. G., & Zanna, M. P. (1985). Trust in close relationships. *Journal of Personality and Social Psychology, 49*, 95-112.

Rumelhart, D. E. (1984). Schemata and the cognitive system. In R. S. Wyer & T. K. Srull (Eds.), *Handbook of Social Cognition, 1* (pp. 161-188). Hillsdale, N. J.: Erlbaum.

Shaw, D. S. & Emery, R. E. (1987). Parental conflict and other correlates of the adjustment of school-age children whose parents have separated. *Journal of Abnormal Child Psychology, 15(2)*, 269-281.

Sinclair, S. L. & Nelson, E. S. (1998). The impact of parental divorce on college students' intimate relationships and relationship beliefs. *Journal of Divorce & Remarriage, 29*, 103-129.

Sprague, H. E. & Kinney, J. M. (1997). The effects of interparental divorce and conflict on college students' romantic relationships. *Journal of Divorce & Remarriage, 27*, 85-104.

Spruijt, A. P. (1995). Adolescents from stepfamilies, single-parent families and (in)stable intact families in The Netherlands. *Journal of Divorce & Remarriage, 24*, 115-132.

Stolberg, A. L. & Anker, J. M. (1984). Cognitive and behavioral changes in children resulting from parental divorce and consequent environmental changes. *Journal of Divorce, 7(2)*, 23-41.

Strauss, A. & Corbin, J. (1990). *Basics of Qualitative Research: Grounded theory procedures and techniques*. Newbury Park, CA: Sage Publications.

Tayler, L., Parker, G., & Roy, K. (1995). Parental divorce and its effects on the quality of intimate relationships in adulthood. *Journal of Divorce & Remarriage, 24*, 181-202.

U. S. Bureau of the Census (1995). *Statistical Abstract of the U. S. (115th edition)*. Washington, D. C.

Walker, T. R. & Ehrenberg, M. F. (1998). An exploratory study of young persons' attachment styles and perceived reasons for parental divorce. *Journal of Adolescent Research, 13*, 320-342.

Wallerstein, J. S. (1983). Children of divorce: Stress and developmental tasks. In N. Garmezy and M. Rutter (Eds.), *Stress, Coping, and Development in Children* (pp. 265-302). New York: McGraw-Hill Book Company.

Wallerstein, J. S. (1991). Long-term effects of divorce on children. *Journal of the American Academy of Child and Adolescent Psychiatry, 30*, 349-360.

Wallerstein, J. S. Blakeslee, S. (1989). *Second Chances: Men, women and children a decade after divorce. Who wins, who loses–and why?* New York: Ticknor & Fields.

Wallerstein, J. S. & Kelley, J. B. (1980). *Surviving the Breakup: How children and parents cope with divorce*. New York: Basic Books, Inc.

Walsh, F. (1993). Conceptualization of normal family processes. In F. Walsh (Ed.), *Normal Family Processes* (pp. 3-69). New York: The Guilford Press.

Walsh, P. E. & Stolberg, A. L. (1989). Parental and environmental determinants of children's behavioral, affective and cognitive adjustment to divorce. *Journal of Divorce, 12*, 265-282.

Warren, N. J., Ilgen, E. R., Grew, R. S., Konanc, J. T., & Amara, I. A. (1985). Time since separation: Another perspective on the NASP study of divorce. *School Psychology Review, 14(3)*, 373-377.

Westervelt, K. & Vandenberg, B. (1997). Parental divorce and intimate relationships of young adults. *Psychological Reports, 80*, 923-926.

EMOTIONAL
AND MENTAL HEALTH ISSUES

Self-Blame and Self-Esteem
in College-Aged Children
from Divorced Families

Clair Goodman
Jeffrey Pickens

SUMMARY. The relationship between self-blame and self-esteem among students from divorced and non-divorced families was compared. Published scales were used to assess current and retrospective reports of self-esteem and self-blame for students from divorced and non-di-

Clair Goodman, BA, is affiliated with the School of Psychology, James Madison University, Harrisonburg, VA. Jeffrey Pickens, PhD, is Director of Research, Family Central, Inc., North Lauderdale, FL.

Address correspondence to: Dr. Jeffrey Pickens, Family Central, Inc., 849 S.W. 81 Avenue, North Lauderdale, FL 33068 (JPickens@familycentral.org).

The authors would like to extend their thanks to all of the participants in this study, and also to Drs. Sharon Lovell and Ashton Trice for their expert assistance.

[Haworth co-indexing entry note]: "Self-Blame and Self-Esteem in College-Aged Children from Divorced Families." Goodman, Clair, and Jeffrey Pickens. Co-published simultaneously in *Journal of Divorce & Remarriage* (The Haworth Clinical Practice Press, an imprint of The Haworth Press, Inc.) Vol. 34, No. 3/4, 2001, pp. 119-135; and: *Divorce and the Next Generation: Perspectives for Young Adults in the New Millennium* (ed: Craig A. Everett) The Haworth Clinical Practice Press, an imprint of The Haworth Press, Inc., 2001, pp. 119-135. Single or multiple copies of this article are available for a fee from The Haworth Document Delivery Service [1-800-342-9678, 9:00 a.m. - 5:00 p.m. (EST). E-mail address: getinfo@haworthpressinc.com].

vorced families. Students from divorced families reported lower retrospective self-esteem and more self-blame than students from non-divorced families. However, self-esteem scores of students from divorced families did appear to recover with time. These results demonstrate that retrospective self-report can be a useful tool for exploring the long-term effects of parental divorce among college students. *[Article copies available for a fee from The Haworth Document Delivery Service: 1-800-342-9678. E-mail address: <getinfo@haworthpressinc.com> Website: <http://www.Haworth Press.com> © 2001 by The Haworth Press, Inc. All rights reserved.]*

KEYWORDS. College students, divorce, self-esteem

For decades, the question of how parental divorce affects children has interested parents and researchers alike. Some researchers have probed concepts related to the 'self' to explore how the divorce process and events associated with it impact a child's self-concept, self-efficacy, self-esteem, and perceived self-competence. Long-term effects are of particular interest, and so researchers have examined the impact of divorce experienced at various points in earlier childhood on the self-esteem and academic performance of college students (e.g., Clifford & Clark, 1995; Giuliani, 1997; Garber, 1991; Gabardi & Rosen, 1991; Kalter, Riemer, Brickman & Chen, 1985; Shook & Jurich, 1992). Age of students at the time of the divorce has typically been found to be an important variable. For example, students who are older at the time of parents' divorce tend to have higher academic performance (Giuliani, 1997). This suggests that the maturity of children, and thus the extent of their developing self-concept, predicts the impact of divorce on self-esteem. However, it is also possible that longer periods of time post-divorce act as a buffer or provide time for a recovery of self-esteem and minimize self-blame. The present study used a retrospective technique to examine the concepts of self-esteem and self-blame and how these were affected by parental divorce.

Self-esteem, as defined by Rosenberg (1965, as cited in Byrne, 1996, p. 141), is the "extent to which a person is generally satisfied with his or her life, considers him- or herself worthy, [and] holds a positive attitude toward him- or herself." Many researchers agree that self-esteem is negatively affected by parental divorce (Amato, 1993; Bynum & Durm, 1996; Clifford & Clark, 1995; Kurtz, 1994). If such effects are long lasting, then as adults the offspring of divorced parents may demonstrate lower levels of self-esteem than individuals from non-divorced families. A recent study did not find differences in measures of global self-worth among college students of divorced versus intact families (Stralka, 1995). However, this study did not examine the students at the time of their parents' divorce, and so it is not known if self-concept suffered and recovered or was not related to self-concept as Stralka concluded. Therefore, studies must either longitudinally follow children of divorced families for many years post-divorce to assess changes in self-concept and self-esteem, or else attempt to assess the effects of divorce over time by using a retrospective approach, as we used in the present study.

Amato (1993) has described an individual's self-esteem as easily altered, especially during stressful life events. Divorce is, undoubtedly, an extremely stressful event for a child. Many other researchers have characterized the negative consequences of divorce as long-term influences (Amato; Clifford & Clark, 1995; Kurdek & Berg, 1987; Wallerstein, 1987; Wyman, Cowen, Hightower, & Pedro-Carroll, 1985). Amato and Keith (1991) concluded that the self-esteem and general well being of children of divorce, even as adults, remains lower than that of children from intact families, although this was not supported by Stralka (1995). It may be also that characteristics of the family environment, such as parental cooperation, nurturance and avoidance of conflict following divorce, may buffer a child's self-esteem and thus can prevent long-term negative effects. For example, inter-parental conflict was found to be significantly related to self-esteem, while overall family structure was not, in a study of college students from divorced families (Garber, 1991). A triadic relationship was defined by Westerman (1987) as one in which "a child is caught between parents who pull the child in opposite directions," often including a constant vying for the child's loyalty. This is a useful way to operationalize family conflict, and for this reason was included in the present study of the effects of divorce on long-term self-esteem.

Researchers have also found an association between self-blame and parental divorce (Healy, Stewart, & Copeland, 1993; Hetherington, 1989; Jenkins & Smith, 1993; Kurdek, Blisk, & Siesky, 1981; Kurdek & Siesky, 1980; Weiss, 1975; Young, 1983). Due to the vulnerable position of children involved in parental divorce, they often feel as though they are to blame for the breakup of the family structure. Healy et al. (1993) reported that many of the negative effects associated with feelings of self-blame are long-lasting, while Kurdek et al. reported that at least six years are necessary for the child to begin to dismiss feelings of responsibility for such an event. Additional research is needed to identify the long-term effects associated with children's attributions of blame for parental divorce.

Some researchers report that individual characteristics such as gender and age at the time of the divorce/separation may affect a child's reaction to the event (Cole, Peeke, & Ingold, 1996; Neemann & Harter, 1986; Wallerstein, 1983; Wyman et al., 1985). However, others have reported no gender or age differences in children's reactions to parental divorce/separation (Allen, Stoltenberg, & Rosko, 1990; Bisnaire, Firestone, & Rynard, 1990; Bynum & Durm, 1996; Mechanic & Hansell, 1989). Clearly, additional research is required to determine what, if any, effects gender, age, and time since parental divorce have on children experiencing parental divorce/separation.

As stated earlier, one way to prospectively examine the long-term effects of parental divorce would be to conduct a longitudinal study measuring the self-esteem and self-blaming tendencies of children immediately following parental divorce, and compare these results with measures of the individuals' self-esteem and self-blame as adults. Although such longitudinal studies yield valuable information, they are often difficult and costly to conduct. A more practical method could be implemented once the children have grown into adulthood by retrospectively measuring the thoughts and feelings of each child at the time that the divorce occurred. Although the use of retrospective methods in research is controversial, Robins (1988) reported that recall of memorable events may be excellent. Maughan and Rutter (1997) reported that individuals' responses to reports about marital dissolution were found to be highly reliable. Fivush (1993) reported that although the amount of information that individuals recall may decrease with time, the accuracy of their recall does not. Thus, memories remain relatively accurate and stable over an individual's lifetime, especially if the memories are of a significant event in one's life. An event such as parental separation/divorce would thus appear to be amenable to retrospective investigation.

The present study compared college-aged students from divorced and non-divorced families on a series of current and retrospective measures of self-esteem, self-blame and parents' marital relationship. We hypothesized that individuals from the divorced group would have significantly lower current and retrospective measures of self-esteem and higher levels of self-blame than participants from the non-divorced families. The self-esteem of children of divorced families was expected to increase from the retrospective to the current measures, while those of the non-divorced group were hypothesized to show minimal change.

Self-blame was hypothesized to be negatively correlated with self-esteem (as self-blame scores increase, self-esteem scores decrease). It was also predicted that there would be a difference in the pattern of retrospective and current self-esteem and self-blame scores for male and female participants, with females having lower self-esteem and higher self-blame scores than males. In this study, we also hypothesized that "triadic" relationships, reflective of levels of conflict during parental divorce, would be correlated with individuals' self-esteem scores. A significant difference was expected to exist in current and retrospective self-esteem and self-blame in individuals who reported a great amount of triadic relations. A positive correlation between the degree of triadic relations and reported conflict over custody was expected in the children of divorced/separated parents.

METHOD

Participants

Two hundred ninety-six undergraduate students from a mid-sized state university were studied. Participants were volunteers selected from a Psychology Department subject pool, as well as others recruited from psychology courses. The mean age of the participants was 19.0 years $(SD = 1.53)$. There were 160 first year participants, 78 sophomores, 27 juniors, 16 seniors, and 2 special students. Thirteen participants failed to report their academic level and/or reported parental death, in which case their data was not utilized. Eighty-four of the participants were males and one hundred ninety-seven were females. Fifteen individuals did not report their gender.

Participants were grouped as follows based on their confidential responses to a demographic survey. Group 1, the "divorced" group, consisted of those participants who reported that their biological parents were divorced or separated. The average number of years since the divorce/separation occurred was 10.11 $(SD = 5.89)$, and ranged from four months to twenty years. Group 2, the "non-divorced" group, consisted of those participants who reported that their parents were never divorced or separated. There was a minimal difference in the mean age of the divorced (M = 19.45, SD = 1.74) and non-divorced (M = 18.84, SD = 1.38) groups. Eighty-nine individuals comprised the "divorced" group and one hundred ninety-four were included in the "non-divorced" group. The data of 13 participants was not included due to omission of responses or parental death.

Materials

All participants received the informed consent form explaining the nature of the study and identifying any possible risks involved with their participation. Each participant was also administered a participant information survey requesting demographic information (i.e., age, gender, academic level, and socioeconomic status–computed using Hollingshead's four-factor index of social status), as well as personal information about each participant's family history.

The participants in each group received a copy of Neemann and Harter's (1986) Self-Perception Profile for College Students entitled "What I Am Like." A second copy of the self-perception measure, named "What I Was Like," consisted of the same questions with instructions to answer these in a retrospective manner (see Procedure, below). To assess participants' self-blaming tendencies, the six-item Self-Blame subscale of Kurdek and Berg's (1987) Children's Beliefs About Parental Divorce Scale (CBAPDS) were added to the retrospective portion of the self-perception measure. A debriefing statement was given to all participants after they completed the experimental session.

Procedure

Participants were administered the informed consent form prior to beginning the experiment. For the participant information survey, those whose parents were not divorced were instructed to respond only to the first set of questions, omitting those in reference to step parents and divorce issues. Participants from divorced families were instructed to respond to all items in the survey. The participants were instructed to answer the items as truthfully as possible, and were reminded that their responses would remain confidential.

Upon completion of the participant information survey, the participants continued on to Neemann and Harter's Self-Perception Profile
for College Students (1986). Participants were instructed to first answer the survey titled What I Am Like, responding to these items
based on their current thoughts and feelings. Upon completion of the
survey, participants continued to record their answers to the What I
Was Like questionnaire. Participants were instructed to answer these
items retrospectively. Children from divorced families were instructed
to base their answers on their thoughts and feelings "at the time that
the parental divorce/separation occurred." Children from non-divorced families responded to the items as they would have "several
years ago, when they were still living at home with their parents."
Participants then completed the self-blame subscale of the Children's
Beliefs About Parental Divorce Scale, and were instructed to answer
these items retrospectively, as well.

RESULTS

Socioeconomic Status. Because the socioeconomic status of individuals from divorced families is often thought to be lower than that of
individuals from non-divorced families, a one-way analysis of variance was performed to compare the Hollingshead socioeconomic status scores of the participants' biological parents as a function of marital status (divorced, non-divorced). The results indicated that there
was no significant difference between the divorced group (M = 51.93,
SD = 8.93) and the non-divorced group (M = 51.77, SD = 8.35) in
terms of their parents' socioeconomic standing, $F(1, 261) = 0.02$, $p >
.05$. Therefore, socioeconomic status did not confound the compari-
sons of the divorced and non-divorced groups in this study.

A correlational analysis revealed no significant relationship between the socioeconomic status of the participants' biological parents
and their What I Am Like scores, $r(261) = .01$, $p > .05$. There was also
no significant relationship between the socioeconomic status of the
participants' biological parents and their What I Was Like scores,
$r(261) = .04$, $p > .05$. Thus, for each group, participants' self-perception scores were not related to the socioeconomic status of their biological parents.

Self-Perception as a Function of Marital Status. A mixed analysis
of variance revealed a significant interaction effect between current

and retrospective self-perception (What I Am Like and What I Was Like) scores as the within subject repeated measures, and parents' marital status as the between groups factor, F(1, 278) = 8.08, p < .01. Current self-perception scores for the members of both groups were higher than their retrospective scores. However, scores on the retrospective (What I Was Like) survey were significantly lower for the divorced versus non-divorced group. The self-esteem scores of individuals from divorced families increased more over time than did those for the non-divorced group. The means for each measure and group are listed in Table 1.

A follow-up independent t-test indicated that the retrospective scores of individuals in the divorced group (*M* = 150.12, *SD* = 27.23) were significantly lower than those in the non-divorced group (*M* = 157.74, *SD* = 27.34), *t*(282) = 2.18, *p* < .05. Thus, individuals from divorced families reported lower retrospective self-perceptions than did participants from non-divorced families. There was no significant difference between the current self-perception scores of individuals from divorced (*M* = 165.57, *SD* = 23.05) and non-divorced (*M* = 162.91, *SD* = 22.77) families, *t*(282) = − 0.91, *p* > .05.

TABLE 1. Mean Current and Retrospective Self-Perception Scores and Self-Blame Scores for Participants from Divorced and Non-Divorced Families

Measure	Divorced	Non-Divorced
Total What I Am Like		
N	89	195
M	165.57	162.91
SD	23.05	22.77
Total What I Was Like		
N	89	195
M*	150.12	157.74
SD	27.23	27.33
Total Self-Blame		
N	88	191
M*	13.15	11.39
SD	4.14	3.60

* *p* < .05

Self-Blame as a Function of Marital Status. An analysis of variance indicated that individuals from the divorced group (M = 13.15, SD = 4.14) and non-divorced group (M = 11.39, SD = 3.60) reported significantly different levels of self-blame, $F(1, 277) = 12.99$, p < .001. Children from divorced families reported more self-blaming tendencies for parental conflict than did children from non-divorced families. There was no significant correlation between the years since the divorce/separation occurred and either the What I Was Like, What I Am Like, or the Self-Blame scores for the divorced group. There was also no significant correlation between Self-Blame scores and What I Was Like scores, or Self-Blame and What I Am Like scores, and only a weak correlation between Self-Blame and What I Was Like approached significance, $r(279) = -0.12$, p = .053.

Gender and Self-Perception. A two-way analysis of variance with gender and marital status as factors revealed a main effect of gender, with males (M = 167.88, SD = 23.73) and females (M = 161.64, SD = 22.39) differing in their current self-perception scores, $F(1, 274) = 7.36$, p < .01. As predicted, male participants reported higher current self-perception scores than did female participants. There were no significant main or interaction effects due to parents' between gender and marital status (p > .05 on both tests).

A similar two-way analysis of variance revealed that there was no significant difference between the males' ($M = 157.02, SD = 29.45$) and females' ($M = 154.24, SD = 26.63$) What I Was Like scores, $F(1,274) = 2.55, p > .05$. in their retrospective "What I Was Like" scores, $F(1, 274) = 2.55, p > .05$. Although there was a considerable difference in the retrospective self-esteem of males ($M = 157.04, SD = 34.45$) and females ($M = 146.83, SD = 23.84$) from divorced families, this difference was not statistically significant. There were also no significant interaction effects between gender and marital status ($p > .05$).

Subscales. The results of a correlational analysis of the What I Am Like and What I Was Like scores, as well as the current and retrospective scores for the social acceptance, global self-worth, appearance, and parent relationships subscales indicated that all of the retrospective measures were positively correlated with their corresponding current measures (see Table 2).

Triadic Relations and Conflict. A Chi-square test of independence indicated that participants in the divorced and non-divorced groups

TABLE 2. Correlations Between Subscale Scores for Current and Retrospective Reports

Current Measures	Retrospective Measures				
	Social Acceptance	Global Self-Worth	Appearance	Parent Relationships	Total Self-Perception
Social Acceptance	.381^c	.256^c	.119^a	.096^a	.271^c
Global Self-Worth	.210^c	.369^c	.245^c	.087^a	.339^c
Appearance	.153^b	.271^c	.435^c	.087^a	.306^c
Parent Relationships	.106^a	.154^b	.122^a	.325^c	.161^b
Total Self-Perception	.313^c	.395^c	.327^c	.163^b	.464^c

Note: Superscripts show p values for two-tailed tests (a = $p < .05$, b = $p < .01$, c = $p < .001$)

were significantly different according to the reported degree of triadic relations between the participants and their biological parents, $X^2(6, N = 283) = 87.09$, $p < .001$. Of the divorced participants, 36.36% rated their relationships with their parents as triadic (values 1-3 on a seven point scale), while 53.41% reported their relationships as not triadic (values 5-7). In the non-divorced group, only 4.10% reported triadic relationships and 92.82% reported non-triadic relationships between themselves and their parents. Thus, as hypothesized, individuals reported triadic relationships more frequently from divorced families than did those from non-divorced families.

A one-way analysis of variance revealed that the self-blame scores of the participants who rated their relationships with their parents as triadic ($M = 15.18$, $SD = 4.26$) were significantly higher than those who reported non-triadic relationships ($M = 11.27$, $SD = 3.45$), $F(1, 261) = 40.29$, $p < .001$. Individuals who viewed their relationships with their parents as triadic reported more feelings of self-blame for parental conflict than those who did not experience triadic relations with their parents.

The relationships between the degree of triadic relations, quality of parents' marital status, parental relationship at the time of the divorce/separation, inter-parental conflict over custody, and both the What I

Am Like and What I Was Like scores were explored using the Spearman correlation statistic. This analysis revealed a strong correlation between the degree of triadic relations and quality of parents' marital relationship, $r(279) = 0.64$, $p < .001$. For the divorced sample, the degree of triadic relations reported was also correlated with the parental relationship at the time of the divorce/separation rating, $r(84) = 0.27$, $p < .05$. The quality of parents' marital relationship was strongly correlated with parental relationship at the time of the divorce/separation, $r(85) = 0.73$, $p < .001$, and with inter-parent conflict over custody, $r(81) = 0.31$, $p < .01$. Parental marital relationships with significant conflict were highly related to unpleasant divorces/separations and a significant amount of conflict concerning custody of the children involved.

Interparental conflict concerning custody was also correlated with degree of triadic relations, $r(81) = 0.50$, $p < .001$, and parental relationship at the time of the divorce/separation, $r(80) = 0.36$, $p = .001$. The What I Was Like scores showed a low positive correlation with the degree of triadic relations, $r(281) = 0.15$, $p = .01$, quality of parents' marital relationship, $r(280) = 0.17$, $p < .01$, and inter-parent conflict over custody, $r(82) = 0.23$, $p < .05$.

DISCUSSION

The significant interaction between the two measures of self-perception and parents' marital status revealed that the self-perception of individuals from divorced families increased dramatically from the time of the divorce to present day, while the self-perception scores of non-divorced individuals increased only slightly with time. Self-perception scores were lower in the divorced group on the retrospective measure, but recovered to levels similar to the non-divorced group in the current measure. This may be an indication of the resiliency of children from divorced families and the recovery of their self-esteem over time.

As predicted, we observed a significant difference in the self-blame scores between divorced and non-divorced individuals. Individuals whose parents were divorced reported higher levels of self-blame regarding parental conflict than did those from non-divorced families. The lack of significant correlations between self-blame scores and self-perception scores indicated that children who blamed themselves for their parents' divorce/separation did not necessarily experience a corresponding decline in self-esteem. Similarly, those who reported low self-perceptions did not blame themselves for their parents' divorce. Thus in contrast to our hypotheses, no significant correlations were found between self-perception and self-blame, and so these data do not support a strong relationship between children's self-blaming tendencies and their perceived self-esteem following a parental divorce.

The absence of a statistically significant effect due to socioeconomic status in the analysis of variance performed on parents' marital status indicated that the participants in each group did not differ in socioeconomic status as a function of being from a divorced/separated or intact family. This result was not surprising given the relative homogeneity of the current sample. Although most of the parents of the college students studied fell within similar levels of social status, the full gamut of scores were represented (i.e., educational levels ranged from not graduating from high school to completing graduate/professional school; parents' occupational levels ranged from unemployed to executives/professionals). Thus, although the sample consisted of a specific group of individuals of relatively high social status, the entire range of possibilities was represented, and no major differences in social status were observed between the divorced/separated and intact families. Therefore, differences due to socioeconomic status as a function of divorce cannot be considered a confounding variable in this study.

Again in accordance with the hypothesis, there was no significant relationship found to exist between parents' socioeconomic status and participants' self-perception scores–current or retrospective. These results indicate that although individuals from divorced families oftentimes find themselves at levels of socioeconomic status below those of their non-divorced counterparts, due to the subsequent loss of the non-custodial parent's income, there will not necessarily be a concurrent decrease in the self-perception of the children involved.

Gender was found to account for some differences in self-perception scores. Males had significantly higher current self-perception scores than did females, in general agreement with Harter's (1993) findings. Females, from both divorced and non-divorced families, had lower levels of current self-esteem than did male participants. Since there was a balance of male and female children in the divorced and non-divorced groups, gender differences in self-esteem did not account for the significant differences in reported self-perceptions between these groups which were the primary analyses of interest in this study. Interestingly, the retrospective self-perception scores did not differ for male and female participants. The mean age of participants at the time of their parent's divorce/separation was approximately ten years. At this young age, children may be less aware of self and other's perceptions, and less able to make such appraisals. Harter (1993) likewise reported similar levels of self-esteem and perceived appearance for males and females throughout their middle childhood years. Thus developmental differences may, in part, account for our data showing that males and females in this study did not differ in terms of their retrospective reporting, but did differ in their current self-perception scores.

The significant correlations that were observed between the current and retrospective scores and subscales of the self-perception measures provide evidence of the consistency of scores produced through the use of this questionnaire. Although the self-perception of both the divorced and non-divorced individuals improved with time, there was a significant positive correlation between the two scores (time 1, time 2) for both groups. This may reflect that for the sample as a whole, individuals' self-perceptions remained relatively stable over time. Current overall self-perception values were significantly correlated with each of the current subscales. Likewise, the retrospective overall self-perception score was significantly correlated to each of the retrospective subscales. This again suggests consistency and stability in the way individuals report self worth and self-esteem, and somewhat supports the validity of retrospective reporting for studying self-perceptions (especially in situations where baseline measurements and longitudinal analyses are not available).

Significantly more individuals in the divorced group reported their relationships with their parents as triadic than did those from the non-divorced group. This finding is not surprising, as parental divorce/separation often involves struggles concerning the child's loyalty and custody. Children are often caught in the middle of a tug-of-war battle between their parents. The results of this study show that this type of situation is reported most frequently by children whose parents are divorced/separated.

As predicted, the individuals reporting triadic relationships with their parents also reported more self-blaming tendencies than did those reporting non-triadic relationships. Oftentimes, parents' disagreements concern their children and differences in child-rearing practices (Westerman, 1987), which may result in the children believing they are to blame for the parental discord. This factor was closely related to the quality of parents' marital relationships. The extent to which the parental relationships were triadic was highly correlated with the degree of disharmony concerning marital relationships. This finding was also in agreement with Westerman's theory of triangulation. In triadic relationships, especially ones involving divorce/separation, there were also reports of poor quality marital relationships.

In accordance with the hypotheses, there were strong correlations between the quality of parents' marital relationship, parents' relationship at the time of the divorce/separation, and inter-parental conflict over custody. Divorce often involves a great deal of conflict, especially between the parents. The reported ratings of the quality of the marital relationship indicated that marriages of poor quality were associated with conflict-ridden divorces, as well as parental conflict concerning custody. Interparental conflict concerning custody was also related to the degree of triadic relations, revealing that many of the participants were caught in what is usually dubbed "custody battles." With both parents fighting for custody, few realize the repercussions of such circumstances for the child. It is important to note these results, and the effects such conflict can have on children's self-perceptions. The current self-perception scores reported by participants were significantly related to the degree of triadic relations, quality of parents' marital relationship, and interparental conflict over custody. This indicates that the conflict that exists between the parents is related to the self-esteem of children experiencing the marital dissolution. Therefore, parents should take care to avoid conflict in the presence of their children.

There was no relationship between the years since the divorce/separation occurred and either of the self-perception or the self-blame scores. This revealed that individuals' self-esteem and self-blaming tendencies in this sample were not closely related to when a divorce/separation occurred or to how much time had passed since the event took place. Therefore, children at any age and at any temporal distance from parental divorce can experience its effects. Although some of the literature has reported age effects in the assessment of adjustment to and effects of parental divorce/separation, children of all ages are susceptible to the impact of divorce on self-perceptions.

Overall, the present study established the use of retrospective self-reporting as a viable means of investigating the effects of divorce on the self-perceptions of the children involved. This study established that college-aged children of divorce report lower self-perceptions than non-divorced controls at the time of their parents' separation. However, the self-perceptions of these individuals recovered over time. This study offers important implications for researchers interested in family systems and measuring the effects of parental divorce on children.

REFERENCES

Allen, S. F., Stoltenberg, C. D., & Rosko, C. K. (1990). Perceived psychological separation of older adolescents and young adults from their parents: A comparison of divorced versus intact families. *Journal of Counseling and Development, 69*(1), 57-61.

Amato, P. R. (1993). Children's adjustment to divorce: Theories, hypotheses, and empirical support. *Journal of Marriage and the Family, 55,* 23-38.

Amato, P. R., & Keith, B. (1991). Parental divorce and adult well-being: A meta-analysis. *Journal of Marriage and the Family, 53,* 43-58.

Bisnaire, L. M. C., Firestone, P., & Rynard, D. (1990). Factors associated with academic achievement in children following parental separation. *American Journal of Orthopsychiatry, 60,* 67-76.

Bynum, M. K., & Durm, M. W. (1996). Children of divorce and its effect on their self-esteem. *Psychological Reports, 79*(2), 447-450.

Byrne, B. M. (1996). *Measuring self-concept across the lifespan.* Washington, D.C.: American Psychological Association.

Clifford, T., & Clark, R. (1995). Family climate, family structure and self-esteem in college females: The physical- vs. psychological-wholeness divorce debate revisited. *Journal of Divorce & Remarriage, 23*(3/4), 97-112.

Cole, D. A., Peeke, L. G., & Ingold, C. (1996). Characterological and behavioral self-blame in children: Assessment and developmental considerations. *Development and Psychopathology, 8,* 381-397.

Fivush, R. (1993). Developmental perspectives on autobiographical recall. In G. S. Goodman & B. L. Bottoms (Eds.), *Child victims, child witnesses: Understanding and improving testimony* (pp. 1-24). New York: Guilford Press.

Gabardi, L. & Rosen, L.A. (1991). Differences between college students from divorced and intact families. *Journal of Divorce & Remarriage, 15*(3-4), 175-191.

Garber, R.J. (1991). Long-term effects of divorce on the self-esteem of young adults. *Journal of Divorce & Remarriage, 17*(1-2), 131-137.

Giuliani, G. A. (1997). The relationship among parental marital status, self-esteem and academic performance in commuter college students. *Dissertation Abstract International, Section B: Sciences & Engineering, 58*(1-B), 0416.

Harter, S. (1993). Causes and consequences of low self-esteem in children and adolescents. In R. F. Baumeister (Ed.), *Self-esteem: The puzzle of low self-regard* (pp. 87-116). New York: Plenum Press.

Healy, J. M., Stewart, A. J., & Copeland, A. P. (1993). The role of self-blame in children's adjustment to parental separation. *Personality and Social Psychology Bulletin, 19*(3), 279-289.

Hetherington, E. M. (1989). Coping with family transitions: Winners, losers, and survivors. *Child Development, 60,* 1-14.

Hollingshead, A. B. (1975). *Four-factor index of social status.* Delaware: Psychological Measurements Inc.

Jenkins, J. M., & Smith, M. A. (1993). A prospective study of behavioral disturbance in children who subsequently experience parental divorce: A research note. *Journal of Divorce & Remarriage, 19*(1/2), 143-160.

Kalter, N., Riemer, B., Brickman, A. & Chen, J.W. (1995). Implications of parental divorce for female development. *Journal of the American Academy of Child Psychiatry, 24*(5), 538-544.

Kurdek, L. A., & Berg, B. (1987). Children's beliefs about parental divorce scale: Psychometric characteristics and concurrent validity. *Journal of Consulting and Clinical Psychology, 55*(5), 712-718.

Kurdek, L. A., Blisk, D., & Siesky, A. E. (1981). Correlates of children's long-term adjustment to their parents' divorce. *Developmental Psychology, 17,* 565-579.

Kurdek, L. A., & Siesky, A. E. (1980). Children's perceptions of their parents' divorce. *Journal of Divorce, 3*(4), 339-378.

Kurtz, L. (1994). Psychosocial coping resources in elementary school-age children of divorce. *American Journal of Orthopsychiatry, 64*(4), 554-562.

Maughan, B. & Rutter, M. (1997). Retrospective reporting of childhood adversity: Issues in assessing long-term recall. *Journal of Personality Disorders, 11*(1), 19-33.

Mechanic, D., & Hansell, S. (1989). Divorce, family conflict, and adolescents' well-being. *Journal of Health and Social Behavior, 30,* 195-116.

Neemann, J., & Harter, S. (1986). Manual for the self-perception profile for college students. University of Denver.

Robins, L. N. (1988). Data gathering and data analysis for prospective and retrospective longitudinal studies. In M. Rutter (Ed.), *Studies of psychosocial risk: The power of longitudinal data* (pp. 318-324). Cambridge: Cambridge University Press.

Shook, N. J. & Jurich, J. (1992). Correlates of self-esteem among college offspring from divorced families: A study of gender differences. *Journal of Divorce & Remarriage, 18*(3-4), 157-176.

Stralka, M. J. D. (1995). Parents' marital status, family adaptability and cohesion, and perceived self-worth of college students. *Dissertation Abstracts International, Section A: Humanities and Social Sciences, 56*(6-A), 2120.

Wallerstein, J. S. (1983) Children of divorce: The psychological tasks of the child. *American Journal of Orthopsychiatry, 53*(2), 230-243.

Wallerstein, J. S. (1987). Children of divorce: Report of a ten-year follow-up of early latency-age children. *American Journal of Orthopsychiatry, 57*(2), 199-211.

Weiss, R. S. (1975). *Marital separation*. New York: Basic Books.

Westerman, M. A. (1987). "Triangulation," marital discord and child behavior problems. *Journal of Social and Personal Relationships, 4*, 87-106.

Wyman, P. A., Cowen, E. L., Hightower, A. D., & Pedro-Carroll, J. L. (1985). Perceived competence, self-esteem, and anxiety in latency-aged children of divorce. *Journal of Clinical Child Psychology, 14*(1), 20-26.

Young, D. M. (1983). Two studies of children of divorce. In L. A. Kurdek (Ed.), *New directions for child development* (No. 19). San Francisco: Jossey-Bass.

Gender Schematization in Adolescents: Differences Based on Rearing in Single-Parent and Intact Families

Michael Lawrence Slavkin

SUMMARY. The study explored three aspects of adolescents' schematization of gender roles: the adolescent's perceptions of socially-idealized gender roles (ideal gender roles), the adolescent's perceptions of their own gender role (personal gender role), and the fit between an adolescent's ideal and personal gender roles. Of the participants sampled, 124 were Caucasian, 31 were African-American, 12 were Asian-American, and 2 were Hispanic-American. Participants' family of origin's current yearly incomes ranged from $10,000 to $150,000, with a median income of $34,000. Because parental gender models in one- and two-parent families differ, the gender roles of adolescents raised in one- versus two-parent families may differ. Differences in personal and idealized gender roles were found between students raised in one- versus two-parent families (students from both types of families valued androgyny, a person who has strong masculine and feminine character-

---

Michael Lawrence Slavkin, PhD, is on the faculty, University of Southern Indiana, 8600 University Boulevard, Evansville, IN 47712.

Address correspondence to: Michael Slavkin, Department of Counseling and Educational Psychology, Indiana University, 201 North Rose Avenue, Bloomington, IN 47405 (E-mail: mslavkin@indiana.edu).

Special thanks to Dr. Wendell Bonner of Saint Louis University for his expertise in editing during earlier phases of this research.

[Haworth co-indexing entry note]: "Gender Schematization in Adolescents: Differences Based on Rearing in Single-Parent and Intact Families." Slavkin, Michael Lawrence. Co-published simultaneously in *Journal of Divorce & Remarriage* (The Haworth Clinical Practice Press, an imprint of The Haworth Press, Inc.) Vol. 34, No. 3/4, 2001, pp. 137-149; and: *Divorce and the Next Generation: Perspectives for Young Adults in the New Millennium* (ed: Craig A. Everett) The Haworth Clinical Practice Press, an imprint of The Haworth Press, Inc., 2001, pp. 137-149. Single or multiple copies of this article are available for a fee from The Haworth Document Delivery Service [1-800-342-9678, 9:00 a.m. - 5:00 p.m. (EST). E-mail address: getinfo@haworthpressinc.com].

istics). A discussion of the results follows. *[Article copies available for a fee from The Haworth Document Delivery Service: 1-800-342-9678. E-mail address: <getinfo@haworthpressinc.com> Website: <http://www.HaworthPress. com> © 2001 by The Haworth Press, Inc. All rights reserved.]*

KEYWORDS. Divorce and adolescents, single parent families, gender and divorce, gender and adolescents

Gender schema are cognitive representations about the way in which individual, familial, community, and societal roles are divided by gender. Gender schema have been historically defined as being either masculine roles or feminine roles (Bem, 1974; Williams, Radin, & Allegro, 1992). Many have stereotyped masculine roles as being independent and dominant, while feminine roles have been traditionally stereotyped as submissive and sensitive (Bem, 1975, 1985). The current study will explore three specifics of gender schema roles: the person's perceptions of their own gender roles (personal gender role schemata), the person's perceptions of socially idealized gender roles (ideal gender role schemata), and the fit between an individual's personal and ideal gender roles (socialized gender role schemata).

Parents are important models of gender schema (Kurdek & Siesky, 1980; Williams et al., 1992). One of the main functions of parents and family is to serve as a socialization system, by which children are taught traditional values, behaviors, and cognitive patterns (Glass, Bengtson, & Dunham, 1986). Parents socialize children by modeling gender-appropriate behaviors and attitudes (Chodorow, 1978; Glass et al., 1986; Williams et al., 1992).

Significant differences exist in the gender schema of family members of single-parent families and intact families (Amato & Booth, 1991; Wallerstein, 1991). Developmental, social, and behavioral changes in children are thought to be the result of changes in economic and caretaking roles for parents in single-parent families (Hess & Camara, 1979; Hetherington, Cox, & Cox, 1977, 1985; Kalter, 1987; Wallerstein & Kelly, 1976, 1980). Being reared in a family with one primary parent may lead children to re-evaluate whether a parent's socialized roles are masculine or feminine. Mothers who used to be primary caregivers are busy with professional careers, and fathers who used to be at their jobs may be found at home more often (Amato & Booth, 1991; Katz, 1989). Differences between personal roles and idealized social roles are also thought to be a result of growing up with one parent (Wallerstein, 1991).

Because adolescents from single-parent families identify their primary parent as being both maternal and paternal, Katz (1989) believes that single-parent family systems lead to more flexible gender schema. Such flexible networks have been defined by Bem (1974, 1981a) as being androgynous in nature, which is the incorporation of masculine and feminine characteristics into a single schematic framework. Androgynous individuals are thought to be more situationally flexible, using a schematic heuristic based on whether or not it is most appropriate for that setting (Bem, 1981a).

Furthermore, social and economic changes experienced by children of single-parent families may affect the ways they perceive the prototype of "parent" (Peck, 1988-89; Wallerstein, 1991; Wallerstein & Kelly, 1976, 1980). Adolescents from single-parent families are typically reared by a mother that works and raises her children, while children from intact homes have two parents that divide these responsibilities based on socially-identified gender roles. Because of these differences, adolescents of single-parent families may hold more flexible gender role schemata when compared to adolescents from intact homes, or even adolescents from father-headed families (Amato & Booth, 1991; Kurdek & Siesky, 1980; Mason & Bumpass, 1975). Since most adolescents of single-parent families live in mother-headed/maternally employed households, they may also be more likely than adolescents in father-headed families to perceive their world based on egalitarian scripts (Amato & Booth, 1991). Single parents are more likely than parents in intact families to have nontraditional prototypes of the family.

Understanding these systemic differences between intact families, mother-headed families and father-headed families is important, in that the changes in gender roles may alter the future cognitive representations of these individuals (Bem, 1981a). The present study examines whether young adults who grew up in intact families, mother-headed families and father-headed families hold different gender role schema.

Five specific questions were asked of gender schema and the structure of the family. In the current study, students reared in single-parent families are expected to hold more androgynous personal gender role schemata that students reared in intact families. Second, students reared in single-parent families are expected to hold more androgynous ideal gender role schemata than students reared in intact families. Third, students reared in single-parent families are thought to be more similar on personal and ideal gender role schema than individuals reared in intact families. Fourth, individuals reared in mother-headed families are believed to hold more androgynous personal gender role schemata than students reared in father-headed households. Finally, individuals reared in mother-headed families are thought to hold more androgynous ideal gender role schemata than students reared in father-headed households.

METHOD

Participants

Participants for the current study were 108 female and 61 male students enrolled in undergraduate psychology courses at a Midwestern university and a community college. Participants completed questionnaires as fulfillment of optional course credits. Participants' ages ranged from 17 years of age to 22 years of age, with the median falling at 19 years. Participants were asked to define their families based on their family of origin. Of the 169 students sampled in this study, 108 were from intact families, while 59 were from single-parent families. The 59 students had all experienced the divorce of their parents prior to adolescence (age 12). Two subjects did not define their family status, and were removed from further analysis (see Table 1). Of the subjects sampled, 125 were Caucasian, 30 were African-American, 12 were Asian-American, and 2 were Hispanic-American.

Participants' socio-economic status was defined based on their family of origin's yearly income. Socio-economic status ranged from $20,000 to $150,000, with a median income of $34,000. In order to assure that differences in gender roles between participants from single-parent families and intact families were attributable to individuals being reared in those families, participants in single-parent and intact families were paired based on gender, age, race, and socio-economic status. 59 pairs resulted (32 female pairs, 27 male pairs; 40 Caucasian pairs, 15 African-American pairs, 4 Asian-American pairs). The pairs ranged in age from 17 to 24, with a median age of 19. Family of origin income ranged from $10,000 to $120,000, with a median of $34,000. The remaining participants were not used in the analyses.

TABLE 1. Frequencies and Percentages for Participants' Gender, Family Status, Ethnicity, and Age

Gender	Frequency	Percent
Female	32	54
Male	27	46
TOTAL	59	100

Ethnicity	Frequency	Percent
Caucasian	40	67
African-American	15	26
Asian-American	4	7
TOTAL	59	100

Age	Frequency	Percent
17-years-old	2	3
18-years-old	22	37
19-years-old	17	29
20-years-old	11	19
21-years-old	3	6
22-years-old	2	3
24-years-old	2	3
TOTAL	59	100

Procedure

Participants were asked to complete two forms of the Bem Sex-Role Inventory (BSRI): one was used to assess how the individual describes their self gender schema (Personal gender role schema), and the other was used to assess how the individual describes the ideal person's gender schema (Ideal gender role schema). Demographic data, such as socio-economic status, status of family (single-parent or intact), and race were assessed via a demographic questionnaire. Each subject completed the questionnaires in the following order: personal gender schema questionnaire, ideal gender schema questionnaire, and finally the demographic questionnaire. The questionnaires were administered to the participants in a group by the researcher in a classroom setting. Most of the students took 30 minutes to complete the questionnaires.

Measures

Personal Gender Role Schema. Participants' perceptions of their personal gender role schemata were assessed using the Bem Sex-Role

Inventory (BSRI, Bem, 1981b). The Bem Sex-Role Inventory-Personal questionnaire asked respondents to rate on a scale of 1 (low) to 7 (high) how much the descriptors were similar to them. Twenty of the adjectives are schematic descriptors that are traditional stereotypes of males, such as ambitious, self-reliant, independent, assertive. An additional 20 items are schematic descriptors that are traditional stereotypes of females, such as affectionate, gentle, understanding, or sensitive to the needs of others. The remaining twenty items are filler items.

Participants' profiles from the Bem Sex-Role Inventory-Personal questionnaire were scored using the total from the Femininity and Masculinity scales (FM scale) (see Table 2). High scores indicate androgynous schematic frameworks, while low scores show sex-typed (masculine or feminine) schematic frameworks.

Alpha scores for the masculinity scale was .84, while alpha scores for the femininity scale was .87.

Ideal Gender Roles. A modified form of the Bem Sex-Role Inventory was used to assess each students' perceptions of socially-stereotyped gender role schemata (ideal gender roles). Respondents were asked to rate each of 20 stereotyped masculine descriptors and 20 stereotyped feminine descriptors based on their perception of the ideal person, rather than for themselves.

Participants' profiles from the Bem Sex-Role Inventory-Ideal questionnaire were scored using the total from the Femininity and Masculinity scales (FM scale). High scores indicate that the societal ideal would have androgynous schematic framing, while low scores show that an ideal person would be schematically sex-typed (masculine or feminine).

TABLE 2. Descriptive Statistics for BSRI Scales

BSRI Scales	N	Minimum	Maximum	Mean	SD
Personal-Feminine	118	3.60	6.35	4.93	.61
Personal-Masculine	118	3.00	6.40	4.88	.90
Ideal-Feminine	114	2.85	6.95	5.16	.79
Ideal-Masculine	114	3.70	6.95	5.49	.81
Personal-Androgynous (FM)	118	39.00	88.00	68.85	8.30
Ideal-Androgynous (FM)	114	30.00	97.00	74.96	10.31

$p = .05$

Alpha scores for the ideal masculinity scale was .89. Alpha scores for the ideal femininity scale was .84.

Demographic Factors. Information on participants was obtained from self-report measures. Participants were asked to define the nature of their family system with an open ended question asking "How would you be most likely to describe the status of your childhood family?"(intact, mother-headed single-parent, father-headed single-parent).

RESULTS

Independent t-tests were run between paired participants from intact and single-parent families on demographic characteristics (gender, age, race, socieo-economic status) to assure that differences in gender roles were attributable to individuals being reared in single-parent or intact families. No significant differences on gender identity were found based on gender, age, race, or socio-economic status.

Results for classifications on personal and ideal gender role schema among the 59 pairs reared in single-parent or intact families can be found in Table 3.

Five sets of analyses were carried out to test the five hypotheses under consideration: (1) that students reared in single-parent families would view their personal gender role schemata as being more androgynous than students reared in intact families, (2) that students reared in single-parent families value androgynous schematization more than students reared in intact families, (3) that students reared in single-parent families would be more similar on personal and ideal

TABLE 3. Descriptive Statistics on Participants' Bem Sex-Role Schematic Classification Based on Status of Family

	Personal Role Schema		Ideal Role Schema	
	Intact	Single	Intact	Single
Feminine	25	14	20	5
Masculine	12	15	11	11
Androgynous	13	18	16	25
Undifferentiated	9	12	8	17
Total	59	59	55	58

gender role schema than individuals reared in intact families, (4) that individuals reared in mother-headed families would view themselves (personal gender role schemata) in more androgynous ways than students reared in father-headed households, and (5) that individuals reared in mother-headed families would view the societal ideal (ideal gender role schemata) in more androgynous ways than students reared in father-headed households.

Differences Between Individuals on Personal Gender Role Schemata

In order to assess whether adolescents reared in single-parent families held more androgynous personal gender role schemata than individuals reared in intact families, a matched sample t-test was performed. A significant difference was found between individuals in intact versus single-parent families with respect to personal gender roles (t (58) = 10.84, p = .01), with adolescents from intact families showing higher levels of androgynous framing (see Table 4). Adolescents reared in single-parent families showed greater personal levels of masculine gender role schematization than adolescents reared in intact families.

TABLE 4. Results of Matched Samples t-Tests (n = 59)

	Pair	Mean	SD	T	DF	Sig.	Sig. Level
Pair 1	BSRI-FM Intact	68.85	8.30				
	BSRI-FM Single-P	53.49	7.25	10.84	58	.01	sig
Pair 2	Ideal-FM Intact	74.96	10.31				
	Ideal-FM Single-P	52.83	7.23	12.76	53	.01	sig
Pair 3	BSRI-FM Intact	53.49	7.25				
	Ideal-FM Intact	52.83	7.23	.90	53	.26	ns
Pair 4	BSRI-FM Single-P	68.85	8.30				
	Ideal-FM Single-P	74.96	10.31	5.97	57	.01	sig
Pair 5	BSRI-FM Mother	49.52	9.40				
	BSRI-FM Father	55.92	9.72	− 2.13	53	.04	sig
Pair 6	Ideal-FM Mother	77.85	6.86				
	Ideal-FM Father	69.54	4.52	− .83	52	.412	ns

p = .05

Differences Between Individuals on Ideal Gender Role Schemata

In order to assess whether adolescents reared in single-parent families held more androgynous ideal gender role schemata than individuals reared in intact families, a matched sample t-test was performed. There was a significant difference in levels of ideal gender role androgyny between students reared in intact versus single-parent families (t (52) = 12.76, p =.01), with individuals from intact families showing higher levels of androgynous framing (see Table 4). Adolescents reared in single-parent families showed greater ideal levels of masculine gender role schematization than adolescents reared in intact families.

Differences Between Personal and Ideal Role Schema

To assess whether adolescents reared in single-parent families had more similar personal and ideal gender role schema than students reared in intact families, two matched t-tests were performed: (1) on data taken from the cumulative scales (BSRI-FM, Ideal-FM) for individuals reared in intact families, and (2) on data taken from the cumulative scales (BSRI-FM, Ideal-FM) for individuals reared in single-parent families. A significant difference between the personal and ideal gender role schematization for individuals reared in single-parent families was found (t (57) = 5.97, p = .01), showing higher levels of idealized androgynous framing for individuals from intact homes. However, there was no difference between personal and ideal role schematization for adolescents reared in intact families (t (53) = .90, p = .26) (see Table 4).

Personal Gender Role Schematic Differences Between Those Reared in Mother-Headed and Father-Headed Families

In order to assess whether adolescents reared in mother-headed families held more androgynous personal gender role schemata than individuals reared in father-headed families, a matched sample t-test was performed. Results showed that there was a significant difference between personal gender role schema scores for adolescents reared in mother-headed and father-headed families (t (53) = 2.13, p = .04) (see Table 4), with individuals from mother-headed families holding more androgynous framing. Adolescents reared in father-headed single-parent families showed greater personal levels of masculine gender role schematization than adolescents reared in intact families, regardless of the individual's sex.

Ideal Gender Role Schematic Differences Between Those Reared in Mother-Headed and Father-Headed Families

In order to assess whether individuals reared in mother-headed families held more androgynous ideal gender role schema than individuals reared in father-headed families, a matched sample t-test was performed. Results showed that there was no significant difference between ideal androgyny scores for students reared in mother-headed and father-headed families (t (52) = .83, p = .41) (see Table 4).

DISCUSSION

Differences for personal and ideal gender role schematization were found between adolescents reared in single-parent and intact families. While adolescents reared in intact homes saw the societal ideal as being evenly divided between sex-typed (masculine-feminine) and androgynous roles, individuals from single-parent homes were more apt to categorize themselves as sex-typed (masculine). That is to say, individuals reared in intact homes were more apt to categorize the societal ideal as androgynous. Upon further examination of the results, both females and males from single-parent families stereotyped the ideal person with a masculine script.

Of further interest in this discussion is the presence of significant differences between personal and ideal role schemata for individuals from single-parent families, but no significant differences for individuals reared in intact families. These results indicate that individuals from single-parent families identify themselves as being different from the script for the societal ideal, whereas individuals from intact homes do not. Since they are identified as schematically sex-typed, individuals from single-parent families could be viewed as not being as flexible in their thinking, in that they were limited in the ways in which they viewed themselves, others, and societal roles.

Individuals from single-parent families also viewed the idealized individual as being schematically sex-typed. Differences between personal and ideal gender role schema for students reared in single-parent homes is an indication that these individuals think of themselves as being different from the societal norm. Such results would appear to be in line with the research on lowered self-esteem in individuals from single-parent families (Wallerstein, 1991; Hetherington, Cox, & Cox, 1985).

The presence of androgynous personal schemas in individuals reared in intact homes may be related to the lack of sexually-stereotyped models in their immediate home environments, or the presence of both male and female models in their home environments. Such nonstereo-typical ways of thinking (the definition of androgyny) may improve adolescents reared in intact homes in their interactions with others and their adaptability in future environments. Sex-typed individuals from single-parent families, faced with changing familial and economic roles in an ever-diversifying world, may have more difficulty adapting to some situations than individuals from intact homes. Sex-typed thinking would challenge those from single-parent families, in that they would become selective of the information they attend to in others (ideal men are masculine, ideal women are feminine–without exception).

Individuals reared in mother-headed families held more androgynous personal gender role scripts than individuals reared in father-headed families. No such differences could be determined for the ideal scales.

In the present sample, only 13 father-headed families were examined. While the results are not highly reliable (due to sample size), individuals in mother-headed families were more apt than individuals from father-headed families to think of themselves from an androgynous framework. It could be that children in mother-headed families break more social stereotypes (and are generally seen negatively by society) in being a single-parent than fathers, who are valued for being both work and family oriented.

Further studies should be performed to identify the relations between a child's personal gender role schema and those gender role scripts modeled in the home. While some of the results of this study were significant, future studies may want to include several measures of gender schema, perhaps even observational data. The expansion of measures may strengthen the validity of the results found, as well as disseminate between the masculine scripts and feminine scripts, between the personal schemata and ideal schemata, and between mother-headed and father-headed families. To further understand how the schematization of gender impacts our relations in society holds promise as a diverse field of study. Future understanding of the dynamics of gender roles could improve the ways in which we relate with others, identify individuals, and discriminate between people.

REFERENCES

Amato, P.R., & Booth, A. (1991). The consequences of divorce for attitudes toward divorce and gender roles. *Journal of Family Issues, 12*, 306-322.

Bem, S.L. (1974). The measurement of psychological androgyny. *Journal of Consulting and Clinical Psychology, 42*, 155-162.

Bem, S.L. (1975). Sex role adaptability: One consequence of psychological androgyny. *Journal of Personality and Social Psychology, 31*, 634-43.

Bem, S.L. (1981a). Gender schema theory: A cognitive account of sex typing. *Psychological Review, 88*, 354-364.

Bem, S.L. (1981b). *Bem Sex-Role Inventory: Sampler Set (Manual, Test Booklet, Scoring Key).* Palo Alto, California: Mind Garden.

Bem, S.L. (1985). If you are gender schematic, all members of the opposite sex look alike. *Journal of Personality and Social Psychology, 49*, 459-468.

Chodorow, N. (1978). *The reproduction of mothering.* Berkley: University of California Press.

Glass, J., Bengtson, V.L., & Dunham, C.C. (1986). Attitude similarity in three-generation families: Socialization, status inheritance, or reciprocal influence. *American Sociological Review, 51*, 685-698.

Grimmell, D., & Stern, G.S. (1992). The relationship between gender role ideals and psychological well-being. *Sex Roles, 27*, 487-497.

Hess, R., & Camara, K. (1979). Post-divorce family relationships as mediating factors in the consequence of divorce for children. *Journal of Social Issues, 35*, 75-96.

Hetherington, E., Cox, M., & Cox, R. (1977). The aftermath of divorce. In J. Stevens, Jr. & M. Matthews (Eds.), *Mother-child, father-child relations.* Washington D.C.: National Association for the Education of Young Children.

Hetherington, E.M., Cox, M., & Cox, R. (1985). Long-term effects of divorce and remarriage on the adjustment of children. *Journal of American Academy of Child Psychology, 24*, 518-530.

Kalter, N. (1987). Long-term effects of divorce on children: A developmental vulnerability model. *American Journal of Orthopsychiatry, 57*, 587-600.

Katz, G.D. (1989). Relations among aspects of children's social environments, gender schematization, gender role knowledge, and flexibility. *Sex Roles, 21*, 803-823.

Kurdek, L.A., & Siesky, A.E. (1980). Sex-role self-concepts of single divorced parents and their children. *Journal of Divorce, 3*, 249-261.

Mason, K.O., & Bumpass, L.L. (1975). U.S. womens' sex-role ideology, 1970. *American Journal of Sociology, 80,* 1212-1219.

Peck, J.S. (1988-89). The impact of divorce on children at various stages of family life cycle. *Journal of Divorce, 12,* 81-106.

Wallerstein, J.S. (1991). The long-term effects of divorce on children. *Journal of the American Academy of Child and Adolescent Psychiatry, 30,* 349-360.

Wallerstein, J., & Kelly, J. (1976). The effects of parental divorce: Experiences of the child in later latency. *American Journal of Orthopsychiatry, 46,* 256-269.

Wallerstein, J., & Kelly, J.B. (1980). *Surviving the breakup: How children and parents cope with divorce.* New York: Basic Books.

Williams, E., Radin, N., & Allegro, T. (1992). Sex role attitudes of adolescents reared primarily by their fathers: An 11-year follow-up. *Merrill-Palmer Quarterly, 38,* 457-477.

The Propensity for Irrational Beliefs Among Young Adults of Divorced Parents

Joseph Guttmann

SUMMARY. Within the framework of Rational Emotive models and the Intergenerational Transmission Theory, the present study tests the hypothesis that the propensity for irrational thinking is greater among young adults of divorced parents than among their counterparts of married parents. Sixty students (30 of married and 30 of divorced parents) responded to the Propensity for Irrational Beliefs (PIB) and Measure of Intimacy questionnaires. The results reveal an opposite trend from the expected direction, that is, subjects of married parents scored higher than the control group on the PIB. Furthermore, the results show no relationship between the two dependent variables: degree of intimacy and propensity for irrational thinking. These results are discussed within the context of other demonstrated effects of parental divorce on children and possible future directions for similar research. *[Article copies available for a fee from The Haworth Document Delivery Service: 1-800-342-9678. E-mail address: <getinfo@haworthpressinc.com> Website: <http://www.HaworthPress.com> © 2001 by The Haworth Press, Inc. All rights reserved.]*

KEYWORDS. Divorce, children of divorce, young adults, irrational beliefs, intergenerational therapy

Intergenerational theory views the factors affecting individual's behavior as originating far and beyond the individual and his/her imme-

---

Joseph Guttmann, PhD, is on the faculty, School of Education, University of Haifa, Mt. Carmel, Haifa, Israel.

[Haworth co-indexing entry note]: "The Propensity for Irrational Beliefs Among Young Adults of Divorced Parents." Guttmann, Joseph. Co-published simultaneously in *Journal of Divorce & Remarriage* (The Haworth Clinical Practice Press, an imprint of The Haworth Press, Inc.) Vol. 34, No. 3/4, 2001, pp. 151-160; and: *Divorce and the Next Generation: Perspectives for Young Adults in the New Millennium* (ed: Craig A. Everett) The Haworth Clinical Practice Press, an imprint of The Haworth Press, Inc., 2001, pp. 151-160. Single or multiple copies of this article are available for a fee from The Haworth Document Delivery Service [1-800-342-9678, 9:00 a.m. - 5:00 p.m. (EST). E-mail address: getinfo@haworthpressinc.com].

151

diate environment. It postulates that legacies from preceding generations, as well as significant experiences and interactions in one's family
of origin, have far-reaching consequences (Boszormenyi-Nagy & Ul-
rich, 1981; William & Bray, 1988; Wolfinger, 1997). Many years ago,
Landis (1956) showed that children of divorced parents are more
likely to divorce than are those of intact families. Pope and Mueller
(1976) later referred to this phenomenon as "intergenerational transmission of marital instability," an element within the larger theory of
the intergenerational model of personal development.

Several studies have analyzed data from large national surveys,
showing support for the intergenerational transmission of divorce theory
(e.g., Amato, 1996; Booth & Edwards, 1989; Bumpass, Martin &
Sweet, 1991; Mueller & Cooper, 1986; Wolfinger, 1997). While demonstrating that to various degrees, children of divorced parents tend to
divorce more than do children of married parents, these studies also
revealed that this relationship is not only a complicated one, but a very
unclear one as well. For example, earlier studies (e.g., Mueller & Pope
et al.; Pope & Mueller et al.) found less of a tendency for divorce to be
transmitted than did later studies (e.g., Glenn & Kramer, 1987; Wolfinger, 1997), and there are conflicting reports on the population most
at risk (Amato, 1996; Wolfinger, 1997). But if there are conflicting
results over the population at risk and the extent of the effect, there is a
real dispute over the reasons for the transmission effect (Amato, 1996).

The term "intergenerational transmission" implies that "something"
is transmitted. When applied to divorce, it infers that "something" is
transmitted to the children by their parents and/or by their parents'
divorce that makes future divorce for the children more likely. However, what that "something" is seems to elude exact definition. Several
theoretical propositions have been offered as to the nature of that
"something": the absence of appropriate modeling of the spouse's
role; a lower threshold to resort to divorce; a lower commitment to
relationships; marriage at a younger age; high-risk mate selection; or
specific values of marriage and intimacy (e.g., Amato, 1996; Glenn &
Kramer, 1987; Greenberg & May, 1982). Of all these hypotheses, the
role model one is the most popular. It suggests that for a successful
and long-lasting marriage, one must learn the appropriate sex and
spousal roles, a task which children of divorced parents may fail to do.
As suggested by Livingston and Kordiak (1990), these children may
fail in one or more of the following three ways: "Parents' interaction

before the divorce may teach an inappropriate spousal role, a role model may be absent after the divorce, or an inappropriate role model may be provided after the divorce" (p. 93). Guttmann and his colleagues (Guttmann, Amir, & Katz, 1987; Guttmann, Ben-Asher and Lazar; 1998) tested the hypothesis that what is being transmitted to children by their parents' divorce is a lower withdrawal threshold in interpersonal conflict situations. Their results did not support this hypothesis.

The present study examines the proposition that intergenerational transmission of divorce may be partially explained by the adoption of irrational beliefs borne of parental divorce. The theoretical frameworks for this hypothesis are those of Alfred Adler (1956) and Albert Ellis' Rational Emotive Therapy (RET) approach (1961; 1995).

RET models are based on the assumption that human beings are born with a potential for both rational and irrational thinking. People have a predisposition for self-preservation, happiness, rational thinking, growth and self-actualization. They also, however, have propensities for self-destruction, procrastination, endless repetition of mistakes, superstition, self-blame, perfectionism, avoidance of thought and of actualizing growth potential. These models also suggest that individuals' emotional response to a situation is largely determined by their perception of the situation. These perceptions are not objective nor entirely situational dependent, but rather determined largely by the person's underlying schemata that is, the unspoken rules of life or basic underlying beliefs, attitudes, and assumptions learned from an individual's early development and henceforth adopted.

Adler ascribes to children a great capacity for logical thinking, yet a poor ability to interpret their experiences (Adler, 1956). Children are capable of reacting in a logical way to traumatic experiences, but the wisdom of those reactions is often questionable. This lack of experience denies the child the possibility of putting the situation in perspective or of taking into an accurate account the often very diverse variables and optional consequences. Thus, irrational beliefs are borne of situations that may have been "understood" well enough by the child, but were poorly interpreted. Such irrational beliefs provide fuel for the developing "private logic" that comes to be a permanent aspect of one's life. One's schemata help children, as well as adults, to make sense of the complicated world around them and of people's behavior and events. Children summarize a number of similar experiences into a set of templates. Once activated, the schemata tend to serve as fast-acting fields and aid the interpretation of both external and internal events. These early, tenuous schemata help to shape incoming information and further confirm preconceived ideas, which, in turn, strengthen the schemata. A specific schema is activated when an event occurs that relates to a relevant rule or theme.

Of special interest are the automatic thoughts that are spontaneously triggered and schemata-based. They are actually an internal dialogue carried out in a private, subjective logic. The automatic thoughts may therefore include inaccurate inferences and/or interpretations about the activating event in a specific situation. Nonetheless, this dialogue and its conclusion have a determining effect on the individual's behavior and emotional responses to the situation. Just as in other events in a child's life, in a case of parental divorce, children may interpret their parents' behavior to activate already tenuously existing schemata and/or to form new ones. The children's lack of experience and information denies them an accurate understanding of the situation and thus reinforces the propensity for irrational beliefs. If so, and irrational beliefs are detrimental to healthy and long-lasting relationships, as asserted by the RET model, then the intergenerational transmission of divorce may be partially explained by the greater tendency towards irrational beliefs among children of divorce.

METHOD

Subjects

Sixty volunteers, 30 of married parents (15 males and 15 females) and 30 of divorced parents (13 males and 17 females) took part in the present study. Fourteen of the subjects (6 of the intact families and 8 of the divorced parents) were married, and 24 (13 of the intact families and 11 of the divorced parents) had steady relationships at the time of the study. The subjects were students at a major university and at a teachers college in northern Israel. Their age ranged from 21-34 ($X =$ 23.6) years old.

Three criteria were applied in choosing the subjects for the divorce group: (1) Parents divorced before the subjects were 16-years-old (range of 2-16; $X = 9.8$ years old). The reason for applying this criterion was the assumption that if parental divorce were to have any effect on the examined dependent variables, then children would have to experience their parents' divorce while living at home for at least two years. (2) After their parents' divorce, the subjects all lived in a single-parent home with their custodial mother. The reason for applying this criterion was to control for any confounding variables due to the attested differences between fathers' and mothers' custody. (3) After their parents' divorce, the subjects "kept in touch" with their non-custodial fathers and none characterized their overall relationship as bad or very bad. This criterion was applied to control for the attested negative effect of total break up and conflictual relationship between the two.

Instruments and Procedure

Subjects were asked to respond to two questionnaires: Sharabany's (1974) Measure of Intimacy and the Propensity for Irrational Beliefs (PIB). Sharabany's test is a self-report questionnaire designed to measure the degree of intimacy attained by young adults in their relationship with a member of the opposite sex. In it subjects are asked to "consider your last (or present) serious-close relationship with a member of the opposite sex" and to rank on a scale of five the degree to which they agree with a series of statements.

The Propensity for Irrational Beliefs (PIB) questionnaire was constructed to measure the propensity to adopt or reject irrational beliefs. The 31 statements included in the questionnaire are based on the 11 basic irrational beliefs (see Table 1) identified by Ellis (1962). PIB was developed in two steps. First, three statements were composed to reflect the idea behind each of the 11 beliefs. Second, three judges (psychology graduate students) were asked to match the unclassified statements to the beliefs. For two of the judges the match was almost perfect, and for the third the match was 91%. In the PIB questionnaire's final form, the items were mixed so that no two statements reflecting the same belief were presented in succession. In it subjects are asked to "read the following statements and consider each as true or false."

Students from two large undergraduate classes were asked to volunteer for the study. Those who did and met the study's criteria filled out both the questionnaires in class following a formal lecture.

TABLE 1. Ellis' Irrational Beliefs and the Corresponding PIB Items

Irrational Beliefs	Questionnaire Items
The idea that it is a direct necessity for an adult human being to be loved or approved by virtually every significant other person in his community.	– One must be loved by all significant others. – One must be appreciated by all significant others. – One's behavior must be approved by all significant others.
The idea that one should be thoroughly competent, adequate, and achieving in all possible respects if one is to consider oneself worthwhile.	– One's inability to succeed in all endeavors must reduce one's self-esteem. – One's inability to achieve all desired goals must reduce one's self-esteem. – One's inability to adjust to all possible situations must reduce one's self-esteem.
The idea that certain people are bad, wicked or villainous and that they should be severely blamed and punished for their villainy.	– In the end, all villains will get what they deserve. – All criminals will be caught and punished. – One's troubles and calamities are deserved punishments for one's bad deeds.
The idea that it is awful and catastrophic when things are not the way one would very much like them to be.	– It is absolutely terrible if things do not turn out to be the way one wants. – It is always a disaster if something important goes sour. – Not getting what one wants is a good reason to get depressed.
The idea that human unhappiness is externally caused and that people have little or no ability to control their sorrows and disturbances.	– One's unhappiness is externally caused. – One has very little control over one's troubles. – One has very little control over one's disturbances.
The idea that if something is or might be dangerous or fearsome, one should be terribly concerned about it and should keep dwelling on the possibility of its occurring.	– Worry is the best way to avoid dangerous situations. – To successfully avoid life's annoyances, one needs only to watch out for them. – Worrying about dangerous situations is the best way to ensure handling them.
The idea that it is easier to avoid than to face certain life difficulties and self-responsibilities.	– Some responsibilities are better to bypass than face. – Some personal difficulties are better not faced than dealt with. – It is better to find a detour to some personal difficulties than to look for their solution.
The idea that one should be dependent on others and needs someone stronger than oneself on whom to rely.	– Everyone needs a strong person to rely on. – To manage life, one must have by one's side a person who is stronger than oneself. – When the going gets tough, one must have a guardian.

Irrational Beliefs	Questionnaire Items
The idea that one's past history is an all-important determiner of one's present behavior and that because something once strongly affected one's life, it should indefinitely have a similar effect.	– If a past event had a strong personal effect, it will always have a similar effect. – One's present behavior is determined by his past history. – If one failed in the past and attempted it again, he would fail again.
The idea that one should become quite upset over other people's problems and disturbances.	– One should feel bad for other people. – Other people's fate should affect one's mood. – One should get upset over others' problems.
The idea that there is virtually a right, precise and perfect solution to human problems and that it is catastrophic if this perfect solution is not found.	– There is a perfect solution for every human problem. One just needs to search hard enough. – At the end of the day, justice will win. – If you think hard enough, you will find the right solution for every personal problem.

RESULTS

The results were analyzed in two steps. First, we examined the strength of the relationship between the two dependent variables, Intimacy and Propensity for Irrational Beliefs. The results of Pearson Correlation Coefficient analysis revealed no significant relationship between the two variables ($r^2 = 0.17$). In light of this, we examined the two dependent variables separately in the next step of the analysis. Two 2×2 ANOVA were performed, one on PIB data (see Table 2) and one on Intimacy data (see Table 3). The results show that for the PIB data, there was a significant Family Type main effect ($F_{(1,59)} = 18.43$; $p < .01$) and a significant Family Type by Gender interaction ($F_{(1,59)} = 9.61$; $p < .01$). No significant Gender main effect was found. That is, contrary to what was expected, on the average, subjects from intact families exhibited a greater propensity for irrational thinking than did those from divorced homes. This group-difference was true for both male and female subjects. However, the difference between females from intact families and those from divorced families was greater than the corresponding difference for males, hence the statistically significant interaction. As for the Intimacy data, the analysis showed only a significant Gender main effect ($F_{(1,59)} = 24.6$; $p < .01$). Neither a significant Family Type main effect nor a significant Family Type by Gender interaction was found. That is, the results show that

TABLE 2. Means and Standard Deviations of "True" and "False" Responses in the PIB by the Subjects' Family Background and Gender

		Divorced Family		Intact Family	
		Men (n = 13)	Women (n = 17)	Men (n = 15)	Women (n = 15)
True	X̲	10.82	11.39	12.23	14.71
	SD	1.43	1.31	0.98	1.08
False	X̲	22.20	21.61	20.77	18.29
	SD	1.21	1.06	1.31	0.89
Total		33	33	33	33

TABLE 3. Means and Standard Deviations of Measure of Intimacy by the Subjects' Family Background and Gender

		Divorced Family	Intact Family
Men	X̲	3.75	3.81
	SD	1.18	0.79
Women	X̲	4.24	4.33
	SD	0.95	1.21

female subjects reported greater intimacy in their cross-sex relationships than did the male subjects, regardless of their parents' marital status.

DISCUSSION

The main results of the present study reveal an opposite trend from the expected direction, that is, young adults of married parents have a greater propensity for irrational beliefs than do those of divorced parents. Thus, the greater divorce rate among children of divorced parents cannot be explained by their propensity for irrational thinking.

In hindsight, this result may make good sense as well. Although traumatic events in one's life may reinforce a schema, it may also shatter it. Parents' divorce may actually force children to rethink and reevaluate their preconceived notions, attitudes and beliefs about romantic love. A trauma of this magnitude may not only change one's life circumstances, but may also have a long-lasting effect on one's schemata and way of thinking. Following divorce a single-parent family becomes less hierarchical, children share adult responsibilities and become more mature and more aware of life's complexities (Guttmann, 1993; Whitehead, 1997). This exposure to big-life problems may have the effect of actually activating rational evaluation and thinking.

It should be noted, however, that in the present study, we tested subjects' propensity for general irrational thinking. It remains an open question as to whether the results would have been different had we tested more situation-specific irrational beliefs. That is, what schemata are present and to what degree are they activated when presented with irrational statements specifically relating to intimate relationships. For example, instead of items such as "One must be loved/appreciated/approved by all significant others." items like "One must be loved/appreciated/approved constantly and at all times by one's intimate partner" would be posed. The idea is to test group-differences in the degree to which irrational beliefs, relevant to their different backgrounds, are triggered and functional in intimate relationships.

The other result of this study shows no relationship between the degree of intimacy and the propensity for irrational thinking. Thus, it seems that, at least at this level of analysis, schemata play no part in the reported level of intimacy. This is surprising because one would expect that general beliefs, attitudes and assumptions would affect the degree to which one is willing to be intimate in a relationship. Yet, it is possible that since PIB is a composite measure tapping the propensity for only general irrational beliefs, then the existing relationship between these two variables may be situation-specific and therefore would not be detected by the PIB. It is also possible that the level of intimacy is determined by the specific partners and by the degree to which they know each other, rather than by preconceived beliefs. Just as the function and effect of stereotypes decrease with knowledge, so it may be with schemata and irrational inner dialogue. The more the partners know each other, the less they rely on automatic thoughts and responses.

In sum, it seems that the propensity for general irrational thinking does not help to explain the intergenerational transmission of divorce. In fact, parental divorce seems to reduce that tendency. It is possible to explain this and the gender differences in intimacy by the fact that PIB measures a general rather than a situation-specific tendency towards false beliefs. This can only be determined by further research.

REFERENCES

Adler, A., (1956). In H.L., Ansbacher, and R.R., Ansbacher (Eds.), *The individual psychology of Alfred Adler.* New York: Basic Books

Amato, P.R. (1996). Explaining the intergenerational transmission of divorce. *Journal of Marriage and the Family*, 58(3), 628-640.

Ellis, A. (1995). Reflection on rational-emotive therapy. In M.J. Mahoney (Ed.), *Cognitive and constractive psychotherapies: Theory, research, and practice* (pp. 69-73): New York: Springer Publishing Co, Inc.

Ellis, A. and Harper, A.H., (1961) *A guide to rational living.* Hollywood, CA: Wilshre Book Co.

Guttmann, (1993). *The Psychosocial Prospective of Divorce: Research and Theory.* Hillsdale. New Jersey: Lawrence Erlbaum Associates. Inc., Publishers.

Guttmann, J., Amir, T. and Katz, M., (1987). Threshold of withdrawal from school-work among children of divorced parents. *Educational Psychology*, 7, 294-303.

Guttmann, J., Ben-Asher, C., and Lazar, A., (1999). Withdrawal threshold in inter-personal conflict of adolescents of divorced parents. *Educational Psychology*, (in print).

Whitehead, B.D., (1997). *The divorce culture.* New York: Alfred A. Knopf.

Family Structure Influences Cardiovascular Reactivity in College Students

Aurora Torres
William D. Evans
Sonali Pathak
Carol Vancil

SUMMARY. While researchers have documented sex differences in the way male and female children behaviorally respond to divorce of their families, data providing information on the impact of this psychosocial stressor on the physiological stress response is lacking. We hypothesized that family structure would affect cardiovascular reactivity in college students describing a frustrating event with students from disrupted families exhibiting greater reactivity. We also predicted we would find sex differences in the responses. Cardiovascular responses in men and women who were college students from Intact (child raised by both biological parents, n = 59) or Disrupted families (divorced,

Aurora Torres, PhD, is Assistant Professor in the Psychology Department, University of Alabama in Huntsville. William D. Evans, Sonali Pathak and Carol Vancil have received their MA from the Psychology Department, University of Alabama in Huntsville.

Address correspondence to: Aurora Torres, PhD, Assistant Professor, Psychology, UAH-Morton Hall 126, Huntsville, AL 35899.

The authors would like to thank Christina Collins, Yoon Kim and Kay Robertson for help with data collection and Michelle Gurley for her help with data entry.

This research was made possible by an equipment loan from Johnson & Johnson Medical, Inc., Tampa, FL, and a minigrant from UAH.

[Haworth co-indexing entry note]: "Family Structure Influences Cardiovascular Reactivity in College Students." Torres, Aurora et al. Co-published simultaneously in *Journal of Divorce & Remarriage* (The Haworth Clinical Practice Press, an imprint of The Haworth Press, Inc.) Vol. 34, No. 3/4, 2001, pp. 161-177; and: *Divorce and the Next Generation: Perspectives for Young Adults in the New Millennium* (ed: Craig A. Everett) The Haworth Clinical Practice Press, an imprint of The Haworth Press, Inc., 2001, pp. 161-177. Single or multiple copies of this article are available for a fee from The Haworth Document Delivery Service [1-800-342-9678, 9:00 a.m. - 5:00 p.m. (EST). E-mail address: getinfo@haworthpressinc.com].

blended families, with one case of single parent, n = 46) were measured in response to three verbal tasks (High Affect provocation, Low Affect provocation and Mental Arithmetic). Significant interactions among Task Content, Sex and Family Structure were found for heart rate despite no significant differences in perceived family stress. The analyses consistently revealed that women from Disrupted families exhibited greater increases in heart rate whereas the men exhibited an attenuated response. This suggests that disruption of family structure may produce long-term changes in cardiovascular responses to stressors. Furthermore, the data suggest that men and women from disrupted families develop cardiovascular stress responses that can be differentiated according to sex, with the men perhaps being able to engage vagal tone. *[Article copies available for a fee from The Haworth Document Delivery Service: 1-800-342-9678. E-mail address: <getinfo@haworthpressinc.com> Website: <http://www.HaworthPress.com> © 2001 by The Haworth Press, Inc. All rights reserved.]*

KEYWORDS. Cardiovascular reactivity, family structure, divorce

Family disruptions can take many forms, but the most common is the divorce of the parents. Portes, Haas and Brown (1991) outlined features that would contribute to the adjustment of a child to divorce, including individual coping skills of the child, family functioning and social support. Others have extended these ideas to include the age at which parental exit occurred (Kot & Shoemaker, 1999). While such reviews have expanded our understanding for positive as well as negative outcomes for children adjusting to divorce, the psychological impact of divorce can last well into adulthood (Heatherington, 1979; Wallerstein, 1991). One cannot ignore the fact that many children experience negative outcomes that affect their own attitudes towards relationships (Mulder & Gunnoe, 1999). Further, the experience may affect how the child who experienced divorce responds to stress, which in turn could make a significant impact in physiological responses; however, data from studies investigating such a relationship is lacking.

Results from the Terman Life Cyclic Study of Children with High Ability revealed a 44% increase in mortality risk for adults whose families had divorced before the child was 21 years of age (Schwartz, Friedman, Tucker, Tomlinson-Keasy, Wingard & Criqui, 1995). Schwartz et al. (1995) translated this into a shorter lifespan of approximately 4 years. Because cardiovascular diseases remain the leading cause of death (U.S. Bureau of the Census, 1990), the identification of social factors that may contribute to the pathogenesis of heart disease, hypertension or stroke is important. An accumulation of life events can influence cardiovascular reactivity, the changes in heart rate and blood pressure in response to an arousing stimulus (e.g., McCann & Matthews, 1988; Ditto, 1993; Jemerin & Boyce, 1992). Cardiovascular responses to stress are individually different, but patterns of responses remain stable throughout one's life (Ditto, 1993). Thus, the structure of a family, either as intact or with disruption (a parental exit in divorce or parental death), may influence the development of that reactivity. The need to investigate the relationship between family disruption and cardiovascular reactivity is evident.

Research pertaining to the physiological responses in children of divorced families has provided data regarding enuresis (Jarvelin, Moilanen, Vikevainen-Tervonen, & Huttunen, 1990) and endocrine changes in adolescent females (Gerra et al., 1993); however, there has been a failure to examine other features of the stress response. Simply experiencing family conflict may affect cardiovascular responses. El-Sheikh (1994) reported increases in blood pressure in children exposed to parental or adult situations expressing anger. These data suggest that the family environment may foster the development of physiological responses to stressors.

The young child or adolescent from a disrupted family system may also display the negative emotions of anger, hostility or depression. Cummings, Pelligrini and Notarius (1989) reported that the manner in which boys and girls respond to divorce is different with girls being more anxious. Spigelman, Spigelman, and Englesson (1991) found that regardless of gender, children from divorced families exhibited significantly greater levels of aggression than those of intact families. This behavioral expression of hostility may be an antecedent for personality risk factors associated with cardiovascular disease such as the Type A behavior pattern (Williams, 1980). Because hostility is considered the toxic element, the possibility exists that social situations that contribute to the behavioral expression of hostility through aggression may produce long-term effects on physiological responses. Potentially the child in a disrupted family may be affected not only by their own cardiovascular reactivity, but by their development of personality characteristics that further promote the stress response.

The two prevailing constructs for cardiovascular reactivity are to view it as an individual difference variable or as an intervening variable for the association between psychosocial variables and disease processes (Manuck, 1994; Blascovish & Katkin, 1993). At present we focused on conceptualizing cardiovascular reactivity as an intervening variable for the influence of family disruptions on stress responses. The cardiovascular responses of college students representing both intact and disrupted families were compared on tasks that would represent social processes aimed at inducing low or high affective content and a more traditional, nonsocial laboratory task. The importance of using tasks that engage interpersonal contexts are currently being emphasized in research (e.g., Smith, Nealy, Kircher & Limon, 1997).

In the present study we engaged students from intact or disrupted families through using three verbal tasks (Lamensdorf & Linden, 1992) as a means of provoking affect to assess the relationship between cardiovascular reactivity and family structure and sex. The majority of parental exits leading to disrupted families were expected to be from the divorce of the biological parents. We hypothesized that college students from disrupted families would display greater cardiovascular reactivity to the experimental stressors. Because of the different behavioral profiles described for boys and girls who have experienced divorce in the family, we also expected to find sex differences in the pattern of responses.

METHOD

Participants

Undergraduate students at the University of Alabama in Huntsville who were enrolled in the introductory psychology courses ($N = 115$) volunteered to participate in exchange for course credit. Participants ranged in age from 18 to 22 years, and with the exception of one, were unmarried and without children. Participants with incomplete data or those with a body mass index over 40 kg/m^2 were removed from the analysis such that the final sample size was 105. Participants were treated in accordance with APA ethical guidelines.

Design

The experimental manipulation of Task Content used a $2 \times 2 \times 4$ (Family Structure $\times$ Sex $\times$ Task Content) design with repeated measures on the last factor by including the baseline and the verbal tasks by content. The experimental manipulation of the content of the verbal tasks (Lamensdorf & Linden, 1992) consisted of the Baseline during which no verbal responses were made by participants, a High Affect provocation task during which the participant described a frustrating event or person, a Low Affect provocation task where the participant described seasonal changes of the local community and a Mental Arithmetic task involving serial 7 subtractions initiated at 1000.

The two levels of family structure required the participants to be classified as being either from an Intact family (n = 59) or Disrupted family (n = 46) family. The criteria for Intact family was that the student had been raised by the biological parents and that there was no legal divorce or death of a parent for 1 year prior to testing (men = 24, women = 35). If these criteria were not met, the students were assigned to the Disrupted family (men = 13, women = 33). Within the Disrupted family group, 7 men and 20 women were from divorced families where the custodial parent had not remarried or where there had never been a marriage and one parent left; 5 men and 12 women were from blended families where the divorced custodial parent had remarried; and 1 man and 1 woman were from families where parental exit was the death of the parent. From the information provided by the student, we determined that the average age of the student at the time of parental exit was 9 and that the typical age of the student at the time of remarriage for those in blended families was 10-13 years. Thus, the Disrupted family group (96%) reflects students who have experienced the divorce of their biological parents. No students who were in families currently experiencing divorce were included in the study.

The dependent variables of the study were cardiovascular responses, inclusive of heart rate in beats per minute (bpm) and systolic (SBP) and diastolic (DBP) blood pressure readings in mm Hg in terms of absolute values. Reactivity for each cardiovascular measure was determined by subtracting BASE from the response achieved for each experimental task by content. The scores on the inventory for family stress were also analyzed by adjusting each scale to its weighted value.

Materials

An inventory developed by the investigators was administered to gain information regarding lifestyle, family structure, diet and health habits. The Family Inventory of Life Events Changes (FILE, McCubbins, Patterson, & Wilson, 1979) was administered to define family stress for the students. The FILE consists of 71 questions which represent 9 categories of family life changes (reliability for each scale is presented in parentheses): intra-family strains (.73), marital strains (.68), pregnancy and childbearing strains (.84), finance and business strains (.64), work-family transitions and strains (.80), illness and family care strains (.66), losses, transitions (.72) and family legal violations (.83). While the FILE was designed for responses from husband-wife, we asked the participants to identify those specific events that had occurred within their family within the last 12 months.

Procedure

After providing consent and completing the questionnaires, we seated the participant in a comfortable armchair facing a wall and placed the blood pressure cuff above the brachial artery of the left arm of the participant. Measures of heart rate and blood pressure were automatically obtained by a Dinamap Vital Signs Monitor (Model 8100, on loan from Johnson & Johnson Medical, Tampa, FL) at 3 min intervals.

During the 15 min Baseline, the participants sat quietly reading nature magazines provided for them. Following the Baseline, each verbal task was prompted for 6 min with the completion of each task followed by a 6 min interval where the participant again quietly read. The content of the verbal tasks were counterbalanced. Experimenters provided verbal prompts (see Lamensdorf & Linden, 1992) during each of the verbal tasks to maintain the flow of each participant's verbal response. The prompts were simple statements such as, "Tell me more about . . ."

Statistical Analyses

The measures recorded at 9, 12 and 15 min were averaged to provide the Baseline. The two measures taken during each 6 min task were averaged for a single measure. Analysis of the effect of the Task Content consisted of a 2 × 2 × 4 (Sex × Family Structure × Task Content) ANOVA with repeated measures on the last factor for the absolute values of Heart Rate, SBP and DBP. Reactivity scores for each of these measures were determined by subtracting the Baseline response from the response achieved during each verbal task as designated by content. This reactivity was then analyzed by a 2 × 2 × 3 (Sex × Family Structure × Task Content) ANOVA with Task Content as a within-subjects factor. The data from the FILE were analyzed by a 2 (Sex) × 2 (Family Structure) ANOVA. Criteria for significance was set at p < .05.

RESULTS

Heart Rate as a Function of Task Content

Figure 1 illustrates that the men from Disrupted families maintained higher Baseline heart rate than their female counterparts; however, the pattern changed with the presentation of the task. Women from Disrupted families exhibited greater heart rate than the men once the verbal task was executed. Within Intact families, women began with higher heart rates, but did not react to the extent that Intact family men did. The 2 × 2 × 4 ANOVA with Task Content as the within-subjects factor for absolute values of Heart Rate revealed a significant three-way interaction among Sex, Family Structure and Task Content, $F(3, 303) = 6.611$, $p < .001$. Additionally, a significant two-way interaction between Sex and Task Content, $F(3, 303) = 4.718$, $p = .003$, and between Family Structure and Sex, $F(3,303) = 5.825$, $p = .001$, was revealed. Finally, Task Content alone made a significant impact on heart rate, $F(3,303) = 5.161$, $p = .002$.

The strongest differences between men and women from Disrupted families occurred during the task designated to have the highest affective content where the student was asked to describe a frustrating event. A 2 (Sex) × 2 (Family Structure) follow-up ANOVA for Heart Rate during the High Affect task produced a significant interaction between Sex and Family Structure, $F(1,101) = 5.09$, $p = .026$. Similar analyses of heart rate during the Low Affect and Mental Arithmetic tasks failed to achieve significance.

Table 1 lists the heart rate reactivity scores for each level of Task Content. The profile of the students from Intact families reflects the not uncommon finding that men were more reactive than women. However, the data from the students of Disrupted families show a very different profile. The women from Disrupted families were as reactive

FIGURE 1. Men (INTACT-M) and women (INTACT-F) from Intact families showed a similar profile (dashed lines) in response to tasks. However, the men (DIS-RUPT-M) and women (DISRUPT-F) from Disrupted families (solid lines) exhibited diverging responses. This illustrates the significant three-way interaction among Family Structure, Sex and Task Content. The tasks included a baseline (BASE), low affect provocation task (LA), a high affect (HA) provocation task, and a mental arithmetic (MA) task.

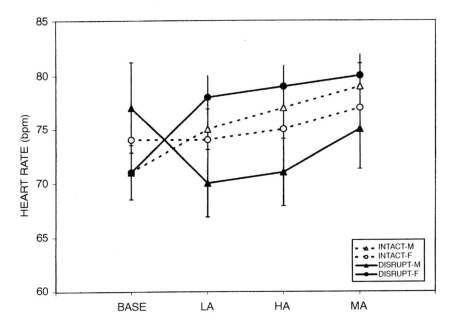

TABLE 1. Mean and Standard Error for Heart Rate Reactivity

Family Structure	Sex	LA		HA		MA	
		M	SE	M	SE	M	SE
INTACT	Male	4.2	3.0	6.5	3.2	8.0	3.2
INTACT	Female	0.4	2.7	1.4	3.0	3.2	2.9
DISRUPT	Male	−6.6	4.6	−6.4	4.6	−2.0	4.9
DISRUPT	Female	7.3	2.6	8.6	2.5	9.6	2.4

LA = Low Affect   HA = High Affect   MA = Mental Arithmetic as the men from Intact families. Further, rather than exhibiting an increase in heart rate, the men from Disrupted families demonstrated a reduction in heart rate. The analyses produced a significant interaction between Sex and Family Structure, $F(1,101) = 7.62$, p = .007, coupled with significant main effects for Sex, $F(1, 101) = 5.45$, p = .022, and Family Structure, $F(1,101) = 6.68$, p = .011. Follow-up ANOVAs provided a significant interaction between Sex and Family Structure in each task with $F(1,101) = 7.212$, p = .008 for Low Affect; $F(1,101) = 8.78$, p = .004 for High Affect; and $F(1,101) = 5.97$, p = .016 for Mental Arithmetic. These interactions capture the significant differences in heart rate reactivity found in men and women from Disrupted families where the Tukey HSD was at p = .038 for Low Affect and p = .027 for Mental Arithmetic.

SBP as a Function of Task Content

Figure 2 illustrates that men, especially those from Disrupted families, began and attained higher SBP than the women. One should note

FIGURE 2. The significant effect of Task Content was seen for SBP. All groups showed increased SBP from baseline; however, men maintained higher SBP.

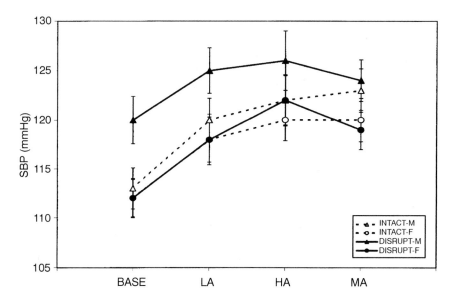

that while the students from Intact families achieved their highest SBP during Mental Arithmetic, the students from Disrupted families had the greatest reactivity to the High Affect task. The results from ANOVA with Task Content as the within-subjects factor indicated only a significant effect for Task Content on SBP, $F(3,303) = 3.31$, $p = .024$, however. A subsequent 2 (Sex) × 2 (Family Structure) ANOVA captured the significant effect of Sex during Baseline for SBP, reflecting the tendency for men to attain higher SBP. No significant effects or interactions were found for the reactivity scores for SBP for task content.

DBP as a Function of Task Content

Figure 3 reveals the similarities in DBP across groups with regard to Task Content. Thus, DBP was not a sensitive measure for the effects of Sex, Family Structure or Task Content on reactivity. Analyses of DBP absolute values or change scores provided no significant effects or interactions for Task Content, Sex or Family Structure, $F < 1$.

FIGURE 3. While reactivity and recovery can be seen in DBP, no significant effects for Task Content, Family Structure or Sex were found.

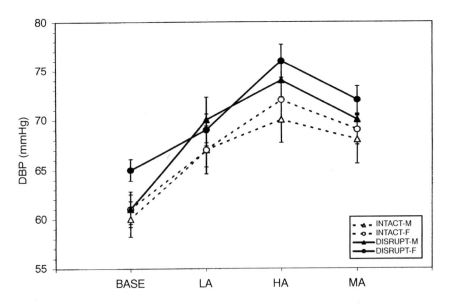

FILE

Although our sample represented students from Intact and Disrupted families, there was no effect of Family Structure or Sex on family stress as reflected by the total weighted scores on the FILE (see Table 2). Likewise, Family Structure and Sex had no effect on the weighted scores of each of the nine subscales; thus, the table provides only the total weighted scores. No group fell within criteria that would be considered high stress.

DISCUSSION

We found significant interactions among Family Structure, Sex and Task Content on the heart rate exhibited by our sample. College students from Intact families exhibited the expected pattern of greater reactivity for men. However, the men and women from Disrupted families not only began at different baselines, they also exhibited dramatic differences in their responses to the verbal tasks. The most striking difference was that whereas the women's heart rate increased from baseline to each task, the men's heart rate was attenuated to a level below their baseline heart rate. Only the response during the traditional, nonsocial task (i.e., mental arithmetic) appeared to produce sufficient reactivity to return the men to their baseline values. These data suggest that men from Disrupted families may have developed a different physiological mechanism for confronting stressors;

TABLE 2. Mean and Standard Error of Family Stress

Reflected in Total Weighted FILE Scores

Family Structure	Sex	FILE	
		M	*SE*
Intact	Male	634	44
Intact	Female	586	49
Disrupted	Male	519	79
Disrupted	Female	642	60

however, the mechanism engaged may be a function of different appraisals for stressful events or engaging different coping skills at a cognitive level. The intervening variable may involve engaging a physiological mechanism such as vagal tone where heart rate will actually be reduced.

The attenuated heart rate of the men from disrupted families is intriguing; however, the data could be clarified with additional information of vagal tone. Stimulation of the vagus nerve produces a decrease in heart rate by activating muscarinic receptors on the heart (Andreassi, 1995). The attenuated cardiovascular response in men could be linked to a sustained vagal tone in response to a stressor or to a dampened stimulation of the sympathetic nervous system. These could be affected by whether the man identifies the particular tasks in the experiment as stressful, whether attention was more focused in the men or whether the adoption of vagal tone responses were adaptive in the way the men learned to respond to conflict. The obvious need for studies that investigate these mechanisms is apparent.

The physiological data gathered from the women from Disrupted families are logical extensions of what would be expected in terms of heart rate for individuals who exhibit greater anxiety. The literature concerning children from divorced families provides documentation of gender differences in behavioral and emotional adjustments to divorce. Cherlin et al. (1991) reported that boys from divorced families were more likely to show acting-out and antisocial behaviors whereas their female counterparts became more helpful, cooperative and quiet; however, the characteristics in boys were antecedents to divorce, not simply a response to the family disruption. Cummings' (1989) described girls from distressed homes as more preoccupied with the angry situation than boys from distressed homes. Mazur, Wolchik and Sandler (1992) reported that girls whose parents had divorced within the previous 24 months made more negative cognitive errors (e.g., catastrophizing, personalizing) than did boys. Girls also appeared to report more symptoms of depression and anxiety. Girls from divorced families may also have a tendency to secrete greater levels of norepinephrine and ACTH when under physical stress, despite no basal differences when compared to girls from intact families (Gerra et al., 1993). These studies provide a basis for the exaggerated cardiovascular response in heart rate described for the women from disrupted families. Not only is the psychological foundation for an anxiety response operating, but these may be linked to increased secretion of stress hormones.

Investigators are beginning to document physiological sex differences in response to family conflicts. El-Sheikh (1994) observed a negative correlation between physical violence in the homes of preschool boys and heart rate reactivity when children were presented a video with adults arguing (i.e., as violence increased, reactivity decreased). One explanation offered by El-Sheikh was that boys may be displaying the physiological responses expected when focusing attention (see Porges, 1995) as boys are more likely to be the targets of physical violence. While our sample of college men did not demonstrate significantly greater family stress as a function of family structure in the past year, their present cardiovascular responses may be a product of interactions with family conflict prior to or concurrent with the time of the parental exit.

In a complementary study, El-Sheikh, Ballard and Cummings (1994) reported a decline in heart rate when preschoolers were presented with videos of adults arguing, regardless of gender. This may indicate that arguments between adults strongly engage the attention of 3-4 year olds. The children were also given a choice as to the intensity level of the video. Lower tonic heart rates were found in the boys who chose to view the videos with the higher intensity (El-Sheikh et al., 1994). Because we asked our college students to describe a frustrating event rather than view an ongoing conflict, making stronger parallels between the present study and El-Sheikh's work is problematic. The research raises questions as to whether aspects of focused attention become classically conditioned for the presentation of any stressor, whether there is some aspect of the developmental delay in cardiovascular responses to stress or whether another mechanism is operating that affects vagal tone.

Another reactive variable in the present study was SBP. Men had higher blood pressures than women, a finding that conforms with previous research (e.g., Stoney, Davis & Mathews, 1987; Smith et al., 1997). While men from families experiencing a parental exit had the highest SBP values, this failed to be a significant difference. The reactivity for women from Disrupted families was likewise exaggerated compared to baseline. Thus, while men from Disrupted families appeared to attenuate their reactivity in terms of heart rate, the SBP indicated exaggerated responses. The arterial response is not reliant on vagal tone. Again, this may indicate a dissociation between autonomic controls for vagal tone, which will decrease heart rate, and stimulation of the sympathetic nervous system which ultimately leads to activation of the alpha adrenergic receptors in the blood vessels. Stimulation of the vagus nerve releases acetylcholine which in turn activates muscarinic receptors on the heart to produce decreases in heart rate whereas activation of the adrenergic receptors produces vasoconstriction (Andreassi, 1995). Thus, the data indicate further support for the attenuated response in heart rate in men from Disrupted families resulting from engaging vagal tone rather than diminishing stimulation of the sympathetic autonomic nervous system.

Taken together, the data indicate that men and women from Disrupted families may develop a different profile of cardiovascular reactivity than students from Intact families even when there are no significant differences in family stress between the two categories of family structure. Given that the majority (96%) of family disruptions in the present study came from the divorce of the biological parents, the further analysis of how divorce influences cardiovascular function is warranted. At no time would the responses be considered excessive or hypertensive, but in these young adults, other variables such as diet and family history could interact to promote the pathogenesis of cardiovascular diseases. Future investigations should include a more detailed inspection of family conflict for, as Cherlin et al. (1991) assert, the dysfunction in children can often precede the family disruption rather than be a product of the legal dissolution of the family. Borrine, Handal, Brown and Searight (1991) reported that adolescents' adjustment was a function of perceived family conflict once the child was beyond the 1 year transitional post-divorce period. Borrine et al.'s (1991) data support the psychological wholeness position versus the physical wholeness position as an explantory variable in that level of family conflict, independent of family structure, predicted maladjustment. The present data, however, is more likely to be interpreted to support the physical wholeness position as there were no differences in our measure of family stress. Obviously, that can only be a tentative conclusion until the data is replicated with more detailed evaluation of family conflict.

The present study adds to the growing data set evaluating psychosocial stressors and health. Divorce of parents prior to reaching the age of 21 has been associated with a decrease in lifespan of 4 years

(Schwartz et al., 1995). Because of the prevalence of cardiovascular diseases, psychosocial events that will affect physiological responses to stressors may be one contributing factor. Furthermore, a broader set of data that includes measures of vagal tone and detailed analysis of family conflict would be valuable in assessing the sex differences reported in the present study for men and women from disrupted families. At this time, one could conclude that special care needs to be taken so that men and women from Disrupted families can express a positive adjustment to family life not only behaviorally, but also psychologically and physiologically. Furthermore, the psychological processes sensitive to family systems that effect the development of physiological mechanisms involved in stress responses need to be delineated so that appropriate interventions can be developed.

REFERENCES

Andreassi, J.L. (1995). *Psychophysiology: Human behavior and physiological response*. Hillsdale, NJ: Lawrence Eerlbaum Associates, Inc.

Blascovich, J., & Katkin, E.S. (1993). *Cardiovascular reactivity to psychological stress and disease*. Washington, DC: American Psychological Association.

Borrine, M.L., Handal, P.J., Brown, N.Y., & Searight, H.R. (1991). Family conflict and adolescent adjustment in intact, divorced and blended families. *Journal of Consulting and Clinical Psychology, 59*, 753-755.

Cherlin, A.J., Furstenberg, Jr. F.F., Chase-Lansdale, R.L., Kierman, K.E., Robins, R.K., Morrison, D.R., & Teitler, J.O. (1991). Longitudinal studies of effects of divorce on children in Great Britain and the United States. *Science, 252*, 1386-1389.

Cummings, J.S., Pellegrini, D.S., & Notarius, C.I. (1989). Children's responses to angry adult behavior as a function of marital distress and history of interparent hostility. *Child Development, 60*, 1035-1043.

Ditto, B. (1993). Familial influences on heart rate, blood pressure, and self-report anxiety responses to stress: Results from 100 twin pairs. *Psychophysiology, 30*, 635-645.

El-Sheikh, M. (1994) Children's emotional and physiological responses to interadult angry behaviors: The role of history of interparental hostility. *Journal of Abnormal Child Psychology, 22*, 661-678.

El-Sheikh, M., Ballard, M., & Cummings, E.M. (1994). Individual differences in preschoolers' physiological and verbal responses to videotaped angry interactions. *Journal of Abnormal Child Psychology, 22*, 303-320.

Gerra, G., Caccavari, R., Delsignore, R., Passeri, M., Affini, G.F., Maestri, D., Monica, C., & Brambilla, F. (1993). Parental divorce and neuroendocrine changes in adolescents. *Acta Psychiatrica Scandinavica, 87*, 350-354.

Hetherington, E.M. (1979). Divorce, a child's perspective. *American Psychologist, 34*, 851-858.

Jarvelin, M.R., Moilanen, I., Vikevainen-Tervonen, L. & Huttunen, N. (1990). Life changes and protective capacities in enuretic and non-enuretic children. *Journal of Child Psychiatry, 34*, 763-774.

Jemerin, J.M. & Boyce, W.G. (1992). Cardiovascular markers of biobehavioral reactivity. *Developmental and Behavioral Pediatrics, 13*, 46-48.

Kot, L., & Shoemaker, H.M. (1999). Children of divorce: An investigation of the developmental effects from infancy through adulthood. *Journal of Divorce & Remarriage, 31*, 161-178.

Lamensdorf, A.M. & Linden, W. (1992) Family history of hypertension and cardiovascular changes during high and low affect provocation. *Psychophysiology, 29*, 558-565.

Manuck, S.B. (1994). Cardiovascular reactivity and cardiovascular disease: "Once more unto the breach." *International Journal of Behavioral Medicine, 1*, 4-31.

Mazur, E., Wolchik, S.A., & Sandler, I.N. (1992). Negative cognitive errors and positive illusions for negative divorce events: predictors of children's psychological adjustment. *Journal of Abnormal Child Psychology, 20*, 523-542.

McCann, B.S. & Matthews, K.A. (1988). Influences of potential for hostility, type A behavior and parental history of hypertension in adolescent's cardiovascular responses during stress. *Psychophysiology, 25*, 503-511.

McCubbin, H., Patterson, J. & Wilson, L. (1979). *Family assessment: Resiliency, coping and adaptation inventories for research and practice.* St. Paul: Family Social Sciences.

Mulder, C., & Gunnoe, M.L. (1999). College students' attitudes toward divorce based on gender, parental divorce, and parental relationships. *Journal of Divorce & Remarriage, 31*, 179-188.

Porges, S.W. (1995). Orienting in a defensive world: Mammalian modifications of our evolutionary heritage. A polyvagal theory. *Psychophysiology, 32*, 301-318.

Portes, P.R., Haas, R.C., & Brown, J. (1991). Identifying family factors that predict children's adjustment to divorce: An analytic synthesis. *Journal of Divorce & Remarriage, 15*, 87-103.

Schwartz, J.E., Friedman, H.S., Tucker, J.S., Tomlinson-Keasy, C., Wingard, D.L. & Criqui, M.H. (1995). Sociodemographic and psychosocial factors in childhood as predictors of adult mortality. *American Journal of Public Health, 85*, 1237-1245.

Kot, L.K. & Shoemaker, H.M. (1999). Children of divorce: An investigation of the developmental effects from infancy through adulthood. *Journal of Divorce & Remarriage, 31*, 161-178.

Smith, T.W., Nealey, J.B., Kircher, J.C., & Limon J.P. (1997). Social determinants of cardiovascular reactivity: Effects of incentive to exert influence and evaluative threat. *Psychophysiology, 34*, 65-73.

Spigelman, G., Spigelman, A., & Englesson, I. (1991). Hostility, aggression, and anxiety levels of divorce and nondivorce children as manifested in their responses to projective tests. *Journal of Personality Assessment, 56*, 438-452.

Stoney, C.M., Davis, M.C., & Mathews, K.A. (1987). Sex differences in physiological responses to stress and in coronary heart disease: A causal link? *Psychophysiology, 24*, 127-131.

U.S. Bureau of Census. (1990). *Statistical abstracts of the United States: 1990* (110th ed.), Washington, DC: U.S. Government Printing Office.

Wallerstein, J.S. (1991). The long-term effects of divorce on children: a review. *Journal of American Academy of Child and Adolescent Psychiatry, 30,* 349-360.

Williams, R.B., Haney, T.L., Lee, K.I., Kong, I.L., Blumenthal, J.A., and Whalen, R.E. (1980). Type A behavior, hostility, and coronary atherosclerosis. *Psychosomatic Medicine, 42,* 539-549.32

Relationships
Between Parents' Marital Status
and University Students' Mental Health,
Views of Mothers and Views of Fathers:
A Study in Bulgaria

Anna L. Christopoulos

SUMMARY. Although the relationships between parental divorce and numerous aspects of psychological adjustment in children have been examined extensively, to date few investigations have included countries outside the Western mainstream. The present study, part of a larger investigation of divorce in the Balkan region, examined relationships between parents' marital status, and the mental health, views of mothers and views of fathers in a sample of Bulgarian University students. One hundred (100) students, 50 from divorced parents, and 50 from intact homes attending the University of Sofia completed the 28-items of the General Health Questionnaire and Parish's Personal Attribute Inventory. Students from divorced homes reported significantly more psychological difficulties in general than their peers from intact homes. Moreover, students whose parents were divorced reported significantly

Anna L. Christopoulos, PhD, is Assistant Professor of Clinical Psychology, Department of Psychology, School of Philosophy, University of Athens.

Address correspondence to: Anna L. Christopoulos, 1 Valaoritou, Street, Athens 10671, Greece.

The author would like to thank Zlatina Touneva for her invaluable assistance in conducting this study.

[Haworth co-indexing entry note]: "Relationships Between Parents' Marital Status and University Students' Mental Health, Views of Mothers and Views of Fathers: A Study in Bulgaria." Christopoulos, Anna L. Co-published simultaneously in *Journal of Divorce & Remarriage* (The Haworth Clinical Practice Press, an imprint of The Haworth Press, Inc.) Vol. 34, No. 3/4, 2001, pp. 179-190; and: *Divorce and the Next Generation: Perspectives for Young Adults in the New Millennium* (ed: Craig A. Everett) The Haworth Clinical Practice Press, an imprint of The Haworth Press, Inc., 2001, pp. 179-190. Single or multiple copies of this article are available for a fee from The Haworth Document Delivery Service [1-800-342-9678, 9:00 a.m. - 5:00 p.m. (EST). E-mail address: getinfo@haworthpressinc.com].

more somatic complaints and problems of depression than students whose parents were married. A significant interaction between parents' marital status and gender was obtained regarding symptoms of anxiety and insomnia: whereas male students from divorced homes reported more difficulties than female students, the reverse was true for students from intact families. Regarding views of fathers, students from divorced homes reported significantly more negative attitudes toward their fathers than students from intact homes. A similar trend was obtained with respect to views of mothers. These findings are discussed with respect to the existing literature. *[Article copies available for a fee from The Haworth Document Delivery Service: 1-800-342-9678. E-mail address: <getinfo@haworthpressinc.com> Website: <http://www.HaworthPress.com>* © *2001 by The Haworth Press, Inc. All rights reserved.]*

KEYWORDS. Young adults' divorce adjustment, young adults' views of divorced parents, divorce in Bulgaria

INTRODUCTION

The increase in divorce during the past forty years has catalyzed considerable clinical and empirical interest regarding relationships between parents' marital status and numerous dimensions of children's psychological development and adjustment. The majority of research has concentrated on children and adolescents, with a relatively sparse literature in comparison on the late adolescent and adult age groups. Recently there has been an increase in interest regarding the relationship between parental divorce and later development, particularly during the college years (Barkley & Procidiano, 1989; Fine, Worley & Schwebel, 1986; Franklin, Janoff-Bulman & Roberts, 1990; Gabardi & Rosen, 1991; Lopez, 1987; Lopez, Campbell & Watkins, 1988; Parish, 1989; Parish & Ostenberg, 1985).

However, virtually all of this work has been based on samples from within the Western mainstream, particularly the United States, Great Britain and Australia. There are no published studies to date in the professional literature published in the English language on the relationship between parental divorce and adjustment in late adolescence or early adulthood from other cultures. Meta-analysis of studies with children worldwide indicates that investigations from other countries have found more problems with children of divorce than studies in the United States (Amato & Keith, 1991a). This raises serious questions regarding generalizability of findings from existing studies on college students to cultures other, and possibly different, than the Western mainstream sampled in the literature to date. Recently, even the applicability of findings from the literature to date to minority groups within mainstream culture has been questioned (Phillips & Asbury, 1991). The need for cross-national studies has also been noted (Amato & Keith, 1991a).

The present study is part of a larger effort to expand investigations of divorce to countries outside the Western mainstream, with a focus on the Balkan area. This effort is based on the consideration that certain cultural parameters may integrally affect the experience of divorce. For example, in cultures that adhere to more traditional values, divorce is far less common, and less socially acceptable than it is in mainstream Western countries. Thus, it may be that the experience of divorce, particularly for children may be considerably different than it is in mainstream Western countries, and may thus have a different impact on their development as well.

More specifically, the aim of the present study was to examine the relationships between parental marital status, and the mental health, views of fathers and views of mothers in a sample of Bulgarian University students. These relationships have been the focus of previous investigations with college students in the United States. With respect to psychological adjustment, studies to date have found few (Amato & Keith, 1991b; Dunlop & Burns, 1995; Phillips & Asbury, 1990; Woo, 1981) or no (Barkley & Procidiano, 1989; Gabardi & Rosen, 1991; Lopez,1987; 1991; Lopez, Campbell & Watkins, 1988; Zill, Morrison & Coiro, 1993) differences between students from divorced homes and their peers from intact homes. Parental divorce has been linked to more negative views of the relationship with the father (Fine, Moreland & Schwabel, 1983; Fine, Worley and Schwabel, 1986) and with the father himself (Parish & Osterberg, 1985; Parish, 1989). However, findings with respect to the mother are inconsistent. Whereas some researchers have found parental divorce to be associated with more negative perceptions of the mother (Boyd, Nunn & Parish, 1983; Parish, 1989; Parish & Wigle, 1985) and of the relationship with her (Fine, Moreland & Schwabel, 1983), other studies have not demonstrated such a relationship (Fine, Worley and Schwabel, 1986; Parish & Osterberg, 1985).

The present study sought to investigate whether, and to what extent these findings are representative of college students in Bulgaria, where the incidence of marriage and divorce, and the economic and legal sequelae of divorce are different than in the United States and other Western countries. Examination of statistics indicates that the incidence of marriage has decreased in recent years, and that the divorce rate is approximately twenty-five percent (Belchewa, 1994; Karamfilov, 1994; Sugareva, 1995). According to a recent study, only ten percent of the population has a favorable attitude toward divorce (Sugareva, 1995). In addition, the legal process of divorce is considered very expensive for the average citizen. Moreover, by law, the parent that is awarded custody of the children is automatically given the right to remain in the house, which is of considerable significance given the extreme shortage of affordable housing. Given such differences in attitudes toward marriage and divorce, as well as in the frequency and in the social and economic consequences of these institutions, it seemed that the experience of divorce in Bulgaria may be quite different than in a mainstream Western country, and may, as a result have a different impact on psychological factors such as psychological adjustment and views of parents.

METHOD

Subjects

One hundred sixty-eight undergraduate students (115 from intact homes, 50 from divorced homes) enrolled in various departments at the University of Sofia initially completed the questionnaires described below. In order to avoid the possible confounding effects of certain demographic variables and potential problems of heterogeneity due to unequal sample sizes, subjects from divorced and intact homes were matched on gender, age, number of siblings, mother's level of education and father's level of education. The final sample that was used in the statistical analyses consisted of 50 students whose parents were divorced, 50 students whose parents were married. Fifty-six were males (28 from intact homes, 28 from divorced homes) and 44 were females (22 from intact homes and 22 from divorced homes).

Measures

Demographic Data Sheet

Subjects completed a series of questions regarding age, gender, major field of study, year of enrollment, parents' marital status, number of siblings, mother's level of education, father's level of education, mother's occupation, and father's occupation.

Psychological Adjustment

The 28-item version of the General Health Questionnaire (Goldberg & Hillyer, 1979) was used to assess students' mental health. This instrument consists of 28 items each of which is answered on a four point scale (0-3), with a higher score indicating greater psychopathology. The scale is comprised of four subscales, which are named according to the domain they assess, namely, (a) somatic symptoms (b) anxiety and insomnia (c) social dysfunction and (d) severe depression. Internal consistency has been shown to be approximately .92 (Goldberg & Hillyer, 1979) and construct validity has been demonstrated for all subscales (Goldberg & Hillyer, 1979). This scale has been translated into Bulgarian by the Higher Medical Institute of Bulgaria (Mutafora, van der Water, Maleshkov, Tonkova, Perenboom & Boshuizen, 1996).

Personal Attribute Inventory (PAI)

The Personal Attribute Inventory (Parish, Bryant & Shirazi, 1976) was used to assess views of fathers and views of mothers. This instrument consists of 50 positive and 50 negative adjectives from which subjects are asked to choose 30 which are most descriptive of the person in question. The total number of negative items chosen is the score for each subject. Test-retest reliability has been estimated to be between .90-.95 (Parish, Bryant & Shirazi, 1976). Criterion-related validity has also been demonstrated (Parish, Bryant & Shirazi, 1976). The PAI was translated into Bulgarian using the method of reverse translation. Each subject completed the PAI for mother and for father separately.

Procedure

The questionnaires were group administered during class time. Subjects were informed that their participation was strictly voluntary and confidential, and that they would be debriefed following completion of the questionnaire.

RESULTS

Psychological Adjustment

A two-way analysis of variance (ANOVA) was performed to test the effects of parents' marital status (intact, divorced) and students' gender (male, female) on the total General Health Questionnaire score. A significant main effect was obtained for parents' marital status, $F(1, 95) = 5.69$, $p < .05$, $\eta^2 = .06$. Students from divorced families reported significantly more total psychological difficulties (M = .74, S.D. = .36) than students from intact homes (M = .58, S.D. = .27). These results are shown in Table 1.

A two-way multivariate analysis of variance (MANOVA) was performed to test the effects of parents' marital status and gender on the four subscale scores of the General Health Questionnaire. Wilks' multivariate criterion indicated that the interaction between parents' marital status and students' gender was not significant. However, examination of univariate statistics indicated a significant interaction of parents' marital status and students' gender on the anxiety-insomnia subscale, $F(1, 96) = 8.24$, $p < .01$, $\eta^2 = .08$.

Female students from intact homes reported more symptoms (M = .82, S.D.= .51) than male students (M = .49, S.D. = .41) whereas male students from divorced homes reported more symptoms (M = 1.05,

TABLE 1. Mean ratings and standard deviations of the General Health Questionnaire (GHQ) subscales by parents' marital status and students' gender

| | Parents' marital status | | | | | Students' gender | | | | |
| | Intact N = 50 | | Divorced N = 50 | | | Male N = 56 | | Female N = 44 | | |
	Mean	(S.D.)	Mean	(S.D.)	p	Mean	(S.D.)	Mean	(S.D.)	p
GHQ subscales										
Somatic symptoms	.69	(.39)	.89	(.47)	.02	.76	(.43)	.82	(.46)	n.s.
Anxiety-insomnia	.65	(.48)	.92	(.56)	.01	.77	(.60)	.80	(.47)	n.s.
Social dysfunction	.73	(.41)	.65	(.44)	n.s.	.70	(.44)	.68	(.42)	n.s.
Severe depression	.26	(.29)	.42	(.43)	.03	.37	(.43)	.31	(.29)	n.s.
Total score	.58	(.27)	.74	(.36)	.02	.65	(.36)	.67	(.29)	n.s.

Note. S.D.: standard deviation; n.s.: not significant; p: probability level; higher scores in the GHQ subscales indicate greater psychopathology.

S.D. = .63) than female students (M = .79, S.D. = .44). These results are shown in Figure 1.

Moreover, Wilks' multivariate criterion indicated that the combined dependent variables were significantly related to parents' marital status, $F(4, 93) = 3.61$, $p < .01$, $\eta^2 = .14$. Examination of the univariate statistics indicated a significant main effect of parents marital status on the somatic symptoms subscale, $F(1, 96) = 5.57$, $p < .05$, $\eta^2 = .06$, on the anxiety–insomnia subscales, $F(1, 96) = 6.84$, $p = .01$, $\eta^2 = .07$, and on the severe depression subscale, $F(1, 96) = 4.79$, $p < .05$, $\eta^2 = .05$. More specifically, these results showed that students from divorced families reported more somatic symptoms (M = .89, S.D. = .47) than students from intact homes (M = .69, S.D. = .39). Students from divorced homes also reported more symptoms of anxiety and insomnia (M = .92, S.D. = .56) than students from intact homes (M = .65, S.D. = .48). Students from divorced homes reported more symptoms of severe depression (M = .43, S.D. = .43) than students whose parents were married (M = .26, S.D. = .29). These results are shown in Table 1.

Personal Attribute Inventory

A two-way multivariate analysis of variance (MANOVA) was conducted to test the effects of parents' marital status and students 'gender on views of fathers and views of mothers. The interaction between

FIGURE 1. Interaction between parents' marital status and students' gender on mean ratings of the Anxiety-Insomnia subscale of the General Health Questionnaire.

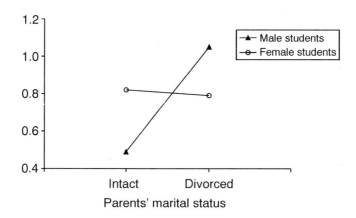

parents' marital status and students' gender on the combined dependent variables was not significant. However, Wilks' multivariate criterion indicated a significant main effect of parents' marital status on the combined dependent variables $F(2, 90) = 5.27$, $p < .01$, $\eta^2 = .10$.

Examination of the univariate statistics indicated a significant main effect of parents' marital status on views of fathers $F(1, 91) = 9.20$, $p < .01$, $\eta^2 = .09$. Students from divorced homes evidenced more negative views of their fathers (M = 12.34, S.D. = 9.32) than students from intact homes (M = 7.27, S.D. = 6.74). A similar trend was obtained for views of mothers, wherein students from divorced parents reported somewhat more negative views of mothers (M = 6.33, S.D. = 6.33) than their peers from intact homes (M = 4.61, S.D. = 4.49). However, this difference did not reach the level of statistical significance (p = .08). These results are shown in Table 2.

DISCUSSION

A major finding of the present study was that students from divorced homes reported significantly more symptoms of psychopathology than their peers from intact homes. These symptoms included somatic complaints, such as feeling run down or ill, having pains or of tightness or pressure in the head, having hot or cold spells, as well as symptoms of depression, such as feeling worthless, hopeless, or having suicidal ideation. These results differ from the findings of most studies with college students in the literature to date; the latter, based

TABLE 2. Mean ratings and standard deviations of the Personal Attribute Inventory (PAI) subscales by parents' marital status and students' gender

	Parents' marital status			Students' gender		
	Intact N = 48	Divorced N = 47		Male N = 51	Female N = 44	
	Mean (S.D.)	Mean (S.D.)	p	Mean (S.D.)	Mean (S.D.)	p
PAI scales						
Views of father	7.27 (6.74)	12.34 (9.32)	.003	10.56 (9.89)	9.04 (8.00)	n.s.
Views of mother	4.61 (4.49)	6.33 (6.33)	n.s.	5.90 (5.00)	5.04 (4.47)	n.s.

Note. S.D.: standard deviation; n.s.: not significant; p: probability level; higher scores in the PAI subscales indicate greater number of negative items.

on college student samples from the United States, have not found differences in psychological adjustment between students from divorced homes and students from intact families. Several factors may be implicated in accounting for this difference. To begin with, the incidence of divorce in Bulgaria was and is, considerably lower than that in the United States. It may be that in Bulgaria, divorce in considered an option only in cases of extreme marital difficulty or conflict, that is, significantly greater difficulty than that associated with divorce in the United States. Thus, it may be that students from divorced homes in Bulgaria have experienced much more inter-parental difficulty than their American peers from divorced families and that this exposure to inter-parental problems is integrally related to the greater incidence of psychopathology reported by the Bulgarian student sample. The relationship between inter-parental discord and difficulties in children's adjustment has been previously demonstrated (Emery, 1982; Emery & O'Leary, 1984).

Another factor that may explain the discrepancy between he findings of the present study and the literature to date concerns possible cultural differences regarding the acceptability of divorce. The lower prevalence of divorce in Bulgaria may in part result from greater social stigma for marital dissolution in accordance with the norms of more traditional, conservative family values. Thus, the differences in reported psychopathology between students from divorced and intact homes in Bulgaria may also reflect the impact of having experienced a family configuration that is stigmatized by the greater societal context, an experience considerably different than that of students from divorced homes in the United States where divorce is more acceptable and commonplace.

Differences in terms of the magnitude of economic changes following divorce in Bulgaria and in the Western mainstream may also be implicated in the discrepancy between the findings of the current study and the literature to date. Economic decline in the standard of living for the family, especially mother-headed families has been noted (Duncan & Hoffman, 1985; Weitzman, 1985) and linked to lowered well-being in the children of divorce (Amato & Keith, 1991a). It is possible that although economic decline is commonplace following divorce across cultures, this decline is of far greater magnitude in Bulgaria than in mainstream Western countries, and consequently with a more deleterious effect on student psychological adjustment.

A second finding of the present study concerns the significant inter-action of gender and parents' marital status with respect to problems of anxiety and insomnia: female students from intact families reported more symptoms than their male counterparts whereas male students from divorced parents reported more difficulties than female students whose parents were divorced. This result is also at odds with the literature to date on college students. Gender differences in psycholog-ical adjustment in students from divorced homes have not been found, with the exception of a study with African-American students, where-in female students from divorced homes reported lower levels of emo-tional health and self-esteem than male students whose parents were divorced (Phillips & Asbury, 1990), a finding opposite in direction from those of the present study.

However, the results of the present study are consistent with find-ings concerning children and adolescents, that is, that boys evidence more psychological difficulty than girls following divorce. As indi-cated by Zaslow (1989) after careful review and analysis of the litera-ture to date, this gender difference appears to be for the most part due to the impact of living with the mother, which is the commonplace custody situation. The effect of such a living arrangement may in part explain the findings of the present study, given that the vast proportion of the divorced sample (83%) was living with the mother at the time of the study. It should be noted that it is the norm rather than the excep-tion for Bulgarian students in general to continue living with their parents during their university studies. Thus, the more protracted ex-posure to maternal custody living arrangements for the divorced group as well as the impact of such living arrangements during later adoles-cence/early adulthood may account for the findings regarding a higher incidence of reported symptoms of anxiety and insomnia for males than females from divorced homes.

Regarding perceptions of parents, the results of the present study indicate that students from divorced homes have significantly more negative views of their fathers than students from intact homes. A similar trend was noted with respect to views of the mother but this was not at a statistically significant level. These findings are in line with the literature to date. Several explanations have been posited to account for these results. To begin with, children of couples who divorce have been exposed to inter-parental difficulties which deleteri-ously affect their views of their parents (Parish & Wiggle, 1985; Fine,

Moreland & Schwabel, 1986). In addition, the non-custodial father may be experienced as abandoning his family, irrespectively of the actual reasons for the divorce (Gardner, 1976). Moreover, non-custodial fathers may find it difficult to remain actively and enthusiastically committed to and involved with their children (Fine, Moreland & Schwebel, 1983, Lopez, 1991).

The results of the present study reveal that relationships between divorce and child outcomes are not uniform across cultures. Thus, it appears that cultural factors play a significant role in the relationship between parental divorce and child adjustment. The findings of this study underscore the need for caution in generalizing from findings from investigations from one culture to another, given that such generalizations may be incorrect. This is especially critical at present given that the majority of conclusions concerning relationships between parental divorce and child outcomes are based on mainstream Western samples, almost entirely from the United States. Further work is clearly needed across cultures in order to investigate possible cultural differences as well as to more specifically examine the ways in which cultural issues affect the experience of parental divorce. Attention to these issues in future studies will enrich and enhance understanding of the experience of divorce in a global context.

REFERENCES

Amato, P. R. & Keith, B. (1991a). Parental divorce and the well-being of children: A meta-analysis. *Psychological Bulletin, 110*, 26-46.

Amato, P. R. & Keith, B. (1991b). Parental divorce and adult well-being: A meta-analysis. *Journal of Marriage and the Family, 53*, 43-58.

Barkely, T. & Procidiano, M. (1989).College-age children of divorce: Are effects evident in early adulthood? *Journal of College Student Psychotherapy, 4*, 77-87.

Belchewa, M. (1994). *We and our children.* Sofia: National Statistical Institute.

Boyd, D., Nunn, G., & Parish, T. (1983). Effects of marital status and parental marital status on evaluation of self and parents. *Journal of Social Psychology, 119*, 229-234.

Duncan, G. J. & Hoffman, S. D. (1985). A reconsideration of the economic consequences of marital disruption. *Demography, 22*, 485-498.

Dunlop, R. & Burns, A. (1995). The sleeper effect: Myth or Reality? *Journal of Marriage and the Family, 57*, 378-386.

Emery, R. E. (1982). Inter-parental conflict and the children of discord and divorce. *Psychological Bulletin, 92*, 310-330.

Emery, R. E., & O'Leary, D. K. (1984). Marital discord and child behavior problems in a non-clinic sample. *Journal of Abnormal Psychology, 12*, 411-420.

Fine, M., Worley, S., & Schwebel, A. (1986). The effects of divorce on parent-child relationships. *Journal of Social Behavior and Personality, 1*, 451-463.

Fine, M., Moreland, J., & Schwebel, A. (1983). The long term effects of divorce on parent-child relationships. *Developmental Psychology, 19*, 703-713.

Franklin, K., Janoff-Bulman, R., & Roberts, J. (1990). Long-term impact of parental divorce on optimism and trust: changes in general assumptions or narrow beliefs? *Journal of Personality and Social Psychology, 59*, 743-755.

Gabardi, L., & Rosen, L. (1991). Differences between college students from divorced and intact families. *Journal of Divorce & Remarriage, 15*, 175-191.

Gardner, R. A. (1976). *Psychotherapy with children of divorce.* New York: Jason Aronson.

Goldberg, D. P., & Hillyer, V. F. (1979). A scaled version of the General Health Questionnaire. *Psychological Medicine, 9*, 139-145.

Karamfilov, Z. (1994). Semeistvoto i promeniastia se sviat. [The family and the changing world.] *Docladi ot nautnospractitseska conferencia str, 16-26*, Sofia: Nationalen statitseski Institut.

Lopez, F. G. (1987). The impact of parental divorce on college student development. *Journal of Counseling and Development, 65*, 484-486.

Lopez, F. G. (1991). The impact of parental divorce on college students. *New Directions for Student Life, 54*, 19-32.

Lopez, F. G., Campbell, V. L., & Watkins, C. E. (1988). The relation of parental divorce. To college student development. *Journal of Divorce, 12*, 83-98.

Mutafora, M., van der Water, H. P., Maleshkov, C., Tonkova, S., Perenboom, R., & Boshuizen, H. (1996). Attempt for assessment of the mental health of the population in Bulgaria. *Paper presented to REVES 9 meeting.* Sofia: Department of social Medicine, Medical University.

Parish, T. (1989). Evaluations of parents: do they vary as a function of parent loss; age at loss, or gender of the respondent? *Journal of Genetic Psychology, 150*, 461-462.

Parish, T., Bryant, W., & Shirazi, A. (1976). The Personal Attribute Inventory. *Perceptual and Motor Skills, 42*, 715-720.

Parish, T. & Ostenberg, J. (1985). Evaluations of self, parents and the family: Variations caused by family structures and personal stress. *Journal of Psychology, 119*, 231-233.

Parish, T. & Wigle, S. E. (1985). A longitudinal study of the impact of parental divorce on adolescents' evaluations of self and parents. *Adolescence, 20*, 239-244.

Phillips, C. P. & Asbury, C. A. (1991). Relationship of parental marital dissolution and sex to selected mental health and self-concept indicators in a sample of black university freshmen. *Journal of Divorce, 13*, 79-90.

Sugereva, M. (1995). Bulgarskoto semeistvo dnes. [The Bulgarian family today.] *Vestnik Az Buki, 42, str. 7.*

Weitzman, L. J. (1995). *The divorce revolution.* New York: Free Press.

Woo, J. (1991). Effects of parental divorce on offspring: A study of a college Population. *Dissertation Abstracts International, 42*, 2557B.

Zaslow, M. (1989). Sex differences in children's response to divorce: 2 samples, variables, ages and sources. *American Journal of Orthopsychiatry, 59*, 118-141.

Zill, N., Morrison, D. R., & Coiro, M. J. (1993). Long-term effects of parental divorce on parent-child-relationships, adjustment and achievement in young adulthood. *Journal of Family Psychology, 7*, 91-103.

Index

Numbers followed by "f" indicate figures; "t" following a page number indicates tabular material.

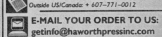